Uncertainty and Operations Research

Decision analysis based on uncertain data is natural in many real-world applications, and sometimes such an analysis is inevitable. In the past years, researchers have proposed many efficient operations research models and methods, which have been widely applied to real-life problems, such as finance, management, manufacturing, supply chain, transportation, among others. This book series aims to provide a global forum for advancing the analysis, understanding, development, and practice of uncertainty theory and operations research for solving economic, engineering, management, and social problems.

More information about this series at http://www.springer.com/series/11709

Dujuan Wang · Yunqiang Yin · Yaochu Jin

Rescheduling Under Disruptions in Manufacturing Systems

Models and Algorithms

Springer

Dujuan Wang
Business School
Sichuan University
Chengdu, Sichuan, China

Yunqiang Yin
School of Management and Economics
University of Electronic Science
and Technology of China
Chengdu, Sichuan, China

Yaochu Jin
Department of Computer Science
University of Surrey
Guildford, UK

ISSN 2195-996X ISSN 2195-9978 (electronic)
Uncertainty and Operations Research
ISBN 978-981-15-3527-7 ISBN 978-981-15-3528-4 (eBook)
https://doi.org/10.1007/978-981-15-3528-4

This Springer imprint is published by the registered company Springer Nature Singapore Pte Ltd.
The registered company address is: 152 Beach Road, #21-01/04 Gateway East, Singapore 189721, Singapore

Preface

This book provides an introduction to the models, methods, and results of some rescheduling problems in the presence of unexpected disruption events, including the machine breakdowns, job unavailability, and arrival of new jobs. The occurrence of these unexpected disruptions may cause a change in the planned schedule, which may render the originally feasible schedule infeasible. Rescheduling, which involves adjusting the previously planned schedule to account for a disruption, is necessary in order to minimize the effect of disruption events on the performance of the system. This involves a trade-off between finding a cost-effective new schedule and avoiding excessive changes to the original schedule.

This book views scheduling theory as practical theory, and it has made sure to emphasize the practical aspects of its topic coverage. Thus, this book considers some scenarios existing in most real-world environments, such as deterioration effect where the actual processing time of a job gets longer along with machine's usage and age. To alleviate the effect of disruption events, some flexible strategies are adopted, including preventive machine maintenance, allocation extra resources to reduce job processing times or job rejection. For each considered scenario, depending on the model settings and the disruption events, this book addresses the complexity, and the design of efficient exact or approximated algorithms. Especially when optimization methods and analytic tools fall short, this book stresses metaheuristics including Improved Elitist non-dominated Sorting Genetic Algorithm and Differential Evolution Algorithm. This book also provides extensive numerical studies to evaluate the performance of the proposed algorithms.

The problem of rescheduling in the presence of unexpected disruption events is of great importance for the successful implementation of real-world scheduling systems. Much work has been reported recently on rescheduling. This book is the first monograph on this topic. Most of the results presented in this book are based on our past research. We freely make use of our published results and acknowledge the sources in the text as and when appropriate. It is written for researchers and Ph. D. students working in scheduling theory and other members of scientific community who are interested in recent scheduling models. Our goal is to enable the reader to know about some new achievements on this topic.

This book is composed of six chapters, organized into three parts.

The first part consists of Chap. 1, in which we introduce rescheduling, and recall the basics of scheduling research and computational complexity.

The second part consists of Chaps. 2 and 3, which deals with rescheduling on identical parallel machines in the presence of machine disruptions and job unavailability, respectively. Chapter 2 focuses on the trade-off between the total completion time of the adjusted schedule and schedule disruption, measured by the maximum time deviation or the total virtual tardiness given that the completion time of any job in the original schedule can be regarded as an implied due date for the job concerned, by finding the set of Pareto-optimal solutions, and develops efficient pseudo-polynomial time algorithms, and two-dimensional fully polynomial-time approximation schemes, if viable. Chapter 3 investigates the rescheduling problem in the presence of job unavailability with the option of rejecting the processing of some jobs, and develops a branch-and-price algorithm to solve the problem to optimality.

The third part consists of Chaps. 4–6, which deals with rescheduling with deterioration effect on a single machine in the presence of the new arrival jobs, and machine breakdown, respectively. To alleviate the effect of disruption events, Chap. 4 adopts the flexible strategies of allocation of extra resources and job rejection, Chap. 5 adopts the flexible strategies of preventive machine maintenance and allocation of extra resources, whereas Chap. 6 adopts the flexible strategy of allocation of extra resources. We develop novel non-dominated Sorting Genetic Algorithms together with some enhancements to solve the problems in Chaps. 4 and 5, whereas devise an efficient Multi-objective Evolutionary Algorithm based on elitist non-dominated sorting together with a support vector regression surrogate model to solve the problem in Chap. 6.

The research presented in this book was supported in part by the National Natural Scsience Foundation of China under grant numbers 71871148 and 71971041; and by the Outstanding Young Scientific and Technological Talents Foundation of Sichuan Province under grant number 20JCQN0281.

While working on this book, we were also supported in different ways by different people. In particular, we would like to thank Prof. Xiang Li (Beijing University of Chemical Technology) for agreeing to publish this monograph in his special series.

Also, we would like to thank our other co-authors of the works that form the basis of this monograph, including T.C.E. Cheng (The Hong Kong Polytechnic University), Feng Liu (Dongbei University of Finance and Economics), and Yanzhang Wang (Dalian University of Technology).

In addition, we would like to thank doctoral students Yongjian Yang and Xiaoyun Xiong, who have helped us greatly in preparing this book.

Finally, we thank the publishers of the various outlets that have published our results for permitting us to reproduce our findings in this book.

Chengdu, China — Dujuan Wang
Chengdu, China — Yunqiang Yin
Guildford, UK — Yaochu Jin

Contents

Chapter 1
Introduction

This chapter introduces the basic concepts and notation in rescheduling under disruptions in manufacturing, and the basic notions related to the complexity of problems and algorithms, which provides a mathematical framework in which computational problems are studied so that they can be classified as "easy" or "hard".

This chapter is composed of three sections. In Sect. 1.1, we present the basic concepts and notation related to rescheduling under disruptions in manufacturing. In Sect. 1.2, we introduce the basic notions related to the complexity of problems and algorithms. We end the chapter in Sect. 1.3 with bibliographic remarks.

1.1 Rescheduling

Most modern production and service systems operate in a dynamic environment in which unexpected *disruptions* may occur, making deviations from the planned schedule inevitable, which may render the previously feasible schedule infeasible. Examples of such disruption events include: the arrival of new orders, order cancellations, changes in order priority, processing delays, changes in release dates, machine breakdowns, and the unavailability of raw materials, personnel, or tools, etc. *Rescheduling*, which involves adjusting the previously planned, possibly optimal, schedule, is then necessary in order to minimize the effect of such disruptions in the performance of the system.

In this book, we mainly focus on the rescheduling problems. Since rescheduling uses the same background and notions as other research domains in the theory of scheduling, we only briefly recall some facts. By *scheduling* we mean all actions that have to be done in order to determine when each activity of a set is to start and to complete. In the field of scheduling, the elements of the set are referred to as *jobs*, which will be used in the sequel. Each job is in competition with the others for the use of time and of resources capacity. The *resources* are regarded as everything what

D. Wang et al., *Rescheduling Under Disruptions in Manufacturing Systems*,
Uncertainty and Operations Research, https://doi.org/10.1007/978-981-15-3528-4_1

is needed for processing a job. Thus, in scheduling we also deal with *allocation of resources* to each job. A *schedule* is determined by a set of start times and of assigned resources, while respecting some predefined requirements, referred to as *constraints*, such as arrival times or due dates of jobs, precedence constraints among the jobs and so on. The quality of a schedule is measured by a function called *optimality criterion* or *objective function* which generally depends on the completion times of jobs.

A problem that has to find a schedule for some given input data is referred to as a *scheduling problem*. A schedule that satisfies all requirements of the considered scheduling problem is referred to as a *feasible schedule*. A feasible schedule that optimizes (i.e., minimizes or maximizes) a certain optimality criterion is referred to as an *optimal schedule*. In the sequel, we describe respectively, the main data concerning job, machine environment and optimality criterion that will be used in this book. For other basic conceptions and notation, the reader is referred to the classical books Brucker [20], Pinedo [119], etc.

1.1.1 Job Characteristics

Assume there is a set of n jobs $J_1, J_2, \ldots, J_n$ to be processed without interruption on m machines $M_1, \ldots, M_m$. Each machine can handle at most one job at a time and job preemption is not allowed. The following pieces of data are associated with job J_j.

- **Processing time** (p_{ij}): the amount of time for the processing of job J_j on machine M_i. The subscript i is omitted if the processing time of job J_j does not depend on the machine or if job J_j is only to be processed on one given machine.
- **Due date** (d_j): the time at which the processing of job J_j is due to be completed representing the committed completion date.
- **Release date** (r_j): the time the job arrives at the system, i.e., the earliest time at which job J_j can start its processing.
- **Weight** (w_j): the weight of job J_j denoting the importance of job J_j relative to the other jobs in the system.

1.1.2 Machine Environments

The possible machine environments involved in this book are:

- **Single machine** (1): There is only one machine, which is the simplest of all possible machine environments and is a special case of all other more complicated machine environments.

- **Identical parallel machines** (Rm): There are m identical machines in parallel with identical processing speed, and each job J_j requires a single operation and may be processed on any one of the m machines or on any one that belongs to a given subset with identical processing time, i.e., $p_{ij} = p_j$.

1.1.3 Optimality Criteria

Denote by C_{ij} the completion time of the operation of job J_j on machine M_i, and C_j the time job J_j exits the system, i.e., its completion time on the last machine on which it requires processing. If in some schedule the completion time of a job is no later than its due date, it is said to be *early* or *on-time*; otherwise, it is said to be *tardy* or *late*. The *tardiness* of job J_j are defined as $T_j = \max\{C_j - d_j, 0\}$.

In this book, we will investigate the following two classical optimality criteria:

- $\sum C_j$: the total completion time of the jobs in a schedule.
- $\sum T_j$: the total tardiness of the jobs in a schedule.

Note that all the above optimality criteria are *regular*, i.e., each of which is non-decreasing with respect to all variables C_j. When an objective function is regular, it is always better to schedule the jobs as early as possible.

As stated earlier, rescheduling involves adjusting a previously planned schedule to account for a disruption, which involves a trade-off between finding a cost efficient new schedule and avoiding excessive changes to the previously planned schedule. Let π^* be an optimal schedule of the original scheduling problem, i.e., the previously planned schedule, and σ any feasible schedule in the presence of disruption. The degree of disruption to the original schedule π^* is often measured as $\Delta_{\max}(\rho) = \max \Delta_j(\rho)$, where $\Delta_j(\rho) = |C_j(\rho) - C_j(\pi^*)|$ denotes the completion time disruption of job J_j, $C_j(\rho)$ and $C_j(\pi^*)$ are the completion times of job J_j in schedules π^* and σ, respectively. Whenever there is no risk of confusion, we drop σ in the notation, and just write C_j, Δ_j and $\Delta_{\max}$ for short in the sequel.

Given two optimality criteria, there are three different optimization problems associated with how the two optimality criteria (γ_1 and γ_2) are treated as objectives and constraints of the corresponding optimization problems as follows.

- **Linear combination optimization problem**: This method consists in defining a linear combination of optimality criteria, $w^1\gamma_1 + w^2\gamma_2$, which has to be optimized. This kind of problem is denoted as $\alpha|\beta|w^1\gamma_1 + w^2\gamma_2$ using the three-field notation for describing scheduling problems introduced by Graham et al. [42], where α field describes the machine environment and contains just on entry, and β field provides details of processing characteristics and constraints and may contain no entry at all, a single entry, or multiple entries.
- **Constrained optimization problem**: This method aims at minimizing γ_1, subject to $\gamma_2 \leq Q$, where Q is a given upper limit on γ_2. This kind of problem is denoted as $\alpha|\beta, \gamma_2 \leq Q|\gamma_1$.

- **Pareto-optimization problem**: This method aims at identifying the set of all the Pareto-optimal points (γ_1^*, γ_2^*), where a schedule π with $\gamma_1^* = \gamma_1^*(\pi)$ and $\gamma_2^* = \gamma_2^*(\pi)$ is called *Pareto-optimal* (or *efficient*) if there does not exist another schedule π' such that $\gamma_1(\pi') \leq \gamma_1^*(\pi)$ and $\gamma_2(\pi') \leq \gamma_2^*(\pi)$ with at least one of these inequalities being strict. This kind of problem is denoted as $\alpha|\beta|(\gamma_1, \gamma_2)$

1.2 Complexity of Problems and Algorithms

Complexity theory, is an important branch of computer science, has a great impact on the scheduling problems, which provides a mathematical framework in which computational problems are investigated so that they can be classified as "easy" or "hard".

1.2.1 The Classes $\mathcal{P}$ and $\mathcal{NP}$

The notion of *complexity* refers to the computing effort required by a solution algorithm, which is measured by the number of elementary operations which must be performed by the algorithm (time complexity) and the total space needed for the execution of the algorithm (space complexity) for finding a solution to any instance of a given problem. The most crucial efficiency measure is the *time complexity*, the function that maps each length of input, denoted as I, into the maximal number of elementary operations needed for finding a solution to any instance of that length. The big-O notation is commonly used to describe this function.

An algorithm that solves a problem is said to be a *polynomial time algorithm* if there exists a polynomial q such that the number of elementary operations performed by the algorithm can be bounded from above by $O(q(n))$ for any instance I of the problem, where $n = size(I)$ is the input length. An algorithm for which this function cannot be bounded by such a polynomial function is called an *exponential time algorithm*. A problem which is so hard that no polynomial time algorithm can possibly solve it is called *intractable*.

An algorithm which is polynomial with respect to both the length of input and the maximum value in the input is called *pseudo-polynomial time algorithm*.

A problem is referred to as *polynomially* (resp., *pseudo-polynomial*) *solvable* if there exists a polynomial (resp., pseudo-polynomial) time algorithm which solves the problem.

A problem is referred to as a *decision problem* that determines whether there exists a solution to the problem. We may associate with each scheduling problem a decision problem by defining a threshold Q for the corresponding optimality criterion γ. This decision problem is: Does there exist a feasible schedule π such that $\gamma(S) \leq Q$?

When a scheduling problem is formulated as a decision problem, there is an important asymmetry between those inputs whose output is "yes" and those whose output is "no". A "yes"-answer can be certified by a small amount of information: the feasible schedule π with $\gamma(S) \leq Q$. Given this certificate, the "yes"-answer can be verified in polynomial time. This is not the case for the "no"-answer.

Two main classes of decision problems exist, i.e., classes $\mathcal{P}$ and $\mathcal{NP}$, depending on the intractability of the problems. The class $\mathcal{P}$ is the class of decision problems that are polynomially solvable. The class $\mathcal{NP}$ is the class of decision problems for which a response "yes" can be verified in polynomial time on a deterministic computer.

Notice that if we know how to solve a decision problem in polynomial time, we can also verify in polynomial time any solution to the problem. Hence, $\mathcal{P} \subset \mathcal{NP}$. However, whether $\mathcal{P} = \mathcal{NP}$ is still one of the major open problems of modern mathematics.

The principal notion in defining $\mathcal{NP}$-completeness is that of a *polynomially reduction*. For two decision problems P_1 and P_2, we say that P_1 *polynomially reduces* to P_2 (denoted $P_1 \propto P_2$) if there exists a polynomial-time computable function g that transforms inputs for P_1 into inputs for P_2 such that x is a "yes"-input for P_1 if and only if $g(x)$ is a "yes"-input for P_2.

The existence of such an algorithm indicates that any instance of problem P_1 can be solved by an algorithm for problem P_2. We say that P_2 is at least as difficult as P_1.

A decision problem P is $\mathcal{NP}$-complete if $P \in \mathcal{NP}$ and $Q \propto P$ for any $Q \in \mathcal{NP}$. In other words, a problem P is $\mathcal{NP}$-complete if any solution to P can be solved by a polynomial time algorithm and any other problem from the $\mathcal{NP}$ class polynomially reduces to P. Therefore, if for a problem P and any $Q \in \mathcal{NP}$, we have $Q \propto P$, the problem P is said to be $\mathcal{NP}$-hard.

If any single $\mathcal{NP}$-complete problem could be solved in polynomial time, then due to the definition of polynomially reduction, all problems in $\mathcal{NP}$ could be solved in polynomial time and we would have $\mathcal{P} = \mathcal{NP}$. It follows that unless $\mathcal{P} = \mathcal{NP}$, the $\mathcal{NP}$-complete problems cannot be solved in polynomial time, which make these problems more "difficult" than those from the class $\mathcal{P}$.

NP-complete problems can further be divided into two subclasses, i.e., $\mathcal{P}$-complete in the strong sense and $\mathcal{P}$-complete in the ordinary sense. An NP-complete problem is said to be *$\mathcal{P}$-complete in the strong* (resp., *ordinary*) *sense*, if the problem cannot (resp., can) be solved by a pseudo-polynomial time algorithm, unless $\mathcal{P} = \mathcal{NP}$.

In what follows, we provide $\mathcal{NP}$-complete problems that will be used in our book.

1.2.1.1 3-Partition

Given an integer E, a finite set A of $3r$ positive integers a_j, $j = 1, \ldots, 3r$, such that $E/4 < a_j < 2/E, \forall j = 1, \ldots, 3r$, and $\sum_{j=1}^{3r} a_j = rE$, can the set $I = \{1, \ldots, 3r\}$ be partitioned into r disjoint subsets $I_1, \ldots, I_r$ such that $\sum_{j \in I_h} a_j = E$ for $h = 1, \ldots, r$?

1.3 Bibliographic Remark

The main notation and definitions of this chapter come from Agnetis et al. [3], Brucker [20], Gawiejnowicz [41], and Pinedo [119]. The basic concepts related to problems and algorithms are presented in Aho et al. [4] and Cormen et al. [29]. More detailed descriptions on rescheduling can be found in the survey papers Ouelhadj and Petrovic [113], and Vieira [145]. A more rigorous presentation of the theory of $\mathcal{NP}$-completeness can be found in Garey and Johnson [43] and Papadimitriou [117].

Chapter 2
Rescheduling on Identical Parallel Machines in the Presence of Machine Breakdowns

This chapter considers a scheduling problem where a set of jobs has already been assigned to identical parallel machines that are subject to machine breakdowns with the objective of minimizing the total completion time. When machine breakdowns occur, the affected jobs need to be rescheduled with a view to not causing excessive schedule disruption with respect to the planned schedule. Schedule disruption is measured by the maximum time deviation or the total virtual tardiness, given that the completion time of any job in the planned schedule can be regarded as an implied due date for the job concerned. We focus on the trade-off between the total completion time of the adjusted schedule and schedule disruption by finding the set of Pareto-optimal solutions. We show that both variants of the problem are $\mathcal{NP}$-hard in the strong sense when the number of machines is considered to be part of the input, and $\mathcal{NP}$-hard when the number of machines is fixed. In addition, we develop pseudo-polynomial time algorithms for the two variants of the problem with a fixed number of machines, establishing that they are $\mathcal{NP}$-hard in the ordinary sense. For the variant where schedule disruption is modelled as the total virtual tardiness, we also show that the case where machine disruptions occur only on one of the machines admits a two-dimensional fully polynomial-time approximation scheme (FPTAS). We conduct extensive numerical studies to evaluate the performance of the proposed algorithms.

This part is composed of six sections. In Sect. 2.1 we formally formulate our problem into two variants. In Sect. 2.2 we analyze the computational complexity and derive structural properties that are useful for tackling the two variants of the problem under study. In Sect. 2.3 we develop a pseudo-polynomial time dynamic programming (DP) algorithm for the variant with the maximum time deviation as the schedule disruption cost and a fixed number of machines, establishing that it is $\mathcal{NP}$-hard in the ordinary sense. In Sect. 2.4 we also develop a pseudo-polynomial time DP algorithm for the variant with the total virtual tardiness as the schedule disruption cost and a fixed number of machines, establishing that it is $\mathcal{NP}$-hard in the ordinary sense, and convert the algorithm into a two-dimensional FPTAS for the case where machine disruptions occur only on one of the machines. We conclude this chapter in Sect. 2.5, and end the chapter in Sect. 2.6 with bibliographic remarks.

D. Wang et al., *Rescheduling Under Disruptions in Manufacturing Systems*,
Uncertainty and Operations Research, https://doi.org/10.1007/978-981-15-3528-4_2

2.1 Problem Formulation

We describe the scheduling problem under study as follows: Assume that a set of non-preemptive jobs $J = \{1, 2, \ldots, n\}$ has been optimally scheduled according to the *shortest processing time (SPT) rule* to minimize the total completion time on m identical parallel machines $\{M_1, \ldots, M_m\}$, which can deal with only one job at a time [10], whereby the jobs are sequenced successively on the m machines, i.e., jobs $i, m+i, \ldots, m\lfloor n/m \rfloor + i$ are successively scheduled on machine i without any idle time, $i = 1, \ldots, m$, where $\lfloor x \rfloor$ denotes the largest integer less than or equal to x. Let π^* denote the sequence in which the jobs are scheduled in this SPT order. All the jobs are available for processing at time zero. However, the processing of most of the jobs has not begun. This situation arises when schedules are planned in advance of their start dates, typically several weeks earlier in practice. Based on the SPT schedule, a lot of preparation work has been made, such as ordering raw materials, tooling the equipment, organizing the workforce, fixing customer delivery dates, etc.

Due to unforeseen disruptions, machine breakdowns may occur on more than one machine, and the disruption start time and the duration of a machine breakdown may differ on different machines. To be precise, each machine M_i, $i = 1, \ldots, m$, may have an unavailable time interval $[B_i, F_i]$ resulting from a machine breakdown with $0 \leq F_i - B_i \leq D$ and $B_i \geq 0$, and at least one of the inequalities $B_1 \leq F_1, B_2 \leq F_2, \ldots, B_m \leq F_m$ is strict, where D denotes an upper limit on the durations of machine breakdowns on each machine, which can be estimated based on past experience. We assume, without loss of generality, that $B_i < F_i$ for $i = 1, \ldots, m_1$, and $B_i = +\infty$ for $i = m_1 + 1, \ldots, m$ for some positive integer m_1, which models the case where machine breakdowns occur only on the first m_1 machines. Let $B_{\max} = \max_{i=1,\ldots,m_1}\{B_i\}$ and $F_{\max} = \max_{i=1,\ldots,m_1}\{F_i\}$. It is clear that $F_{\max} \leq B_{\max} + D$. During job processing, machine breakdowns occur so that the original SPT schedule is no longer optimal, or worse, no longer feasible. As a consequence, we wish to reschedule all the uncompleted jobs in response to the disruptions. We assume that B_i and F_i, $i = 1, \ldots, m$, are known at time zero, prior to processing but after scheduling the jobs of J, and focus on the non-resumable case with the following assumption: If B_i and F_i, $i = 1, \ldots, m$ are all known after time zero, then the jobs of J having already been processed are removed from the problem, while the partially processed jobs, at most one on each machine, can either be processed to completion and removed, or processing can be halted immediately and started again from the beginning at a later time, with J and n updated accordingly. In this case, we reset the time index such that machine M_i, $i = 1, \ldots, m$, is available from τ_i onwards with at least one of the τ_i's equal to 0. Here, τ_i can be regarded as the release time of machine M_i, $i = 1, \ldots, m$.

This necessitates rescheduling the remaining jobs in the original SPT schedule. However, doing so will disrupt the SPT schedule, causing havoc on the preparative work already undertaken. Thus, on rescheduling, it is important to adhere to the original scheduling criterion, say, the total completion time $\sum C_j$ while minimizing the disruption cost with respect to the SPT schedule. In this chapter we use the maximum time deviation $\Delta_{\max}$ or the total virtual tardiness $\sum T_j$, where the completion time of a job in the SPT schedule can be regarded as an implied due date for the job concerned here, to model the disruption cost with respect to the SPT schedule. We focus on the *trade-off* between the total completion time of the adjusted schedule and schedule disruption by finding the set of Pareto-optimal solutions for this bicriterion scheduling problem.

Using the three-field notation $\alpha|\beta|\gamma$ introduced in Graham et al. [42], we denoted the problems under study as $Px, h_{m_1 1}|\tau, [B_i, F_i]_{1\le i\le m_1}|(\sum C_j, \Delta_{\max})$ and $Px, h_{m_1 1}|\tau, [B_i, F_i]_{1\le i\le m_1}|(\sum C_j, \sum T_j)$, in which $\alpha = Px, h_{m_1 1}$ denotes that there are m identical parallel machines, where x is empty when m is considered to be part of the input and $x = m$ when m is fixed, and that there is a single unavailable time interval on the first m_1 machines; $\tau = (\tau_1, \ldots, \tau_m)$ denotes the release time vector of the m machines, and $\beta = [B_i, F_i]_{1\le i\le m_1}$ represents that machine disruptions occur only on the first m_1 machines and the unavailable time interval on machine M_i is $[B_i, F_i], i = 1, \ldots, m_1$; and (v_1, v_2) in the third field indicates a Pareto-optimization problem with two criteria v_1 and v_2.

2.2 Problem Analysis

In this section we address the computational complexity issues of the considered problems and derive several structural properties of the optimal schedules that will be used later in the design of solution algorithms for the problems.

We first show that both problems $P, h_{m_1 1}|\tau, [B_i, F_i]_{1\le i\le m_1}|(\sum C_j, \Delta_{\max})$ and $P, h_{m_1 1}|\tau, [B_i, F_i]_{1\le i\le m_1}|(\sum C_j, \sum T_j)$ are $\mathcal{NP}$-hard in the strong sense.

Theorem 2.2.1 *The problem $P, h_{m_1 1}|\tau, [B_i, F_i]_{1\le i\le m_1}|(\sum C_j, \Delta_{max})$ is $\mathcal{NP}$-hard in the strong sense.*

Proof We establish the proof by making a reduction from 3-**PARTITION** to the problem $P, h_{m_1 1}|\tau, [B_i, F_i]_{1\le i\le m_1}|\sum C_j \le Q_A, \Delta_{\max} \le Q^B$. Given an instance of 3-**PARTITION**, construct an instance of the scheduling problem as follows:

- The number of jobs: $n = 3r$;
- The number of machines: $m = r$;
- The number of disrupted machines: $m_1 = r$;
- Job processing times: $p_j = a_j, j = 1, \ldots, 3r$;
- The release times of the machines: $\tau_i = 0, j = 1, \ldots, r$;
- The disruption start times: $B_i = E, j = 1, \ldots, r$;
- The disruption finish times: $F_i = (3r + 2)E, j = 1, \ldots, r$;
- The threshold value for $\sum C_j$: $Q_A = 3rE$;
- The threshold value for $\Delta_{\max}$: $Q_B = (6r + 2)E$.

Analogous to the proof of Theorem 2 in Levin et al. [81], it is easy to see that there is a solution to the 3-**PARTITION** instance if and only if there is a feasible schedule for the constructed instance of the problem $P, h_{m_1 1}|\tau, [B_i, F_i]_{1 \le i \le m_1}|\sum C_j \le Q_A, \Delta_{\max} \le Q^B$. □

In a similar way, we can establish the following result.

Theorem 2.2.2 *The problem* $P, h_{m_1 1}|\tau, [B_i, F_i]_{1 \le i \le m_1}|(\sum C_j, \sum T_j)$ *is* $\mathcal{NP}$*-hard in the strong sense.*

As a result of Theorems 2.2.1 and 2.2.2, we focus only on the case with a fixed number of machines m in the sequel. Note that even the single-machine case with a known future machine unavailability, denoted as $1, h_1||\sum_{j=1}^n C_j$, is $\mathcal{NP}$-hard [1]. Hence both of our problems $Pm, h_{m_1 1}|\tau, [B_i, F_i]_{1 \le i \le m_1}|(\sum_{j=1}^n C_j, \Delta_{\max})$ and $Pm, h_{m_1 1}|\tau, [B_i, F_i]_{1 \le i \le m_1}|(\sum_{j=1}^n C_j, \sum_{j=1}^n T_j)$ are $\mathcal{NP}$-hard, too, which have been further shown to be $\mathcal{NP}$-hard in the ordinary sense by developing pseudo-polynomial time algorithms for them in the subsequent sections.

The following lemma provides an easy-to-prove property of the original SPT schedule for the problem $Pm||\sum C_j$.

Lemma 2.2.3 *For any two jobs* j *and* k *in the original SPT schedule* π^* *for the problem* $Pm||\sum_{j=1}^n C_j$, $j < k$ *implies* $C_j(\pi^*) - p_j \le C_k(\pi^*) - p_k$.

After rescheduling, we refer to the partial schedule of jobs finished no later than B_i on machine $M_i, i = 1, \ldots, m_1$, as the earlier schedule on machine M_i; the partial schedule of jobs in the earlier schedules on all the machine $M_i, i = 1, \ldots, m_1$, as the earlier schedule; and the partial schedule of jobs that begin their processing at time F_i or later on machine $M_i, i = 1, \ldots, m_1$, and that are processed on machine $M_i, i = m_1 + 1, \ldots, m$, as the later schedule. The next result establishes the order of the jobs in the earlier schedule on each machine $M_i, i = 1, \ldots, m_1$, and the order of the jobs in the later schedule.

Lemma 2.2.4 *For each of the problems* $Pm, h_{m_1 1}|\tau, [B_i, F_i]_{1 \le i \le m_1}|(\sum_{j=1}^n C_j, \Delta_{max})$ *and* $Pm, h_{m_1 1}|\tau, [B_i, F_i]_{1 \le i \le m_1}|(\sum_{j=1}^n C_j, \sum_{j=1}^n T_j)$, *there exists an optimal schedule* ρ^* *in which*

(1) *the jobs in the earlier schedule on each machine* $M_i, i = 1, \ldots, m_1$, *follow the SPT order; and*
(2) *the jobs in the later schedule follow the SPT order.*

Proof (1) Consider first the earlier schedule in ρ^* on any machine $M_i, i = 1, 2, \ldots, m_1$. If property (1) does not hold, let k and j be the first pair of jobs for which j precedes k in π^*, implying that $p_j \le p_k$, but k immediately precedes j in ρ^* on machine M_i. Constructing a new schedule ρ' from ρ^* by swapping jobs k and j while leaving the other jobs unchanged. Furthermore, let t denote the processing start time of job k in schedule ρ^*. Then we have $C_k(\rho^*) = t + p_k \geq t + p_j = C_j(\rho')$ and $C_j(\rho^*) = C_k(\rho') = t + p_j + p_k$. Hence, $C_j(\rho') + C_k(\rho') = 2t + 2p_j + p_k \leq 2t + p_j + 2p_k = C_k(\rho^*) + C_j(\rho^*)$, making $\sum_{j=1}^n C_j(\rho') \leq \sum_{j=1}^n C_j(\rho^*)$. To show that ρ' is no worse than ρ^*, it suffices to show that $\Delta_{\max}(\rho^*) \geq \Delta_{\max}(\rho')$ for the problem $Pm, h_{m_1 1}|\tau, [B_i, F_i]_{1\leq i\leq m_1}|(\sum C_j, \Delta_{\max})$ and $\sum T_i(\rho^*) \geq \sum T_i(\rho')$ for the problem $Pm, h_{m_1 1}|\tau, [B_i, F_i]_{1\leq i\leq m_1}|(\sum C_j, \sum T_j)$. Indeed, by Lemma 2.2.3, $p_j \leq p_k$ implies that $C_j(\pi^*) \leq C_k(\pi^*)$. Thus, it follows from the proof of Lemma 1 in [88] that $\Delta_{\max}(\rho^*) \geq \Delta_{\max}(\rho')$ and from Emmons [38] that $\sum T_i(\rho^*) \geq \sum T_i(\rho')$. Repeating this argument a finite number of times establishes property (1).

(2) Denote by I the set of jobs in the later schedule with $|I| = n'$. Re-index the jobs in I as $1', 2', \ldots, n'$ such that $p_{1'} \leq p_{2'} \leq \cdots \leq p_{n'}$. In what follows, we show that it is optimal to sequence the jobs in I in SPT order. To achieve this, it suffices to show that there exists an optimal schedule in which job n' among the jobs in I has the latest processing start time. If this is the case, then the problem can be decomposed into a problem of scheduling the first $n' - 1$ jobs on machine M_i after F_i, $i = 1, \ldots, m_1$, and on machine M_i, $i = m_1 + 1, \ldots, m$, and then inserting job n' at the earliest possible time when any one of the machines becomes available. Similarly, the problem with the first $n' - 1$ jobs can be further decomposed into a problem with the first $n' - 2$ jobs and scheduling job $n' - 1$, and so on. Thus property (2) follows.

Since job n' has the largest processing time among the jobs in the set I, analogous to the proof of property (1), we can show that it must be the last job on machine M_{i_1} to which it was assigned. Now suppose that there exists an optimal schedule ρ^* in which there is a job j', other than job n', assigned to a different machine M_{i_2} but with a later processing start time than that of job n'. Let t_1 be the processing start time of job n' on machine M_{i_1} and t_2 be the processing start time of job j' on machine M_{i_2} with $t_1 < t_2$. We construct a new schedule ρ' by letting job j' start its processing at t_1 on machine M_{i_1} and job n' start its processing at t_2 on machine M_{i_2}, while leaving the other jobs unchanged. Such an exchange makes job j' start earlier by $t_2 - t_1$ and job n' start later by $t_2 - t_1$. The total completion time, however, does not change. Now we show that ρ' is no worse than ρ^*. There are two cases to consider.

Case 1: Job j' is early in ρ', i.e., $t_1 + p_{j'} \leq C_{j'}(\pi^*)$. It follows from $t_1 \leq C_{j'}(\pi^*) - p_{j'} \leq C_{n'}(\pi^*) - p_{n'}$ that job n' is early in ρ^*. Hence,

$$\Delta_{j'}(\rho') = C_{j'}(\pi^*) - p_{j'} - t_1, \ \Delta_{n'}(\rho^*) = C_{n'}(\pi^*) - p_{n'} - t_1, \ T_{j'}(\rho') = T_{n'}(\rho^*) = 0.$$

Furthermore, if job n' is tardy in ρ', i.e., $t_2 + p_{n'} \geq C_{n'}(\pi^*)$. It follows from $t_2 \geq C_{n'}(\pi^*) - p_{n'} \geq C_{j'}(\pi^*) - p_{j'}$ that job j' is also late in ρ^*. Hence,

$$\Delta_{n'}(\rho') = T_{n'}(\rho') = t_2 + p_{n'} - C_{n'}(\pi^*), \ \Delta_{j'}(\rho^*) = T_{j'}(\rho^*) = t_2 + p_{j'} - C_{j'}(\pi^*).$$

Thus, it follows from $C_{j'}(\pi^*) - p_{j'} \leq C_{n'}(\pi^*) - p_{n'}$ that $\Delta_{j'}(\rho') \leq \Delta_{n'}(\rho^*)$, $\Delta_{n'}(\rho') \leq \Delta_{j'}(\rho^*)$ and $T_{n'}(\rho') + T_{j'}(\rho') = T_{n'}(\rho') \leq T_{j'}(\rho^*) = T_{j'}(\rho^*) + T_{n'}(\rho^*)$.

If job n' is early in ρ', i.e., $t_2 + p_{n'} \le C_{n'}(\pi^*)$, we have

$$\Delta_{n'}(\rho') = C_{n'}(\pi^*) - p_{n'} - t_2,\ T_{n'}(\rho') = 0,$$

$$\Delta_{j'}(\rho^*) = |t_2 + p_{j'} - C_{j'}(\pi^*)|,\ T_{j'}(\rho^*) = \max\{t_2 + p_{j'} - C_{j'}(\pi^*), 0\}.$$

Thus, it follows from $C_{j'}(\pi^*) - p_{j'} \le C_{n'}(\pi^*) - p_{n'}$ and $t_1 < t_2$ that $\Delta_{j'}(\rho') \le \Delta_{n'}(\rho^*)$, $\Delta_{n'}(\rho') \le \Delta_{n'}(\rho^*)$ and $T_{n'}(\rho') + T_{j'}(\rho') = 0 \le T_{j'}(\rho^*) + T_{n'}(\rho^*)$.

Case 2: Job j' is tardy in ρ', i.e., $t_1 + p_{j'} \ge C_{j'}(\pi^*)$. It follows from $t_1 < t_2$ that job j' is also tardy in ρ^*. Hence,

$$\Delta_{j'}(\rho') = T_{j'}(\rho') = t_1 + p_{j'} - C_{j'}(\pi^*),\ \Delta_{j'}(\rho^*) = T_{j'}(\rho^*) = t_2 + p_{j'} - C_{j'}(\pi^*).$$

Furthermore, if job n' is tardy in ρ', i.e., $t_2 + p_{n'} \ge C_{n'}(\pi^*)$, we have

$$\Delta_{n'}(\rho') = T_{n'}(\rho') = t_2 + p_{n'} - C_{n'}(\pi^*),$$

$$\Delta_{n'}(\rho^*) = |t_1 + p_{n'} - C_{n'}(\pi^*)|,\ T_{n'}(\rho^*) = \max\{t_1 + p_{n'} - C_{n'}(\pi^*), 0\}.$$

Thus, it follows from $C_{j'}(\pi^*) - p_{j'} \le C_{n'}(\pi^*) - p_{n'}$ and $t_1 < t_2$ that $\Delta_{j'}(\rho') \le \Delta_{j'}(\rho^*)$, $\Delta_{n'}(\rho') \le \Delta_{j'}(\rho^*)$ and that $T_{n'}(\rho') + T_{j'}(\rho') \le T_{j'}(\rho^*) + T_{n'}(\rho^*)$.

If job n' is early in ρ', i.e., $t_2 + p_{n'} \le C_{n'}(\pi^*)$, it follows from $t_1 < t_2$ that n' is also early in ρ^*. Hence

$$\Delta_{n'}(\rho') = C_{n'}(\pi^*) - p_{n'} - t_2,\ \Delta_{n'}(\rho^*) = C_{n'}(\pi^*) - p_{n'} - t_1,\ T_{n'}(\rho') = T_{n'}(\rho^*) = 0.$$

Thus, it follows from $C_{j'}(\pi^*) - p_{j'} \le C_{n'}(\pi^*) - p_{n'}$ that $\Delta_{n'}(\rho') \le \Delta_{n'}(\rho^*)$, $T_{n'}(\rho') + T_{j'}(\rho') = \Delta_{j'}(\rho') \le \Delta_{j'}(\rho^*) = T_{j'}(\rho^*) + T_{n'}(\rho^*)$.

Thus, in any case, schedule ρ' is no worse than ρ^* for the two problems under consideration. The result follows. □

It is worth noting that scheduling the jobs in the earlier schedule in the SPT order, each as early as possible, is not necessarily optimal even for the case without the schedule disruption cost. This is because such rescheduling may waste a long period of machine idle time immediately preceding the start time of each machine disruption, which we illustrate in the following example.

Example 2.2.5 Let $n = 3, m = 2;\ \ p_1 = 2, p_2 = 3, p_3 = 4;\ \ \tau_1 = \tau_2 = 0;\ B_1 = B_2 = 5;$ *and* $F_1 = F_2 = 6$. If the jobs are scheduled in the same sequence as π^*, each as early as possible, then jobs 1 and 3 are scheduled in the intervals [0, 2] and [6, 10], respectively, on machine M_1, while job 2 is scheduled in the interval [0, 3] on machine M_2, yielding an objective value of 15. In an optimal schedule, however, jobs

1 and 2 are scheduled in the intervals [0, 2] and [2, 5], respectively, on machine M_1, while job 3 is scheduled in the interval [0, 4] on machine M_2, yielding an objective value of 11.

2.3 Problem $Pm, h_{m_1 1}|\tau, [B_i, F_i]_{1\le i\le m_1}|\left(\sum_{j=1}^{n} C_j, \Delta_{\max}\right)$

In this section we consider the problem $Pm, h_{m_1 1}|\tau, [B_i, F_i]_{1\le i\le m_1}|(\sum_{j=1}^{n} C_j, \Delta_{\max})$. We first develop a pseudo-polynomial time DP algorithm to solve it, followed by an experimental study to evaluate the effectiveness of the DP-based solution algorithm.

2.3.1 A Pseudo-Polynomial Time Algorithm for the Problem $Pm, h_{m_1 1}| \tau, [B_i, F_i]_{1\le i\le m_1}|\left(\sum_{j=1}^{n} C_j, \Delta_{\max}\right)$

We start with providing an auxiliary result.

Lemma 2.3.1 *For the problem* $Pm, h_{m_1 1}|\tau, [B_i, F_i]_{1\le i\le m_1}|(\sum_{j=1}^{n} C_j, \Delta_{max})$*, the maximum time disruption* Δ_{max} *is upper-bounded by* $\max\{\min\{B_{max}, P\} + D, C_S - p_{min}\}$.

Proof It suffices to show that $\Delta_{\max}(\rho^*)$ is less than $\max\{\min\{B_{\max}, P\} + D, C_S - p_{\min}\}$, where ρ^* is an optimal schedule for the problem $Pm, h_{m_1 1}|\tau, [B_i, F_i]_{1\le i\le m_1}| \sum_{j=1}^{n} C_j$ that satisfies Lemma 2.2.4. We first consider the jobs with $C_j(\rho^*) > C_j(\pi^*)$. If $C_j(\rho^*) \le \min\{B_{\max}, P\} + D$, then $\Delta_j \le \min\{B_{\max}, P\} + D$; otherwise, Lemma 2.2.4 indicates that all the jobs completed after time $\min\{B_{\max}, P\} + D$ and before job j in ρ^* are processed before job j in π^*, so $\Delta_j \le \min\{B_{\max}, P\} + D$. Alternatively, when $C_j(\rho^*) \le C_j(\pi^*)$, we have $\Delta_j \le C_S - p_{\min}$ since C_S is the maximum completion time of the jobs in π^*. Thus, $\Delta_{\max}(\rho^*) \le \max\{\min\{B_{\max}, P\} + D, C_S - p_{\min}\}$. □

Our DP-based solution algorithm *SMDP* for the problem $Pm, h_{m_1 1}|\tau, [B_i, F_i]_{1\le i\le m_1}|(\sum_{j=1}^{n} C_j, \Delta_{\max})$ relies strongly on Lemmas 2.2.4 and 2.3.1. Note that after rescheduling, a job in the earlier schedule might be completed earlier than in π^*. In this case, as $\Delta_{\max}$ is defined as $\max_{j\in J} |C_j - C_j(\pi^*)|$, the job might be immediately preceded by an idle time period. Thus, we design Algorithm *SMDP* on the basis of solving a series of the constrained optimization problem $Pm, h_{m_1 1}|\tau, [B_i, F_i]_{1\le i\le m_1}, \Delta_{\max} \le Q| \sum_{j=1}^{n} C_j$ with $0 \le Q \le \max\{\min\{B_{\max}, P\} + D, C_S - p_{\min}\}$. The constraint $\Delta_{\max} \le Q$ implies that, in a feasible schedule ρ, $C_j(\rho) \ge C_j(\pi^*) - Q$ and $C_j(\rho) \le C_j(\pi^*) + Q$, for $j = 1, \ldots, n$. Accordingly, each job j has an implied release time $r_j^Q = C_j(\pi^*) - p_j - Q$ and an implied deadline $\overline{d}_j^Q = C_j(\pi^*) + Q$.

Let $(j, \mathcal{B}, \mathcal{F}, \mathcal{T}, v)_Q$ be a state corresponding to a partial schedule for the jobs $\{1, \ldots, j\}$ such that the maximum time deviation is less than Q, where

- $\mathcal{B} = (t_{1'}, t_{2'}, \ldots, t_{m_1'})$: $t_{k'}$, $k = 1, \ldots, m_1$, denotes the completion time of the last job scheduled before B_k on machine M_k;
- $\mathcal{F} = (t_1, t_2, \ldots, t_{m_1})$: t_k, $k = 1, \ldots, m_1$, stands for the total processing time of the jobs scheduled after F_k on machine M_k;
- $\mathcal{T} = (t_{m_1+1}, t_{m_1+2}, \ldots, t_m)$: t_{m_1+k}, $k = 1, \ldots, m - m_1$, measures the completion time of the last job scheduled on machine M_k;
- v: the total completion time of the partial schedule.

Algorithm *SMDP* follows the framework of forward recursive state generation and starts with the empty state in which no job has been scheduled yet, i.e., $j = 0$. The set $\mathcal{S}_j^Q$ contains the states for all the generated sub-schedules for jobs $\{1, \ldots, j\}$. The algorithm recursively generates the states for the partial schedules by adding a job to a previous state. Naturally, the construction of $\mathcal{S}_j^Q$ may generate more than a single state that will not lead to a complete optimal schedule. The following result shows how to reduce the state set $\mathcal{S}_j^Q$.

Lemma 2.3.2 *For any two states $(j, \mathcal{B}, \mathcal{F}, \mathcal{T}, v)_Q$ and $(j, \mathcal{B}' = (t'_{1'}, \ldots, t'_{m'_1}), \mathcal{F}' = (t'_1, \ldots, t'_{m_1}), \mathcal{T}' = (t'_{m_1+1}, \ldots, t'_m), v')$ in $\mathcal{S}_j^Q$, if $t_{k'} \leq t'_{k'}$ for $k = 1, \ldots, m_1$, $t_k \leq t'_k$ for $k = 1, \ldots, m$, and $v \leq v'$, we can eliminate the latter state.*

Proof Let S_1 and S_2 be two sub-schedules corresponding to the states $(j, \mathcal{B}, \mathcal{F}, \mathcal{T}, v)_Q$ and $(j, \mathcal{B}', \mathcal{F}', \mathcal{T}', v')_Q$, respectively. And let $\widetilde{S}_2$ be a sub-schedule of the jobs $\{j+1, \ldots, n\}$ that is appended to the sub-schedule S_2 so as to create a feasible schedule $\widehat{S}_2$. In the resulting feasible schedule $\widehat{S}_2$, the total completion time is given as follows:

$$\sum C_j(\widehat{S}_2) = v' + \sum_{k=j+1}^{n} C_k(\widetilde{S}_2).$$

Since $t_{k'} \leq t'_{k'}$ for $k = 1, \ldots, m_1$ and $t_k \leq t'_k$ for $k = 1, \ldots, m$, set $\{j+1, \ldots, n\}$ can also be added to the sub-schedule S_1 in an analogous way as $\widetilde{S}_2$, denoting the resulting sub-schedule as $\widetilde{S}_1$, to form a feasible schedule $\widehat{S}_1$, and we have $C_k(\widetilde{S}_1) \leq C_k(\widetilde{S}_2)$ for $k = j+1, \ldots, n$. In the resulting feasible schedule $\widehat{S}_1$, the total completion time is given as follows:

$$\sum C_j(\widehat{S}_1) = v + \sum_{k=j+1}^{n} C_k(\widetilde{S}_1).$$

It follows from $v \leq v'$ that $\sum C_j(\widehat{S}_1) \leq \sum C_j(\widehat{S}_2)$. Therefore, sub-schedule S_1 dominates S_2, so the result follows. □

We provide a formal description of Algorithm *SMDP* as follows:

Sum-Max-DP Algorithm *SMDP*

Step 1. [*Preprocessing*] Re-index the jobs in the SPT order.

Step 2. [*Initialization*] For each $j = 1, \ldots, n$, set $i = j - m\lfloor j/m \rfloor$ and $C_j(\pi^*) = \sum_{k=i,m+i,\ldots,m\lfloor j/m\rfloor+i} p_k$;

for each $Q \in [0, \max\{\min\{B_{\max}, P\} + D, C_S - p_{\min}\}]$, set $\mathcal{S}_0^Q = \{(0, \mathcal{B}, \mathcal{F}, \mathcal{T}, 0)_Q\}$, where $\mathcal{B} = (\tau_1, \ldots, \tau_{m_1})$, $\mathcal{F} = \underbrace{(0, \ldots, 0)}_{m_1}$ and $\mathcal{T} = (\tau_{m_1+1}, \ldots, \tau_m)$, and set $r_j^Q = C_j(\pi^*) - p_j - Q$ and $\bar{d}_j^Q = C_j(\pi^*) + Q$.

Step 3. [*Generation*] Generate $\mathcal{S}_j^Q$ from $\mathcal{S}_{j-1}^Q$.

For each $Q \in [0, \max\{\min\{B_{\max}, P\} + D, C_S - p_{\min}\}]$ do

For $j = 1$ to n do

Set $\mathcal{S}_j^Q = \emptyset$;

For each $(j-1, \mathcal{B}, \mathcal{F}, \mathcal{T}, v)_Q \in \mathcal{S}_{j-1}^Q$ do

Set $t = \min\left\{\min_{k=1,\ldots,m_1}\{F_k + t_k\}, \min_{k=m_1+1,\ldots,m} t_k\right\}$ and

$k^* = \arg\min\left\{\min_{k=1,\ldots,m_1}\{F_k + t_k\}, \min_{k=m_1+1,\ldots,m} t_k\right\}$;

For $i = 1$ to m_1 do

/*Alternative 1: schedule job j before B_i:

If $\max\{t_{i'}, r_j^Q\} + p_j \le \min\{\bar{d}_j^Q, B_i\}$, then

set $\mathcal{S}_j^Q \leftarrow \mathcal{S}_j^Q \cup \{(j, \mathcal{B}', \mathcal{F}, \mathcal{T}, v + \max\{t_{i'}, r_j^Q\} + p_j)_Q\}$,

where $\mathcal{B}' = (t_{1'}, \ldots, t_{(i-1)'}, \max\{t_{i'}, r_j^Q\} + p_j, t_{(i+1)'}, \ldots, t_{m_1'})$;

Endif

Endfor

/*Alternative 2: assign job j to the later schedule:

If $t + p_j \le d_j^Q$, then

set $\mathcal{S}_j^Q \leftarrow \mathcal{S}_j^Q \cup \{(j, \mathcal{B}, \mathcal{F}', \mathcal{T}', v + t + p_j)_Q\}$,

where $\mathcal{F}' = (t_1, \ldots, t_{k^*-1}, t + p_j - F_{k^*}, t_{k^*+1}, \ldots, t_{m_1})$ and $\mathcal{T}' = \mathcal{T}$ if $1 \le k^* \le m_1$, otherwise $\mathcal{F}' = \mathcal{F}$ and $\mathcal{T}' = (t_{m_1+1}, \ldots, t_{k^*-1}, t + p_j, t_{k^*+1}, \ldots, t_m)$;

Endif

Endfor

Endfor

[*Elimination*] /* Update set $\mathcal{S}_j^Q$ */

1. For any two states $(j, \mathcal{B}, \mathcal{F}, \mathcal{T}, v)_Q$ and $(j, \mathcal{B}, \mathcal{F}, \mathcal{T}, v')_Q$ with $v \le v'$, eliminate the latter state from set $\mathcal{S}_j^Q$;
2. For any two states $(j, \mathcal{B} = (t_{1'}, \ldots, t_{(i-1)'}, t_{i'}, t_{(i+1)'}, \ldots, t_{m_1'}), \mathcal{F}, \mathcal{T}, v)_Q$ and $(j, \mathcal{B} = (t_{1'}, \ldots, t_{(i-1)'}, t'_{i'}, t_{(i+1)'}, \ldots, t_{m_1'}), \mathcal{F}, \mathcal{T}, v)_Q$ with $t_{i'} \le t'_{i'}$, eliminate the latter state from set $\mathcal{S}_j^Q$;
3. For any two states $(j, \mathcal{B}, \mathcal{F} = (t_1, \ldots, t_{i-1}, t_i, t_{i+1}, \ldots, t_{m_1}), \mathcal{T}, v)_Q$ and $(j, \mathcal{B}, \mathcal{F} = (t_1, \ldots, t_{i-1}, t'_i, t_{i+1}, \ldots, t_{m_1}), \mathcal{T}, v)_Q$ with $t_i \le t'_i$, eliminate the latter state from set $\mathcal{S}_j^Q$;
4. For any two states $(j, \mathcal{B}, \mathcal{F}, \mathcal{T} = (t_{m_1+1}, \ldots, t_{k-1}, t_k, t_{k+1}, \ldots, t_m), v)_Q$ and $(j, \mathcal{B}, \mathcal{F}, \mathcal{T} = (t_{m_1+1}, \ldots, t_{k-1}, t'_k, t_{k+1}, \ldots, t_m), v)_Q$ with $t_k \le t'_k$, eliminate the latter state from set $\mathcal{S}_j^Q$;

Endfor

Step 4. [*Return all the Pareto-optimal points*]

Set $\overline{Q} = \max\{\min\{B_{\max}, P\} + D, C_S - p_{\min}\}$ and $i = 1$;

While $\mathcal{S}_n^{\overline{Q}} \ne \emptyset$ do

Select $(\mathcal{V}_i, \mathcal{Q}_i) = (v, Q)$ that corresponds to the state $(n, \mathcal{B}, \mathcal{F}, \mathcal{T}, v)_Q$ with the minimum v value among all the states in $\mathcal{S}_n^Q$ such that $Q \le \overline{Q}$ as a Pareto-optimal point;

Set $\overline{Q} = \mathcal{Q}_i - 1$ and $i = i + 1$;
End while
Return $(\mathcal{V}_1, \mathcal{Q}_1), \ldots, (\mathcal{V}_{i-1}, \mathcal{Q}_{i-1})$ and the corresponding Pareto-optimal schedules can be found by backtracking.

Justification for algorithm SMDP. After the [Preprocessing] procedure, for each $Q \in [0, \max\{\min\{B_{\max}, P\} + D, C_S - p_{\min}\}]$, the algorithm goes through n phases. The jth phase, $j = 1, \ldots, n$, takes care of job j and produces a set $\mathcal{S}_j^Q$. Suppose that the state set $\mathcal{S}_{j-1}^Q$ has been constructed and we try to assign job j now. Due to Lemma 2.2.4, it is optimal to assign j either to the last position of any machine $M_i, i = 1, \ldots, m_1$, that is finished no later than B_i, or to the later schedule on some machine $M_i, i = 1, \ldots, m$, at the earliest possible time when the machine becomes available. Note that after rescheduling, a job might be completed earlier than in π^*. In this case, due to the maximum time deviation constraint, the job might be immediately preceded by an idle time period. Thus, if job j is assigned to the last position of machine $M_i, i = 1, \ldots, m_1$, that is finished no later than B_i, its processing start time is $\max\{t_{i'}, r_j^Q\}$, where $t_{i'} > r_j^Q$, i.e., $t_{i'} + p_j - C_j(\pi^*) > -Q$, implying that job j has a time deviation strictly less than Q, while $t_{i'} \le r_j^Q$ implies that there may be an idle time immediately preceding job j and that job j has a time deviation of Q time units, and that $\max\{t_{i'}, r_j^Q\} + p_j \le \min\{\overline{d}_j^Q, B_i\}$, which guarantees that job j has a time deviation no more than Q and can be completed before B_i. In this case, we update $t_{i'}$ as $\max\{t_{i'}, r_j^Q\} + p_j$ and the contribution of job j to the scheduling objective is $\max\{t_{i'}, r_j^Q\} + p_j$, so $v' = v + \max\{t_{i'}, r_j^Q\} + p_j$. If job j is assigned to the later schedule on some machine M_i, we have $i = k^*$ by Lemma 2.2.4 and its processing start time is t, where the condition $t + p_j \le d_j^Q$ guarantees that job j has a time deviation less than Q. In this case, the contribution of job j to the scheduling objective is $t + p_j$, so $v' = v + t + p_j$. Naturally, the construction process of $\mathcal{S}_j^Q$ may generate more than a single state $(j, \mathcal{B}, \mathcal{F}, \mathcal{T}, v)_Q$ with the same $\mathcal{B}$, $\mathcal{F}$, and $\mathcal{T}$. Among all these states, by the elimination rule 1 in Algorithm *SMDP*, we keep in $\mathcal{S}_j^Q$ only the state with the minimum v value to ensure the finding of the minimum objective value. By Lemma 2.3.2, the elimination rules 2–4 in Algorithm *SMDP* can also be used to eliminate the non-dominated states. It is easy to see that for each $\overline{Q} \in [0, \max\{\min\{B_{\max}, P\} + D, P - p_{\min}\}]$, an efficient solution is given by the pair $(\mathcal{V}, \mathcal{Q}) = (v, Q)$, which corresponds to the state $(n, \mathcal{B}, \mathcal{F}, \mathcal{T}, v)_Q$ with the minimum v value among all the states in $\mathcal{S}_n^Q$ such that $Q \le \overline{Q}$.

Theorem 2.3.3 *Algorithm* SMDP *solves the problem* $Pm, h_{m_1 1}|\tau, [B_i, F_i]_{1\le i\le m_1}|(\sum_{j=1}^n C_j, \Delta_{max})$ *in* $O(n \max\{\min\{\min\{B_{max}, P\} + D, C_S - p_{min}\} P^m \prod_{i=1}^{m_1} B_i)$ *time.*

Proof The optimality of Algorithm *SMDP* is guaranteed by Lemmas 2.2.4, 2.3.1 and 2.3.2, and the above analysis. We now work out the time complexity of the algorithm. Step 1 implements a sorting procedure that needs $O(n \log n)$ time. In Step 3, for each Q, before each iteration j, the total number of possible states $(j - 1, \mathcal{B}, \mathcal{F}, \mathcal{T}, v)_Q \in \mathcal{S}_{j-1}^Q$ can be calculated in the following way: there are at most B_i possible values for $t_{i'}$, $i = 1, \ldots, m_1$, and at most P possible values for t_i, $i = 1, \ldots, m$. Because of the elimination rule, the total number of different states at the beginning of each iteration is at most $O(P^m \prod_{i=1}^{m_1} B_i)$. In each iteration j, there are at most $m_1 + 1$ new states generated from each state in $\mathcal{S}_{j-1}^{Q}$ for each candidate job. Thus, the number of new states generated is at most $(m_1 + 1)O(P^m \prod_{i=1}^{m_1} B_i)$. However, due to the elimination rules, the number of new states generated in $\mathcal{S}_j^Q$ is upper-bounded by $O(P^m \prod_{i=1}^{m_1} B_i)$ after the elimination step. Thus, after $n \max\{\min\{B_{\max}, P\} + D, C_S - p_{\min}\}$ iterations, Step 3 can be executed in $O(n \max\{\min\{B_{\max}, P\} + D, C_S - p_{\min}\}P^m \prod_{i=1}^{m_1} B_i)$ time, as required. Step 4 takes $O(\max\{\min\{B_{\max}, P\} + D, C_S - p_{\min}\}P^m \prod_{i=1}^{m_1} B_i)$ time. Therefore, the overall time complexity of the algorithm is $O(n \max\{\min\{B_{\max}, P\} + D, C_S - p_{\min}\}P^m \prod_{i=1}^{m_1} B_i)$. □

The proof of Theorem 2.3.3 also implies that the problem $Pm, h_{m_1 1}|\tau, [B_i, F_i]_{1\le i\le m_1}, \Delta_{\max} \le Q|\sum_{j=1}^{n} C_j$ can be solved in $O(nP^m \prod_{i=1}^{m_1} B_i)$ time. In particular, when $m = m_1 = 1$, the corresponding problem, denoted as $1, h_1|\Delta_{\max} \le Q|\sum C_j$, can be solved in $O(nPB_1)$ time. In what follows, we develop an alternative algorithm for the problem $1, h_1|\Delta_{\max} \le Q|\sum C_j$ by exploiting the following stronger results on the optimal schedule, the proofs of which are analogous to those of Lemmas 2 and 3 in Liu and Ro [88], respectively.

Lemma 2.3.4 *For the problem* $1, h_1|\Delta_{max} \le Q|\sum C_j$, *there exists an optimal schedule* ρ^* *in which:*

(1) *the jobs in the earlier schedule are processed with at most one inserted idle time period;*
(2) *each job processed in the earlier schedule after an inserted idle time period starts processing exactly at its induced release time;*
(3) *the jobs processed in the earlier schedule after an inserted idle time period are processed consecutively in* π^*.

Lemma 2.3.5 *For the problem* $1, h_1|\Delta_{max} \le Q|\sum C_j$, *there exists an optimal schedule* ρ^* *in which if a job is immediately preceded by an idle time period in the earlier schedule, then in* π^* *the job has a start time later than* F_1.

Combining Lemmas 2.2.4, 2.3.4, and 2.3.5, we can apply algorithm *ML* in Liu and Ro [88] with a slight modification to solve the problem $1, h_1|\Delta_{\max} \le Q|\sum C_j$. As a result, the problem $1, h_1|\Delta_{\max} \le Q|\sum C_j$ can also be solved in $O(n^2 B_1 Q)$ time (see Theorem 2 in Liu and Ro [88]).

2.3.2 *The Performance of Algorithm* SMDP

We performed numerical studies by varying the problem size to assess the performance of Algorithm *SMDP*. We coded the algorithm in Java and conducted the experiments on a Dell OptiPlex 7010 with a 3.40 GHz, 4 GB memory Intel core i5-3570 CPU. For simplicity, we only studied the two-machine case with $m_1 = 1$. The number of jobs considered was $n \in \{10, 15, 20, 25\}$. For each value of n, we randomly generated 30 instances for each combination of the specifications for the two parameters B_1 and $\mathcal{D} = F_1 - B_1$. Randomly generating the job processing times p_j from the uniform distribution (1, 20), we considered the case where $B_1 \in \{\lfloor P/8 \rfloor, \lfloor P/6 \rfloor, \lfloor P/4 \rfloor\}$, and $\mathcal{D} \in \{\lfloor P/80 \rfloor, \lfloor P/50 \rfloor, \lfloor P/30 \rfloor\}$. For each value of n, we recorded the average number of Pareto-optimal points, the maximum number of Pareto-optimal points, and the average time required to construct the entire Pareto set for a single instance. For each of the $4 * 3 * 3 = 36$ parameter combinations, we generated 30 instances, i.e., we tested a total of 1,080 instances. Table 2.1 summarizes the results. The main observations from Table 2.1 are as follows:

- As expected beforehand, the number of Pareto-optimal points increases as the number of machines increases;
- The number of Pareto-optimal points is insensitive to the duration of the machine disruption and the disruption start time;
- The average time required to construct the entire Pareto-set decreases as the disruption start time increases;
- In most cases the algorithm fails to solve instances with up to 25 jobs due to space capacity limitation.

2.4 Problem $Pm, h_{m_1 1}|\tau, [B_i, F_i]_{1 \le i \le m_1}| \left(\sum_{j=1}^n C_j, \sum_{j=1}^n T_j\right)$

In this section we consider the problem $Pm, h_{m_1 1}|\tau, [B_i, F_i]_{1 \le i \le m_1}|(\sum_{j=1}^n C_j, \sum_{j=1}^n T_j)$. We first develop a pseudo-polynomial time DP algorithm to solve the problem, and then show that the special case with $m_1 = 1$ admits a two-dimensional FPTAS, which is the strongest approximation result for a bicriterion $\mathcal{NP}$-hard problem. Recall that an algorithm A_ε for a bicriterion problem is a $(1+\varepsilon)$-approximation algorithm if it always delivers an approximate solution pair (Z, T) with $Z \le (1+\varepsilon)Z^*$ and $T \le (1+\varepsilon)T^*$ for all the instances, where (Z^*, T^*) is a Pareto-optimal solution. A family of approximation algorithms $\{A_\varepsilon\}$ defines a two-dimensional FPTAS for the considered problem, if for any $\varepsilon > 0$, A_ε is a $(1+\varepsilon)$-approximation algorithm that is polynomial in n, L, and $1/\varepsilon$, where $L = \log \max\{n, \tau_{\max}, B_{\max}, D, p_{\max}\}$ is the number of bits in binary encoding for the largest numerical parameter in the input.

Table 2.1 The performances of the Algorithm $SMDP$

n	B_1	D	Avg. number of Pareto-optimization points	Max. number of Pareto-optimization points	Avg. running time (s)
10	$\lfloor p/8 \rfloor$	$\lfloor p/80 \rfloor$	57.30	74	9.30
		$\lfloor p/50 \rfloor$	54.77	70	8.50
		$\lfloor p/30 \rfloor$	56.27	75	8.30
	$\lfloor p/6 \rfloor$	$\lfloor p/80 \rfloor$	58.90	74	9.06
		$\lfloor p/50 \rfloor$	50.07	69	7.45
		$\lfloor p/30 \rfloor$	56.93	72	8.11
	$\lfloor p/4 \rfloor$	$\lfloor p/80 \rfloor$	54.93	75	7.14
		$\lfloor p/50 \rfloor$	51.37	69	6.54
		$\lfloor p/30 \rfloor$	55.27	72	7.19
15	$\lfloor p/8 \rfloor$	$\lfloor p/80 \rfloor$	81.63	101	82.17
		$\lfloor p/50 \rfloor$	79.73	101	75.79
		$\lfloor p/30 \rfloor$	79.73	101	75.79
	$\lfloor p/6 \rfloor$	$\lfloor p/80 \rfloor$	81.27	110	65.79
		$\lfloor p/50 \rfloor$	85.23	108	62.90
		$\lfloor p/30 \rfloor$	84.87	115	57.31
	$\lfloor p/4 \rfloor$	$\lfloor p/80 \rfloor$	84.47	106	36.87
		$\lfloor p/50 \rfloor$	85.73	108	38.02
		$\lfloor p/30 \rfloor$	84.10	104	31.88
20	$\lfloor p/8 \rfloor$	$\lfloor p/80 \rfloor$	110.17	132	685.17
		$\lfloor p/50 \rfloor$	107.63	126	567.76
		$\lfloor p/30 \rfloor$	105.63	133	489.43
	$\lfloor p/6 \rfloor$	$\lfloor p/80 \rfloor$	108.40	138	465.83
		$\lfloor p/50 \rfloor$	110.20	129	402.12
		$\lfloor p/30 \rfloor$	108.10	135	329.70
	$\lfloor p/4 \rfloor$	$\lfloor p/80 \rfloor$	106.53	126	161.83
		$\lfloor p/50 \rfloor$	104.83	132	156.22
		$\lfloor p/30 \rfloor$	108.53	135	166.08
25	$\lfloor p/8 \rfloor$	$\lfloor p/80 \rfloor$	131.00	142	6145.25
		$\lfloor p/50 \rfloor$	133.25	162	5602.20
		$\lfloor p/30 \rfloor$	132.25	160	4820.60
	$\lfloor p/6 \rfloor$	$\lfloor p/80 \rfloor$	116.75	131	2287.93
		$\lfloor p/50 \rfloor$	134.50	142	3508.21
		$\lfloor p/30 \rfloor$	133.75	141	3426.92
	$\lfloor p/4 \rfloor$	$\lfloor p/80 \rfloor$	135.50	155	1651.32
		$\lfloor p/50 \rfloor$	138.00	143	1889.25
		$\lfloor p/30 \rfloor$	131.75	141	1544.08

2.4.1 A Pseudo-Polynomial Time Algorithm for the Problem $Pm, h_{m_1 1}|\tau, [B_i, F_i]_{1\le i\le m_1}|\left(\sum_{j=1}^n C_j, \sum_{j=1}^n T_j\right)$

We can easily derive the following result by Lemma 2.4.1.

Lemma 2.4.1 *For the problem* $Pm, h_{m_1 1}|\tau, [B_i, F_i]_{1\le i\le m_1}|(\sum_{j=1}^n C_j, \sum_{j=1}^n T_j)$, *the total virtual tardiness* $\sum_{j=1}^n T_j$ *is upper-bounded by* $n \max\{\min\{B_{max}, P\} + D, C_S - p_{min}\}$.

Our DP-based solution Algorithm *STDP* for the problem $Pm, h_{m_1 1}|\tau, [B_i, F_i]_{1\le i\le m_1}|(\sum_{j=1}^n C_j, \sum_{j=1}^n T_j)$ follows the framework of forward recursive state generation and relies strongly on Lemma 2.2.4. Algorithm *STDP* contains n phases. In each phase $j, j = 0, 1, \ldots, n$, a state space $\mathcal{S}_j$ is generated. Any state in $\mathcal{S}_j$ is a vector $(j, \mathcal{B}, \mathcal{F}, \mathcal{T}, v_1, v_2)$ corresponding to a partial schedule for the jobs $\{1, \ldots, j\}$, where $\mathcal{B}$, $\mathcal{F}$, and $\mathcal{T}$ are defined as those in Sect. 2.1, and v_1 denotes the total completion time of the partial schedule, while v_2 represents the total virtual tardiness of the partial schedule. The state spaces $\mathcal{S}_j$, $j = 0, 1, \ldots, n$ are constructed iteratively. The initial space $\mathcal{S}_0$ contains $(0, \mathcal{B}, \mathcal{F}, \mathcal{T}, 0, 0)$ as its only element, where $\mathcal{B} = (\tau_1, \ldots, \tau_{m_1})$, $\mathcal{F} = (\underbrace{0, \ldots, 0}_{m_1})$, and $\mathcal{T} = (\tau_{m_1+1}, \ldots, \tau_m)$. In the jth phase, $j = 1, \ldots, n$, we build a state by adding a single job J_j to a previous state, if it is possible for the given state. That is, for any state $(j, \mathcal{B}, \mathcal{F}, \mathcal{T}, v_1, v_2) \in \mathcal{S}_{j-1}$, by Lemma 2.2.4, we include $m_1 + 1$ possibly generated states in $\mathcal{S}_j$ as follows:

(1) Schedule job J_j before B_i on machine M_i, $i = 1, \ldots, m_1$. This is possible only when $t_{i'} + p_j \le B_i$. In this case, the contributions of job J_j to the total completion time objective and the total virtual objective are $t_{i'} + p_j$ and $\max\{t_{i'} + p_j - C_j(\pi^*), 0\}$, respectively. Thus, if $t_{i'} + p_j \le B_i$, we include $(j, \mathcal{B}', \mathcal{F}, \mathcal{T}, v_1 + t_{i'} + p_j, v_2 + \max\{t_{i'} + p_j - C_j(\pi^*), 0\})$ in $\mathcal{S}_j$.
(2) Assign job J_j to the later schedule. In this case, set $t = \min\left\{\min_{k=1,\ldots,m_1}\{F_k + t_k\}, \min_{k=m_1+1,\ldots,m} t_k\right\}$ and $k^* = \arg\min\left\{\min_{k=1,\ldots,m_1}\{F_k + t_k\}, \min_{k=m_1+1,\ldots,m} t_k\right\}$, which denote the earliest possible time when the machine becomes available after disruption and the corresponding machine with the earliest available time, respectively. Then the contributions of job J_j to the total completion time objective and the total virtual objective are $t + p_j$ and $\max\{t + p_j - C_j(\pi^*), 0\}$, respectively. Thus, we include $(j, \mathcal{B}, \mathcal{F}', \mathcal{T}', v_1 + t + p_j, v_2 + \max\{t + p_j - C_j(\pi^*), 0\})$ in $\mathcal{S}_j$, where $\mathcal{F}' = (t_1, \ldots, t_{k^*-1}, t + p_j - F_{k^*}, t_{k^*+1}, \ldots, t_{m_1})$ and $\mathcal{T}' = \mathcal{T}$ if $1 \le k^* \le m_1$; otherwise, $\mathcal{F}' = \mathcal{F}$ and $\mathcal{T}' = (t_{m_1+1}, \ldots, t_{k^*-1}, t + p_j, t_{k^*+1}, \ldots, t_m)$.

Before presenting Algorithm *STDP* in detail, we introduce the following elimination property to reduce the state set $\mathcal{S}_j$.

Lemma 2.4.2 *For any two states* $(j, \mathcal{B}, \mathcal{F}, \mathcal{T}, v_1, v_2)$ *and* $(j, \mathcal{B}' = (t'_{1'}, \ldots, t'_{m'_1})$, $\mathcal{F}' = (t'_1, \ldots, t'_{m_1})$, $\mathcal{T}' = (t'_{m_1+1}, \ldots, t'_m)$, $v'_1, v'_2)$ *in* $\mathcal{S}_j$, *if* $t_{k'} \le t'_{k'}$ *for* $k = 1, \ldots, m_1$, $t_k \le t'_k$ *for* $k = 1, \ldots, m$, $v_1 \le v'_1$ *and* $v_2 \le v'_2$, *we can eliminate the latter state.*

Proof The proof is analogous to that of Lemma 2.3.2. □

We give a formal description of Algorithm *STDP* as follows:

Sum-Tardiness-DP Algorithm *STDP*

Step 1. [*Preprocessing*] Re-index the jobs in the SPT order.
Step 2. [*Initialization*] Set $\mathcal{S}_0 = \{(0, \mathcal{B}, \mathcal{F}, \mathcal{T}, 0, 0)\}$, where $\mathcal{B} = (\tau_1, \ldots, \tau_{m_1})$, $\mathcal{F} = \underbrace{(0, \ldots, 0)}_{m_1}$ and
$\mathcal{T} = (\tau_{m_1+1}, \ldots, \tau_m)$; For each $j = 1, \ldots, n$, set $i = j - m\lfloor j/m \rfloor$ and $C_j(\pi^*) = \sum_{k=i,m+i,\ldots,m\lfloor j/m\rfloor+i} p_k$.
Step 3. [*Generation*] Generate $\mathcal{S}_j$ from $\mathcal{S}_{j-1}$.
For $j = 1$ to n do
Set $\mathcal{S}_j = \emptyset$;
For each $(j-1, \mathcal{B}, \mathcal{F}, \mathcal{T}, v_1, v_2) \in \mathcal{S}_{j-1}$ do
Set $t = \min\left\{\min_{k=1,\ldots,m_1}\{F_k + t_k\}, \min_{k=m_1+1,\ldots,m} t_k\right\}$ and
$k^* = \arg\min\left\{\min_{k=1,\ldots,m_1}\{F_k + t_k\}, \min_{k=m_1+1,\ldots,m} t_k\right\}$;
For $i = 1$ to m_1 do
/*Alternative 1: schedule job j before B_i:
If $t_{i'} + p_j \le B_i$, then
set $\mathcal{S}_j \leftarrow \mathcal{S}_j \cup \{(j, \mathcal{B}', \mathcal{F}, \mathcal{T}, v_1 + t_{i'} + p_j, v_2 + \max\{t_{i'} + p_j - C_j(\pi^*), 0\})\}$,
where $\mathcal{B}' = (t_{1'}, \ldots, t_{(i-1)'}, t_{i'} + p_j, t_{(i+1)'}, \ldots, t_{m_1'})$;
Endif
Endfor
/*Alternative 2: assign job j to the later schedule:
set $\mathcal{S}_j \leftarrow \mathcal{S}_j \cup \{(j, \mathcal{B}, \mathcal{F}', \mathcal{T}', v_1 + t + p_j, v_2 + \max\{t + p_j - C_j(\pi^*), 0\})\}$,
where $\mathcal{F}' = (t_1, \ldots, t_{k^*-1}, t + p_j - F_{k^*}, t_{k^*+1}, \ldots, t_{m_1})$ and $\mathcal{T}' = \mathcal{T}$ if $1 \le k^* \le m_1$, otherwise $\mathcal{F}' = \mathcal{F}$ and $\mathcal{T}' = (t_{m_1+1}, \ldots, t_{k^*-1}, t + p_j, t_{k^*+1}, \ldots, t_m)$;
Endfor
[*Elimination*] /* Update set $\mathcal{S}_j$ */
1. For any two states $(j, \mathcal{B}, \mathcal{F}, \mathcal{T}, v_1, v_2)$ and $(j, \mathcal{B}, \mathcal{F}, \mathcal{T}, v_1, v_2')$ with $v_2 \le v_2'$, eliminate the second state from set $\mathcal{S}_j$;
2. For any two states $(j, \mathcal{B}, \mathcal{F}, \mathcal{T}, v_1, v_2)$ and $(j, \mathcal{B}, \mathcal{F}, \mathcal{T}, v_1', v_2)$ with $v_1 \le v_1'$, eliminate the second state from set $\mathcal{S}_j$;
3. For any two states $(j, \mathcal{B} = (t_{1'}, \ldots, t_{(i-1)'}, t_{i'}, t_{(i+1)'}, \ldots, t_{m_1'}), \mathcal{F}, \mathcal{T}, v_1, v_2)$ and $(j, \mathcal{B} = (t_{1'}, \ldots, t_{(i-1)'}, t_{i'}', t_{(i+1)'}, \ldots, t_{m_1'}), \mathcal{F}, \mathcal{T}, v_1, v_2)$ with $t_{i'} \le t_{i'}'$, eliminate the latter state from set $\mathcal{S}_j$;
4. For any two states $(j, \mathcal{B}, \mathcal{F} = (t_1, \ldots, t_{i-1}, t_i, t_{i+1}, \ldots, t_{m_1}), \mathcal{T}, v_1, v_2)$ and $(j, \mathcal{B}, \mathcal{F} = (t_1, \ldots, t_{i-1}, t_i', t_{i+1}, \ldots, t_{m_1}), \mathcal{T}, v_1, v_2)$ with $t_i \le t_i'$, eliminate the latter state from set $\mathcal{S}_j$;
5. For any two states $(j, \mathcal{B}, \mathcal{F}, \mathcal{T} = (t_{m_1+1}, \ldots, t_{k-1}, t_k, t_{k+1}, \ldots, t_m), v_1, v_2)$ and $(j, \mathcal{B}, \mathcal{F}, \mathcal{T} = (t_{m_1+1}, \ldots, t_{k-1}, t_k', t_{k+1}, \ldots, t_m), v_1, v_2)$ with $t_k \le t_k'$, eliminate the latter state from set $\mathcal{S}_j$;
Endfor
Step 4. [*Return all the Pareto-optimal points*]
Set $\overline{Q} = n\max\{\min\{B_{\max}, P\} + D, C_S - p_{\min}\}$ and $i = 1$;
While $\overline{Q} \ge 0$ do
Select $(\mathcal{V}_i, \mathfrak{V}_i) = (v_1, v_2)$ that corresponds to the state $(n, \mathcal{B}, \mathcal{F}, \mathcal{T}, v_1, v_2)$ with the minimum v_1 value among all the states in $\mathcal{S}_n$ such that $v_2 \le \overline{Q}$ as a Pareto-optimal point;
Set $\overline{Q} = \mathfrak{V}_i - 1$ and $i = i + 1$;

End while
Return $(\mathcal{V}_1, \mathfrak{V}_1), \ldots, (\mathcal{V}_{i-1}, \mathfrak{V}_{i-1})$ and the corresponding Pareto-optimal schedules can be found by backtracking.

Theorem 2.4.3 *Algorithm STDP solves the problem* $Pm, h_{m_1 1}|\tau, [B_i, F_i]_{1\le i\le m_1}|(\sum_{j=1}^n C_j, \sum_{j=1}^n T_j)$ *in* $O(n^2 \max\{\min\{B_{max}, P\} + D, C_S - p_{min}\}P^{m-1}\prod_{i=1}^{m_1} B_i)$ *time.*

Proof Given that Algorithm *STDP* implicitly enumerates all the schedules satisfying the properties given in Lemma 2.2.4, the DP-based algorithm finds an efficient solution for each possible $\overline{Q}$ through state transition. Verification of the time complexity of the algorithm is analogous to that of Algorithm *SMDP*, where the difference lies in that before each iteration j, the total number of different possible combinations of $(\mathcal{B}, \mathcal{F}, \mathcal{T})$ is upper-bounded by $P^{m-1}\prod_{i=1}^{m_1} B_i$ due to the fact that $\sum_{k=1}^{m_1}(t_{k'} + t_k) + \sum_{k=m_1+1}^{m} t_k = \sum_{k=1}^{j} p_k$, while the total number of different possible combinations of v_1 and v_2 is upper-bounded by $n\max\{\min\{B_{\max}, P\} + D, C_S - p_{\min}\}$ due to the elimination rules and the fact that v_2 is upper-bounded by $n\max\{\min\{B_{\max}, P\} + D, C_S - p_{\min}\}$. □

2.4.2 A Two-Dimensional FPTAS for Finding a Pareto Optimal Solution

In this section we show how to obtain a good approximation of an efficient point on the trade-off curve by using the trimming-the-solution-space approach for the special case with $m_1 = 1$. It is based on an approximate DP algorithm *STAA* with a slight modification of Algorithm *STDP*. We present the idea as follows: For any $\delta > 1$ and $\varepsilon > 0$, partition the interval $\mathcal{I}_1 = [0, P]$ into $L_1 = \lceil \log_\delta P \rceil$ subintervals

$$I_1^{(1)} = [0, 0],\ I_k^{(1)} = [\delta^{k-1}, \delta^k), k = 1, \ldots, L_1 - 1,\ I_{L_1}^{(1)} = [\delta^{L_1-1}, P];$$

and partition the intervals $\mathcal{I}_2 = [0, n(F_1 + P)(1+\varepsilon)]$ and $\mathcal{I}_3 = [0, n\max\{F_1, C_S - p_{\min}\}(1+\varepsilon)]$ into $L_2 = \lceil \log_\delta n(F_1 + P)(1+\varepsilon) \rceil$ subintervals

$$I_1^{(2)} = [0, 0],\ I_k^{(2)} = [\delta^{k-1}, \delta^k), k = 1, \ldots, L_2 - 1,\ I_{L_2}^{(2)} = [\delta^{L_2-1}, n(F_1 + P)(1+\varepsilon)],$$

and $L_3 = \lceil \log_\delta n\max\{F_1, C_S - p_{\min}\}(1+\varepsilon) \rceil$ subintervals

$$I_1^{(3)} = [0, 0],\ I_k^{(3)} = [\delta^{k-1}, \delta^k), k = 1, \ldots, L_3 - 1,$$
$$I_{L_3}^{(3)} = [\delta^{L_3-1}, n\max\{F_1, C_s - p_{\min}\}(1+\varepsilon)],$$

respectively. This will divide $\underbrace{\mathcal{I}_1 \times \cdots \times \mathcal{I}_1}_{m} \times \mathcal{I}_2 \times \mathcal{I}_3$ into a set of $L_1^m L_2 L_3$ $(m+2)$-dimensional subintervals. We develop an alternative dynamic programming Algorithm *STAA* that differs from Algorithm *STDP* in that out of all the states such that $(t_1, \ldots, t_m, v_1, v_2)$ falls within the same $(m+2)$-dimensional subinterval, only the state with the smallest $t_{1'}$ value is kept, while all the other states are eliminated. We formally describe the resulting procedure as follows:

Sum-Tardiness-AA Algorithm *STAA*

Step 1. [*Preprocessing*] The same as that in Algorithm *STDP*.
Step 2. [*Partitioning*] Partition the interval $\mathcal{I}_1 = [0, P]$ into $L_1 = \lceil \log_\delta P \rceil$ subintervals

$$I_1^{(1)} = [0, 0],\ I_k^{(1)} = [\delta^{k-1}, \delta^k),\ k = 1, \ldots, L_1 - 1,\ I_{L_1}^{(1)} = [\delta^{L_1 - 1}, P];$$

and partition the intervals $\mathcal{I}_2 = [0, n(F_1 + P)(1+\varepsilon)]$ and $\mathcal{I}_3 = [0, n\max\{F_1, C_S - p_{\min}\}(1+\varepsilon)]$ into $L_2 = \lceil \log_\delta n(F_1 + P)(1+\varepsilon) \rceil$ subintervals

$$I_1^{(2)} = [0, 0],\ I_k^{(2)} = [\delta^{k-1}, \delta^k),\ k = 1, \ldots, L_2 - 1,\ I_{L_2}^{(2)} = [\delta^{L_2 - 1}, n(F_1 + P)(1+\varepsilon)],$$

and $L_3 = \lceil \log_\delta n\max\{F_1, C_S - p_{\min}\}(1+\varepsilon) \rceil$ subintervals

$$I_1^{(3)} = [0, 0],\ I_k^{(3)} = [\delta^{k-1}, \delta^k),\ k = 1, \ldots, L_3 - 1,\ I_{L_3}^{(3)} = [\delta^{L_3 - 1}, n\max\{F_1, C_S - p_{\min}\}(1+\varepsilon)],$$

respectively.
Step 3. [*Initialization*]: The same as that in Algorithm *STDP*.
Step 4. [*Generation*]: Generate $\mathcal{S}_j$ from $\mathcal{S}_{j-1}$

For $j = 1$ to n do
  Set $\mathcal{S}_j = \emptyset$;
  /*the exact dynamic program:
  For each $(j-1, t_{1'}, t_1, \mathcal{T} = (t_2, \ldots, t_m), v_1, v_2) \in \mathcal{S}_{j-1}$ do
    /*Alternative 1: schedule job j on machine M_1 before B_1:
    If $t_{1'} + p_j \le B_1$, then
      set $\mathcal{S}_j \leftarrow \mathcal{S}_j \cup \{(j, t_{1'} + p_j, t_1, \mathcal{T}, v_1 + t_{1'} + p_j, v_2 + \max\{t_{1'} + p_j - C_j(\pi^*), 0\})\}$;
    Endif
    /*Alternative 2: assign job j to machine M_1 after F_1:
      set $\mathcal{S}_j \leftarrow \mathcal{S}_j \cup \{(j, t_{1'}, t_1 + p_j, \mathcal{T}, v_1 + F_1 + t_1 + p_j, v_2 + \max\{F_1 + t_1 + p_j - C_j(\pi^*), 0\})\}$;
    For $i = 2$ to m do
      /*Alternative 3: schedule job j on machine M_i:
      set $\mathcal{S}_j \leftarrow \mathcal{S}_j \cup \{(j, t_{1'}, t_1, \mathcal{T}', v_1 + t_i + p_j, v_2 + \max\{t_i + p_j - C_j(\pi^*), 0\})\}$,
        where $\mathcal{T}' = (t_2, \ldots, t_{i-1}, t_i + p_j, t_{i+1}, \ldots, t_m)$;
    Endfor
  Endfor
  [*Elimination*] /* Update set $\mathcal{S}_j$ */
  1. For any two states $(j, t_{1'}, t_1, \mathcal{T} = (t_2, \ldots, t_m), v_1, v_2)$ and $(j, t'_{1'}, t'_1, \mathcal{T}' = (t'_2, \ldots, t'_m), v'_1, v'_2)$ in $\mathcal{S}_j$, where $(t_1, t_2, \ldots, t_m, v_1, v_2)$ and $(t'_1, t'_2, \ldots, t'_m, v'_1, v'_2)$ fall within the same $(m+2)$-dimensional subinterval with $t_{1'} \le t'_{1'}$, eliminate the latter state from set $\mathcal{S}_j$;
  2. For any two states $(j, t_{1'}, t_1, \mathcal{T}, v_1, v_2)$ and $(j, t_{1'}, t_1, \mathcal{T}, v_1, v'_2)$ with $v_2 \le v'_2$, eliminate the second state from set $\mathcal{S}_j$;
  3. For any two states $(j, t_{1'}, t_1, \mathcal{T}, v_1, v_2)$ and $(j, t_{1'}, t_1, \mathcal{T}, v'_1, v_2)$ with $v_1 \le v'_1$, eliminate the second state from set $\mathcal{S}_j$;
  4. For any two states $(j, t_{1'}, t_1, \mathcal{T}, v_1, v_2)$ and $(j, \mathcal{B}, t_{1'}, t'_1, \mathcal{T}, v_1, v_2)$ with $t_1 \le t'_1$, eliminate the latter state from set $\mathcal{S}_j$;
  5. For any two states $(j, t_{1'}, t_1, \mathcal{T} = (t_{m_1+1}, \ldots, t_{k-1}, t_k, t_{k+1}, \ldots, t_m), v_1, v_2)$ and $(j, t_{1'}, t_1, \mathcal{T} = (t_{m_1+1}, \ldots, t_{k-1}, t'_k, t_{k+1}, \ldots, t_m), v_1, v_2)$ with $t_k \le t'_k$, eliminate the latter state from set $\mathcal{S}_j$;
Endfor

Step 4. [*Result*] The same as that in Algorithm *STDP*.

Lemma 2.4.4 *For any eliminated state* $(j, t_{1'}, t_1, \mathcal{T} = (t_2, \ldots, t_m), v_1, v_2) \in \mathcal{S}_j$, *there exists a non-dominated state* $(j, t'_{1'}, t'_1, \mathcal{T}' = (t'_2, \ldots, t'_m), v'_1, v'_2)$ *such that* $t'_{1'} \leq t_{1'}$, $t'_k \leq \delta^j t_k$, $k = 1, \ldots, m$, $v'_1 \leq \delta^j v_1$, *and* $v'_2 \leq \delta^j v_2$.

Proof The proof is by induction on j. It is clear that the lemma holds for $j = 1$. As the induction hypothesis, we assume that the lemma holds for any $j = l - 1$, i.e., for any eliminated state $(l - 1, t_{1'}, t_1, \mathcal{T} = (t_2, \ldots, t_m), v_1, v_2) \in \mathcal{S}_{l-1}$, there exists a non-dominated state $(l - 1, t'_{1'}, t'_1, \mathcal{T}' = (t'_2, \ldots, t'_m), v'_1, v'_2)$ such that $t'_{1'} \leq t_{1'}$, $t'_k \leq \delta^{l-1} t_k$, $k = 1, \ldots, m$, $v'_1 \leq \delta^{l-1} v_1$, and $v'_2 \leq \delta^{l-1} v_2$. We show that the lemma holds for $j = l$.

Consider an arbitrary state $(l, t_{1'}, t_1, (t_2, \ldots, t_m), v_1, v_2) \in \mathcal{S}_l$. First, we assume that job l appears in the earlier schedule obtained under the exact dynamic program, where $t_{1'} \leq B_1$. While implementing Algorithm *STAA*, the state $(l, t_{1'}, t_1, \mathcal{T} = (t_2, \ldots, t_m), v_1, v_2)$ is constructed from $(l - 1, t_{1'} - p_l, t_1, (t_2, \ldots, t_m), v_1 - t_{1'}, v_2 - \max\{t_{1'} - C_l(\pi^*), 0\}) \in \mathcal{S}_{l-1}$. According to the induction assumption, there exists a state $(l - 1, t'_{1'}, t'_1, \mathcal{T}' = (t'_2, \ldots, t'_m), v'_1, v'_2)$ such that $t'_{1'} \leq t_{1'} - p_l$, $t'_k \leq \delta^{l-1} t_k, k = 1, \ldots, m, v'_1 \leq \delta^{l-1}(v_1 - t_{1'})$, and $v'_2 \leq \delta^{l-1}(v_2 - \max\{t_{1'} - C_l(\pi^*), 0\})$. On the other hand, since $t'_{1'} + p_l \leq t_{1'} \leq B_1$, the state $(l - 1, t'_{1'} + p_l, t'_1, \mathcal{T}', v'_1 + t'_{1'} + p_l, v'_2 + \max\{t'_{1'} + p_l - C_l(\pi^*), 0\})$ is generated under the exact dynamic program. It follows directly from the elimination procedure that there exists a state $(l - 1, \widetilde{t_{1'}}, \widetilde{t_1}, \widetilde{\mathcal{T}} = (\widetilde{t_2}, \ldots, \widetilde{t_m}), \widetilde{v_1}, \widetilde{v_2})$ such that

(a) $\widetilde{t_{1'}} \leq t'_{1'} + p_l \leq t_{1'}$,
(b) $\widetilde{t_k} \leq \delta t'_k \leq \delta^l t_k, k = 1, \ldots, m$,
(c) $\widetilde{v_1} \leq \delta(v'_1 + t'_{1'} + p_l) \leq \delta(v'_1 + t_{1'}) \leq \delta(v'_1 + \delta^{l-1} t_{1'}) \leq \delta\delta^{l-1} v_1 = \delta^l v_1$, and
(d) $\widetilde{v_2} \leq \delta(v'_2 + \max\{t'_{1'} + p_l - C_l(\pi^*), 0\}) \leq$
$\delta(v'_2 + \max\{t_{1'} - C_l(\pi^*), 0\}) \leq \delta(v'_2 + \delta^{l-1} \max\{t_{1'} - C_l(\pi^*), 0\}) \leq \delta^l v_2$.

It follows that the induction hypothesis holds for $j = l$ when job l appears in the earlier schedule obtained under the exact dynamic program.

We now assume, without loss of generality, that job l appears in the later schedule on machine M_1 obtained under the exact dynamic program. While implementing Algorithm *STAA*, the state $(l, t_{1'}, t_1, \mathcal{T} = (t_2, \ldots, t_m), v_1, v_2)$ is constructed from $(l - 1, t_{1'}, t_1 - p_l, \mathcal{T}, v_1 - t_1 - F_1, v_2 - \max\{F_1 + t_1 - C_l(\pi^*), 0\}) \in \mathcal{S}_{l-1}$. According to the induction assumption, there exists a state $(l - 1, t'_{1'}, t'_1, \mathcal{T}' = (t'_2, \ldots, t'_m), v'_1, v'_2)$ such that $t'_{1'} \leq t_{1'}, t'_1 \leq \delta^{l-1}(t_1 - p_l), t'_k \leq \delta^{l-1} t_k, k = 2, \ldots, m$, $v'_1 \leq \delta^{l-1}(v_1 - t_1 - F_1)$, and $v'_2 \leq \delta^{l-1}(v_2 - \max\{F_1 + t_1 - C_l(\pi^*), 0\})$. On the other hand, the state $(l - 1, t'_{1'}, t'_1 + p_l, \mathcal{T}', v'_1 + F_1 + t'_1 + p_l, v'_2 + \max\{F_1 + t'_1 + p_l - C_l(\pi^*), 0\})$ is generated under the exact dynamic program. It follows directly from the elimination procedure that there exists a state $(l - 1, \widetilde{t_{1'}}, \widetilde{t_1}, \widetilde{\mathcal{T}} = (\widetilde{t_2}, \ldots, \widetilde{t_m}), \widetilde{v_1}, \widetilde{v_2})$ such that

(a) $\widetilde{t_{1'}} \leq t'_{1'} \leq t_{1'}$,
(b) $\widetilde{t_1} \leq \delta(t'_1 + p_l) \leq \delta(t'_1 + \delta^{l-1} p_l) \leq \delta\delta^{l-1} t_1 = \delta^l t_1$,
(c) $\widetilde{t_k} \leq \delta t'_k \leq \delta^l t_k, k = 2, \ldots, m$,
(d) $\widetilde{v_1} \leq \delta(v'_1 + F_1 + t'_1 + p_l) \leq \delta(v'_1 + \delta^{l-1} F_1 + (t'_1 + \delta^{l-1} p_l)) \leq \delta(v'_1 + \delta^{l-1} F_1 + \delta^{l-1} t_1) \leq \delta\delta^{l-1} v_1 = \delta^l v_1$, and

(e) $\widetilde{v_2} \le \delta(v_2' + \max\{F_1 + t_1' + p_l - C_l(\pi^*), 0\}) \le \delta(v_2' + \delta^{l-1}\max\{F_1 + t_1 - C_l(\pi^*), 0\}) \le \delta^l v_2$.

This establishes that the induction hypothesis holds for $l = j$ when job j appears in the later schedule on machine M_1 obtained under the exact dynamic program. The case where job l appears in the later schedule on each of the other machines obtained under the exact dynamic program can be similarly proved. Thus, the result follows. □

Theorem 2.4.5 *For any $\varepsilon > 0$ and a Pareto-optimal point $(\overline{\mathcal{V}}, \overline{\mathfrak{V}})$, algorithm STAA finds in $O\left(\frac{n^{m+3}L^{m+2}}{\varepsilon^{m+2}}\right)$ time a solution pair $(\mathcal{V}, \mathfrak{V})$ such that $\mathcal{V} \le (1+\varepsilon)\overline{\mathcal{V}}$ and $\mathfrak{V} \le (1+\varepsilon)\overline{\mathfrak{V}}$.*

Proof Let $\delta = 1 + \frac{\varepsilon}{2(1+\varepsilon)n}$ and $(n, t_{1'}, t_1, (t_2, \ldots, t_m), \overline{\mathcal{V}}, \overline{\mathfrak{V}})$ be a state corresponding to the Pareto-optimal point $(\overline{\mathcal{V}}, \overline{\mathfrak{V}})$. By the proof of Lemma 2.4.4, for $(n, t_{1'}, t_1, (t_2, \ldots, t_m), \overline{\mathcal{V}}, \overline{\mathfrak{V}})$, there exists a non-eliminated state $(n, \widetilde{t_{1'}}, \widetilde{t_1}, (\widetilde{t_2}, \ldots, \widetilde{t_m}), \mathcal{V}, \mathfrak{V})$ such that $\mathcal{V} \le \delta^n\overline{\mathcal{V}}$ and $\mathfrak{V} \le \delta^n\overline{\mathfrak{V}}$. It follows from $\left(1 + \frac{x}{n}\right)^n \le 1 + 2x$, for any $0 \le x \le 1$, that $\left(1 + \frac{\varepsilon}{2(1+\varepsilon)n}\right)^n \le 1 + \frac{\varepsilon}{1+\varepsilon} \le 1 + \varepsilon$, so $\mathcal{V} \le \delta^n\overline{\mathcal{V}} \le (1+\varepsilon)\overline{\mathcal{V}}$ and $\mathfrak{V} \le \delta^n\overline{\mathfrak{V}} \le (1+\varepsilon)\overline{\mathfrak{V}}$.

For the time complexity of Algorithm *STAA*, Step 1 requires $O(1)$ time. For each iteration j, note that we partition the interval $\mathcal{I}_1$ into $L_1 = \lceil \log_\delta P \rceil = \lceil \ln P / \ln \delta \le \lceil (1 + 2n(1+\varepsilon)/\varepsilon) \ln P \rceil$ subintervals, where the last inequality is obtained from the well-known inequality $\ln x \ge (x-1)/x$ for all $x \ge 1$, and we partition the intervals $\mathcal{I}_2$ and $\mathcal{I}_3$ into $L_2 = \lceil \log_\delta(n(F_1 + P)(1+\varepsilon)) \rceil \le \lceil (1 + 2n(1+\varepsilon)/\varepsilon) \ln(n(F_1 + P)(1+\varepsilon)) \rceil$ subintervals and $L_3 = \lceil \log_\delta(n \max\{F_1, C_S - p_{\min}\}(1+\varepsilon)) \rceil \le \lceil (1 + 2n(1+\varepsilon)/\varepsilon) \ln(n \max\{F_1, P - p_{\min}\}(1+\varepsilon)) \rceil$ subintervals, respectively. So we have $|S_j| \le (\lceil (1 + 2n(1+\varepsilon)/\varepsilon) \ln P \rceil)^m \lceil (1 + 2n(1+\varepsilon)/\varepsilon) \ln(n(F_1 + P)(1+\varepsilon)) \rceil \lceil (1 + 2n(1+\varepsilon)/\varepsilon) \ln(n \max\{F_1, P - p_{\min}\}(1+\varepsilon)) \rceil = O\left(\frac{n^{m+2}L^{m+2}}{\varepsilon^{m+2}}\right)$ after the elimination process, while Step 2 takes $O\left(\frac{n^{m+3}L^{m+2}}{\varepsilon^{m+2}}\right)$ time. Thus, the overall time complexity of Algorithm *STAA* is $O\left(\frac{n^{m+3}L^{m+2}}{\varepsilon^{m+2}}\right)$ indeed. □

2.4.3 *The Performance of Algorithms* STDP *and* STAA

We performed numerical studies by varying the problem size to evaluate the performance of Algorithms *STDP* and *STAA*. We carried out an experimental study analogous to the one conducted for assessing the performance of Algorithm *SMDP* in Sect. 2.3.2. In this experiment we focused on finding a Pareto-optimal solution by applying Algorithm *STDP* and an approximate Pareto solution by applying Algorithm *STAA* for a given $\overline{Q}$ in various parameter settings. We tested our algorithms on three classes of randomly generated instances:

(i) $m = 2$ and $m_1 = 1$, the job processing times p_j were randomly drawn from the uniform distribution (1, 20), $B_1 = \lfloor P/8 \rfloor, \lfloor P/6 \rfloor$, and $\lfloor P/4 \rfloor$, $\mathcal{D} = \lfloor P/80 \rfloor$, $\lfloor P/50 \rfloor$, and $\lfloor P/30 \rfloor$, and $\varepsilon = 0.3, 0.5$, and 0.8;
(ii) $m > 2$ and $m_1 = 1$, the job processing times p_j were randomly drawn from the uniform distribution (1, 20), and B_1, $\mathcal{D}$, and ε were chosen randomly from the sets $\{\lfloor P/8 \rfloor, \lfloor P/6 \rfloor, \lfloor P/4 \rfloor\}$, $\{\lfloor P/80 \rfloor, \lfloor P/50 \rfloor, \lfloor P/30 \rfloor\}$, and $\{0.3, 0.5, 0.8\}$, respectively;
(iii) $m = 3$ and $m_1 = 1, 2, 3$, the job processing times p_j were randomly drawn from the uniform distribution (1, 20), and B_1 and $\mathcal{D}$ were chosen randomly from the sets $\{\lfloor P/8 \rfloor, \lfloor P/6 \rfloor, \lfloor P/4 \rfloor\}$ and $\{\lfloor P/80 \rfloor, \lfloor P/50 \rfloor, \lfloor P/30 \rfloor\}$, respectively.

Instance classes (i) and (ii) are used to analyze the impacts of disruption start time, disruption duration, and ε, and the impact of number of machines on the performance of Algorithms *STDP* and *STAA*, respectively, while instance class (iii) is used to analyze the impact of number of disrupted machines on the performance of Algorithm *STDP*. For instance class (i), we tested our algorithms on instances with $n = 50, 80$, and 100 jobs; and for instance classes (ii) and (iii), we went no further than instances with 70 jobs, since larger instances took too much time to solve. For each combination of n and instance class (i), we generated 30 instances; and for each combination of n and instance classes (ii) and (iii), we generated 20 instances.

Let $(\mathcal{V}^i, \mathfrak{V}^i)$ be a Pareto-optimal solution and $(\widetilde{\mathcal{V}}^i, \widetilde{\mathfrak{V}}^i)$ be an approximate Pareto solution for instance i, where $i = 1, \ldots, 20$ or 30. For instance i, $i = 1, \ldots, 20$ or 30, we define $\Delta_i^{v_1} = \frac{\widetilde{\mathcal{V}}^i - \mathcal{V}^i}{\mathcal{V}^i} \leq \varepsilon$ and $\Delta_i^{v_2} = \frac{\widetilde{\mathfrak{V}}^i - \mathfrak{V}^i}{\mathfrak{V}^i} \leq \varepsilon$ as the relative deviation of the approximate solution from the efficient solution with respect to the total completion time and total virtual tardiness, respectively. For each combination of n, B_1, D, and ε, we recorded the average and maximum numbers of states generated by both Algorithms *STDP* and *STAA*, the average times required to obtain the Pareto-optimal and approximate Pareto solutions, and the average and maximum relative deviations.

Tables 2.2, 2.3 and 2.4 summarize the results of the experimental study for instance class (i) with $n = 50$, $n = 80$, and $n = 100$, respectively.

We make the following observations from Tables 2.2, 2.3 and 2.4.

- As the disruption start time increases, the number of states increases, so the time required to solve an instance also increases for both algorithms;
- Algorithm *STAA* does not perform better than Algorithm *STDP* as expected. The reasons are twofold. One is that in each iteration j, there are two new states generated from each state in $\mathcal{S}_j$ in Algorithm *STDP*, while in Algorithm *STAA* there are three new states generated. Another is that δ becomes small as the problem size increases, so it becomes more difficult for the quaternarys (t_1, t_2, v_1, v_2) to fall within the same 4-dimensional subinterval, implying that the elimination rule 1 in Algorithm *STAA* cannot efficiently eliminate the dominated states;
- The benefits of Algorithm *STAA* are particularly evident when the number of jobs is large.

Tables 2.5 and 2.6 summarize the results of the experimental study for instance classes (ii) and (iii), respectively. Different from Tables 2.1, 2.2, 2.3 and 2.4,

Table 2.2 A comparison between algorithm STDP and Algorithm STAA for $m = 2$ and $n = 50$

B_1	D	ε	Performances of the Algorithm *STDP*			Performances of the Algorithm *STAA*			Δ_i^{v1}		Δ_i^{v2}		Number of infeasible solution
			Avg. number of triples	Max. number of triples	Avg. running time (s)	Avg. number of triples	Max. number of triples	Avg. running time (s)	Avg.	Max.	Avg.	Max.	
$\lfloor p/8 \rfloor$	$\lfloor p/80 \rfloor$	0.3	14671.60	20,297	25.172	13653.80	18,862	23.07	4.45E−05	2.23E−04	8.84E−03	3.45E−02	0
		0.5	15717.20	19,747	23.76	14323.00	16,600	21.13	3.64E−05	1.82E−04	9.49E−03	1.72E−02	1
		0.8	13724.40	18,732	21.29	12082.60	15,119	18.09	0	0	1.06E−02	1.28E−02	0
	$\lfloor p/50 \rfloor$	0.3	12849.60	15,676	16.62	12275.60	15,476	16.52	0	0	3.25E−03	8.33E−03	0
		0.5	13638.40	14,609	18.82	12662.40	13,903	17.69	0	0	4.69E−03	8.55E−03	1
		0.8	13829.80	16,843	19.71	12671.00	14,882	17.96	4.11E−05	2.05E−04	1.06E−02	2.31E−02	0
	$\lfloor p/30 \rfloor$	0.3	14715.00	17,258	21.54	13590.60	14,917	19.74	3.97E−05	1.99E−04	2.56E−03	4.59E−03	0
		0.5	14890.00	17,455	21.60	13874.00	16,103	20.25	0	0	4.68E−03	5.78E−03	1
		0.8	13715.80	15,767	19.03	12462.40	14,338	17.31	3.49E−05	1.74E−04	5.98E−03	1.61E−02	1
$\lfloor p/6 \rfloor$	$\lfloor p/80 \rfloor$	0.3	17812.60	23,076	37.59	16537.00	20,647	33.63	4.68E−05	2.34E−04	2.16E−02	6.06E−02	1
		0.5	18386.60	26,200	41.70	16557.60	21,866	35.04	0	0	1.97E−02	5.63E−02	0
		0.8	18824.60	22,800	41.99	16744.80	20,301	34.74	8.91E−05	2.32E−04	1.77E−02	5.26E−02	0
	$\lfloor p/50 \rfloor$	0.3	16375.60	20,513	34.53	14988.00	18,926	30.20	0	0	5.17E−03	9.09E−03	0
		0.5	18669.20	23,497	40.76	16622.80	20,288	33.94	8.65E−05	4.32E−04	1.44E−02	5.51E−02	1
		0.8	20775.00	24,285	48.84	17892.80	19,172	37.80	0	0	6.93E−03	1.11E−02	0
	$\lfloor p/30 \rfloor$	0.3	18806.40	20,936	42.39	17423.80	19,841	37.62	0	0	4.50E−03	6.49E−03	0
		0.5	14754.80	19,210	27.67	13893.60	17,006	25.52	3.89E−05	1.94E−04	7.61E−03	2.14E−02	0
		0.8	16879.40	22,685	37.98	15453.80	21,153	33.25	3.68E−05	1.84E−04	6.27E−03	1.52E−02	0
$\lfloor p/4 \rfloor$	$\lfloor p/80 \rfloor$	0.3	24345.20	29,529	92.09	22554.60	27,692	79.26	3.70E−05	1.85E−04	1.49E−02	3.75E−02	1
		0.5	23275.80	31,540	87.14	21276.20	27,945	72.674	3.77E−05	1.89E−04	2.54E−02	3.80E−02	0
		0.8	22523.40	27,464	80.54	20678.40	24,233	68.75	0	0	1.39E−02	2.86E−02	0
	$\lfloor p/50 \rfloor$	0.3	14605.60	24,622	48.26	13870.80	23,246	44.26	4.40E−05	2.20E−04	1.67E−02	4.76E−02	0
		0.5	20046.40	30,280	63.84	19005.00	28,960	59.10	0	0	9.26E−03	1.85E−02	1
		0.8	25112.80	29,892	101.68	22649.80	25,949	82.73	1.95E−04	7.64E−04	5.96E−02	2.19E−01	0
	$\lfloor p/30 \rfloor$	0.3	23668.80	25,967	89.25	21962.60	24,246	77.09	4.23E−05	2.11E−04	7.52E−03	2.27E−02	0
		0.5	25729.80	30,160	104.09	24229.80	28,520	92.92	3.27E−05	1.63E−04	5.61E−03	1.60E−02	0
		0.8	22790.00	31,202	83.28	20658.00	27,495	69.64	0	0	6.70E−03	9.62E−03	1

Table 2.3 A comparison between Algorithm STDP and Algorithm STAA for $m = 2$ and $n = 80$

B_1	D	ε	Performances of the Algorithm *STDP*			Performances of the Algorithm *STAA*			Δ_i^{v1}		Δ_i^{v2}		Number of infeasible solution
			Avg. number of triples	Max. number of triples	Avg. running time (s)	Avg. number of triples	Max. number of triples	Avg. running time (s)	Avg.	Max.	Avg.	Max.	
$\lfloor p/8 \rfloor$	$\lfloor p/80 \rfloor$	0.3	48853.20	57,393	166.06	43531.80	49,634	134.17	3.41E−05	8.64E−05	5.52E−03	1.29E−02	0
		0.5	56176.80	71,089	225.20	48104.60	57,299	165.42	0	0	4.89E−03	5.41E−03	0
		0.8	57833.60	69,299	225.96	50089.20	61,360	175.05	0	0	4.55E−03	5.24E−03	0
	$\lfloor p/50 \rfloor$	0.3	56251.60	65,603	224.44	49379.40	54,662	173.33	0	0	1.84E−03	3.39E−03	0
		0.5	53262.20	68,947	203.91	44873.80	50,467	144.58	0	0	1.95E−03	3.53E−03	0
		0.8	55434.60	64,209	212.57	45714.60	51,411	149.85	3.15E−05	8.06E−05	5.92E−03	1.17E−02	0
	$\lfloor p/30 \rfloor$	0.3	56969.80	65,982	227.09	50915.00	56,388	182.00	6.22E−05	2.34E−04	2.76E−03	5.21E−03	0
		0.5	44785.40	51,804	143.58	39352.00	45,530	115.03	0	0	1.88E−03	2.03E−03	0
		0.8	52984.20	60,350	201.41	45333.80	50,582	148.92	1.56E−05	7.78E−05	3.13E−03	6.84E−03	0
$\lfloor p/6 \rfloor$	$\lfloor p/80 \rfloor$	0.3	69871.80	80,951	415.71	58774.40	62,439	288.90	0	0	6.22E−03	7.14E−03	0
		0.5	72365.00	86,473	443.95	61678.40	69,756	319.30	0	0	5.49E−03	6.71E−03	0
		0.8	75316.20	90,732	475.43	60162.80	69,494	296.69	0	0	4.51E−03	6.02E−03	0
	$\lfloor p/50 \rfloor$	0.3	76450.60	90,437	491.30	66127.60	80,463	362.72	0	0	2.78E−03	3.75E−03	0
		0.5	66111.80	90,064	444.85	55291.20	79,949	311.38	0	0	1.99E−03	3.70E−03	1
		0.8	76312.60	83,662	490.08	65324.80	72,065	354.24	0	0	2.61E−03	3.52E−03	0
	$\lfloor p/30 \rfloor$	0.3	69035.20	81,815	411.65	60201.80	67,929	309.39	0	0	2.03E−03	2.42E−03	0
		0.5	74708.00	91,732	485.20	62780.00	76,907	338.08	3.06E−05	8.06E−05	1.24E−03	2.35E−03	0
		0.8	62540.20	77,919	371.73	50996.40	61,362	237.89	0	0	1.64E−03	2.16E−03	0
$\lfloor p/4 \rfloor$	$\lfloor p/80 \rfloor$	0.3	92613.60	99,770	942.91	79931.80	82,783	686.51	1.73E−05	8.67E−05	1.46E−02	4.19E−02	0
		0.5	72072.40	98,556	686.42	61905.80	83,686	492.64	3.42E−05	9.59E−05	1.34E−02	3.82E−02	0
		0.8	89633.00	138,368	1035.73	72876.00	111,634	660.78	3.38E−05	1.05E−04	1.35E−02	3.78E−02	0
	$\lfloor p/50 \rfloor$	0.3	100733.80	111,183	1115.05	86193.40	92,564	793.27	0	0	1.76E−03	4.50E−03	0
		0.5	64352.00	103,409	622.11	53385.80	85,747	411.01	0	0	5.11E−03	5.35E−03	0
		0.8	92696.80	141,811	1016.62	77378.00	108,900	675.21	0	0	4.63E−03	4.93E−03	0
	$\lfloor p/30 \rfloor$	0.3	92520.20	103,670	960.48	79750.20	89,232	701.34	1.57E−05	7.83E−05	3.98E−03	1.17E−02	0
		0.5	87923.60	104,571	879.50	76995.60	93,838	661.79	0	0	2.83E−03	3.23E−03	0
		0.8	79774.60	95,863	730.30	66392.40	81,873	494.18	0	0	3.21E−03	3.57E−03	0

Table 2.4 A comparison between Algorithm STDP and Algorithm STAA for $m = 2$ and $n = 100$

B_1	D	ε	Performances of the Algorithm *STDP*			Performances of the Algorithm *STAA*			Δ_i^{v1}		Δ_i^{v2}		Number of infeasible solution
			Avg. number of triples	Max. number of triples	Avg. running time (s)	Avg. number of triples	Max. number of triples	Avg. running time (s)	Avg.	Max.	Avg.	Max.	
$\lfloor p/8 \rfloor$	$\lfloor p/80 \rfloor$	0.3	102384.80	112,750	623.77	84596.00	89941	422.41	9.87E−06	4.93E−05	4.75E−03	1.11E−02	0
		0.5	111313.20	135675	740.53	88817.80	104,351	463.16	0	0	2.37E−03	3.79E−03	0
		0.8	107853.40	120,754	673.86	85827.20	92,366	421.28	0	0	2.86E−03	3.02E−03	1
	$\lfloor p/50 \rfloor$	0.3	88003.20	97,860	473.21	71309.40	77,460	308.48	0	0	2.13E−03	2.49E−03	1
		0.5	90375.20	101,640	492.24	78220.40	81,812	368.34	0	0	1.91E−03	2.02E−03	0
		0.8	96500.40	103,211	552.75	77956.20	83,086	358.41	0	0	1.85E−03	1.95E−03	0
	$\lfloor p/30 \rfloor$	0.3	85251.40	117,752	490.01	69745.00	91,530	326.86	3.28E−05	5.91E−05	2.63E−03	7.41E−03	0
		0.5	84709.60	105,162	467.94	69518.80	83,528	310.66	9.77E−06	4.88E−05	1.75E−03	4.26E−03	0
		0.8	87061.40	92,097	462.68	72286.00	79,603	323.30	3.10E−05	1.00E−04	1.22E−03	1.38E−03	0
$\lfloor p/6 \rfloor$	$\lfloor p/80 \rfloor$	0.3	127267.40	140,259	1133.82	106142.20	113,152	794.57	4.31E−05	1.59E−04	1.70E−02	6.63E−02	0
		0.5	134547.60	160,433	1323.18	105713.80	120,795	798.04	1.17E−05	5.87E−05	6.64E−03	1.87E−02	0
		0.8	145354.60	169,646	1518.93	111685.60	121,502	862.63	1.93E−05	5.08E−05	4.09E−03	9.68E−03	0
	$\lfloor p/50 \rfloor$	0.3	132494.20	154,301	1269.80	110590.40	122,296	865.57	2.08E−05	5.78E−05	6.14E−03	1.25E−02	1
		0.5	123410.60	131,286	1098.35	101660.80	111,610	734.74	1.04E−05	5.22E−05	4.37E−03	1.27E−02	2
		0.8	108277.40	138,856	893.62	84539.40	104,328	551.41	1.12E−05	5.59E−05	1.94E−03	2.81E−03	0
	$\lfloor p/30 \rfloor$	0.3	101112.20	131,326	836.69	82791.20	109,556	543.87	2.02E−05	1.01E−04	3.03E−03	9.88E−03	0
		0.5	115060.60	128,438	1010.72	92650.80	98,661	640.74	1.08E−05	5.40E−05	1.12E−03	1.58E−03	1
		0.8	125590.00	145,032	1149.10	102462.60	110,347	748.20	1.01E−05	5.04E−05	8.26E−04	1.48E−03	0
$\lfloor p/4 \rfloor$	$\lfloor p/80 \rfloor$	0.3	156900.60	174,772	2332.13	127149.80	150,739	1468.45	1.07E−05	5.33E−05	4.97E−03	5.13E−03	0
		0.5	139667.00	165,600	1779.92	116461.20	141,117	1201.93	0	0	5.16E−03	5.92E−03	0
		0.8	174297.40	200,929	2800.72	134702.20	148,204	1564.48	9.91E−06	4.96E−05	6.03E−03	1.52E−02	0
	$\lfloor p/50 \rfloor$	0.3	135820.20	202311	2083.66	113193.20	171,235	1419.31	2.12E−05	6.08E−05	6.67E−03	1.38E−02	1
		0.5	165788.00	195037	2543.35	136933.60	149,168	1661.57	2.32E−05	1.16E−04	3.59E−03	6.23E−03	0
		0.8	142354.20	153,697	1917.58	118787.60	127,067	1281.90	0	0	3.30E−03	3.57E−03	0
	$\lfloor p/30 \rfloor$	0.3	153036.40	176,658	2275.56	126913.80	147,437	1498.56	1.03E−05	5.16E−05	1.56E−03	2.10E−03	0
		0.5	125955.33	133,073	104956.33	112331.00	1539.75	1037.60	0	0	1.99E−03	2.14E−03	0
		0.8	153468.20	164422	2210.93	125777.20	129,604	1434.12	1.00E−05	5.02E−05	2.63E−03	5.21E−03	1

Tables 2.5 and 2.6 also report the number of jobs in a problem that the corresponding algorithm cannot solve within 3,600 s.

We make the following observations from Tables 2.5 and 2.6.

- When there is only one disrupted machine, i.e., $m_1 = 1$, the number of jobs that Algorithms *STDP* and *STAA* are capable of solving within 3,600 s decreases and Algorithm *STAA* generates more Pareto-optimal points as the number of machines increases;
- As stated above, Algorithm *STAA* does not perform better than Algorithm *STDP* as expected;
- As expected, Algorithm *STDP* performs poorly as the number of disrupted machines increases.

2.5 Summary

In this chapter we introduce a rescheduling model in which both the original scheduling criterion, i.e., the total completion time, and the deviation cost associated with a disruption of the planned schedule in the presence of machine breakdowns are taken into account. The disruption cost is measured as the maximum time deviation or the total virtual tardiness with respect to the planned schedule. For each variant, we show that the case where the number of machines is considered to be part of the input is $\mathcal{NP}$-hard in the strong sense, and develop a pseudo-polynomial time algorithm for finding the set of Pareto-optimal solutions for the case with a fixed number of machines, establishing that it is $\mathcal{NP}$-hard in the ordinary sense. For the variant where the disruption cost is modelled as the total virtual tardiness and the machine disruption occurs only on one of the machines, we also develop a two-dimensional FPTAS. Several important issues are interesting for future research. However, whether there is a two-dimensional FPTAS or a constant ratio approximation algorithm for the problems $Pm, h_{m_1 1}|\tau, [B_i, F_i]_{1\leq i\leq m_1}|(\sum_{j=1}^{n} C_j, \Delta_{\max})$ and $Pm, h_{m_1 1}|\tau, [B_i, F_i]_{1\leq i\leq m_1}|(\sum_{j=1}^{n} C_j, \sum_{j=1}^{n} T_j)$ is still unclear.

2.6 Bibliographic Remarks

In recent years rescheduling in dynamic environments has attracted much attention in scheduling research. The optimal baseline schedule for the jobs with respect to a given system performance measure (such as the makespan, total completion time etc) can easily be interrupted by the occurrence of unexpected events (disruptions), which renders the existing schedule no longer optimal or even infeasible. The need for rescheduling in response to unexpected changes that take place in the production environment is commonplace in modern flexible manufacturing systems. Managers and production planners must not only generate high quality schedules, but also react

Table 2.5 A comparison between Algorithm STDP and Algorithm STAA for $m \geq 3$ and $m_1 = 1$

	n	Performances of the Algorithm *STDP*			Performances of the Algorithm *STAA*			Δ_i^{v1}		Δ_i^{v2}		Number of infeasible solution
		Avg. number of triples	Max. number of triples	Avg. running time (s)	Avg. number of triples	Max. number of triples	Avg. running time (s)	Avg.	Max.	Avg.	Max.	
3	10	189.20	331	0.61	161.40	331	0.74	0	0	2.00E−01	5.00E−01	0
	20	3153.20	5233	2.75	2545.20	5047	2.72	0	0	1.25E−02	6.25E−02	0
	30	11303.40	13575	15.08	9655.80	11515	12.51	1.45E−04	7.26E−04	7.39E−02	2.08E−01	0
	40	30987.00	39949	102.26	26735.80	37746	81.01	8.83E−05	4.42E−04	4.01E−02	1.20E−01	0
	50	66465.17	125348	553.88	58672.47	105025	430.07	8.75E−06	2.63E−04	1.07E−01	2.14E−01	1
	60	113994.60	1373.39	105033.20	110060	1169.13	0	0	1.88E−02	3.57E−02	0	
	70	–	–	–	–	–	–	–	–	–	–	–
4	10	129.80	213	0.64	88.00	205	0.80	0	0	5.71E−02	2.86E−01	1
	20	6609.40	13905	10.95	5048.80	9294	6.45	4.82E−04	2.41E−03	6.33E−01	3.00E+00	0
	30	45481.20	74698	357.94	33280.20	56087	207.57	0	0	2.50E−02	1.25E−01	0
	40	100693.40	140254	1076.71	72664.00	114804	635.56	0	0	2.04E−01	5.71E−01	0
	50	157583.60	192774	2560.24	136377.80	193625	2135.09	0	0	1.80E−02	4.17E−02	2
	60	–	–	–	–	–	–	–	–	–	–	–
5	10	163.00	203	0.70	104.80	203	0.89	1.53E−03	7.63E−03	0	0	0
	20	10804.60	24128	28.09	5383.20	13339	8.79	0	0	0	0	0
	30	73022.60	138175	1438.16	68594.60	155146	1276.06	2.29E−04	1.15E−03	3.45E−01	1.50E+00	1
	40	144347.40	181805	2485.44	129444.00	179408	1907.24	0	0	5.00E−02	2.50E−01	2
	50	–	–	–	–	–	–	–	–	–	–	–
6	10	208.20	355	0.78	134.60	182	0.99	0.00	0.00	0.00	0.00	0
	20	9595.20	35323	43.10	5616.00	20069	15.63	0.00	0.00	0.00	0.00	0
	30	71310.80	151696	1723.63	73947.40	156208	1699.88	0.00	0.00	5.56E−02	1.67E−01	2
	40	–	–	–	–	–	–	–	–	–	–	–
7	10	163.80	229	0.81	125.20	229	1.09	0.00	0.00	0.00	0.00	0
	20	8283.40	21096	17.92	5432.40	11653	8.66	0.00	0.00	0.00	0.00	0
	30	110707.40	134262	2349.56	84714.40	175177	1867.76	0.00	0.00	0.00	0.00	2
	40	–	–	–	–	–	–	–	–	–	–	–
8	10	160.60	209	0.91	143.00	209	1.21	0.00	0.00	0.00	0.00	0
	20	3340.80	3999	2.80	2221.60	3758	2.85	0.00	0.00	0.00	0.00	0
	30	99627.60	126664	2412.54	87502.40	154268	1859.12	0.00	0.00	0.00	0.00	2
	40	–	–	–	–	–	–	–	–	–	–	–

Table 2.6 A comparison between Algorithm STDP for $m = 3$ and $m_1 = 1, 2, 3$

m_1	n	Avg. number of triples	Max. number of triples	Avg. running time (s)
1	10	167.80	368	0.76
	15	838.60	1987	1.34
	20	2661.60	3907	2.57
	25	5164.40	8641	5.39
	30	11994.60	19,195	19.63
	40	42503.80	65,917	249.49
	50	86342.40	104,628	703.19
	60	113994.60	122,645	1373.39
	70	186330.00	208,293	3557.40
	$\geq$	–	–	–
2	10	1540.20	2143	1.36
	15	11621.80	21,681	44.08
	20	48947.80	62,809	480.62
	25	81454.80	93,116	3343.68
	30	–	–	–
3	10	8976.20	18,967	32.23
	15	60762.80	91,876	3503.86
	20	–	–	–

quickly to disruptions and revise their schedules in a cost-effective manner (Hall and Potts [53], Vieira et al. [145]). Examples of possible disruptions include changes in component release dates (Hall and Potts [55]), arrivals of new orders (Hall and Potts [54], Hall et al. [53], Hoogeveena et al. [63], Wang et al. [146, 147]), machine breakdowns (Huo and Zhao [64], Liu and Ro [88], Luo and Liu [93], Qi et al. [120], Rustogi and Strusevich [123], Xu et al. [159], Yin et al. [176, 177]), changes in job characteristics (Wu et al. [155]), and so on.

Rescheduling, which involves adjusting the original schedule to account for a disruption, is necessary in order to minimize the effects of the disruption on the performance of the system. This involves a trade-off between finding a cost-effective new schedule and avoiding excessive changes to the original schedule. The degree of disruption to the original schedule is often modelled as a constraint or part of the original scheduling objective (Hall and Potts [54], Hall et al. [53], Hoogeveena et al. [63], Liu and Ro [88], Jain and Foley [65], Qi et al. [120], Unal et al. [143], Yan et al. [160], Yang [161], Yuan and Mu [179]. Variants of the rescheduling problem can be found in many real-world applications such as automotive manufacturing (Bean et al. [14]), space shuttle missions (Zweben et al. [195]), shipbuilding (Clausen et al. [27]), short-range airline planning (Yu et al. [178]), deregulated power market (Dahal et al. [30]) etc.

The literature on rescheduling abounds. For recent reviews, the reader may refer to Aytug et al. [8], Billaut et al. [15], Ouelhadj and Petrovic [113], and Vieira et al. [145]. We review only studies on machine rescheduling with unexpected disruptions arising from machine breakdowns that are directly related to our work. Leon et al. [79] developed robustness measures and robust scheduling to deal with machine breakdowns and processing time variability when a right-shift repair strategy is used. Robustness is defined as the minimization of the bicriterion objective function comprising the expected makespan and expected delay, where the expected delay is the deviation between the deterministic makespan in the original and adjusted schedules. Their experimental results showed that robust schedules significantly outperform schedules based on the makespan alone. Ozlen and Azizoğlu [114] considered a rescheduling problem on unrelated parallel machines, where a disruption occurs on one of the machines. The scheduling measure is the total completion time and the deviation cost, which is the total disruption caused by the differences between the original and adjusted schedules. They developed polynomial-time algorithms to solve the following hierarchical optimization problems: minimizing the total disruption cost among the minimum total completion time schedules and minimizing the total completion time among the minimum total disruption cost schedules. Qi et al. [120] considered a rescheduling problem in the presence of a machine breakdown in both the single-machine and two parallel-machine settings with the objective of minimizing the total completion time plus different measures of time disruption. They provided polynomial-time algorithms and pseudo-polynomial-time algorithms for the problems under consideration. Zhao and Tang [186] extended some of their results to the case with linear deteriorating jobs. Liu and Ro [88] considered a rescheduling problem with machine unavailability on a single machine, where disruption is measured as the maximum time deviation between the original and adjusted schedules. Studying a general model where the maximum time disruption appears both as a constraint and as part of the scheduling objective, they provided a pseudo-polynomial-time algorithm, a constant factor approximation algorithm, and a fully polynomial-time approximation scheme when the scheduling objective is to minimize the makespan or maximum lateness.

In this chapter we address the issue of how to reschedule jobs in the presence of machine breakdowns. Compared with the problem in Ozlen and Azizoğlu [114], we consider the situation where machine breakdowns may occur on more than one machine, and the disruption start time and the duration of a machine disruption may differ on different machines. In addition, compared with the studies aforementioned which model the degree of disruption to the original schedule either as a constraint or part of the original scheduling objective, we focus on the trade-off between the total completion time of the adjusted schedule and schedule disruption by finding the set of Pareto-optimal solutions.

It is worth noting that the main results of this chapter come from Yin et al. [174].

Chapter 3
Parallel-Machine Rescheduling with Job Rejection in the Presence of Job Unavailability

This chapter focuses on a scheduling problem on identical parallel machines to minimize the total completion time under the assumption that all the jobs are available at time zero. However, before processing begins, some jobs are delayed and become unavailable at time zero, so all the jobs need to be rescheduled with a view to not causing excessive schedule disruption with respect to the planned schedule. To reduce the negative impact of job unavailability and achieve an acceptable service level, one option in rescheduling the jobs is to reject a subset of the jobs at a cost (the rejection cost). Three criteria are thus involved: the total completion time of the accepted jobs in the adjusted schedule, the degree of disruption measured by the maximum completion time disruption to any accepted job between the planned and adjusted schedules, and the total rejection cost. The overall objective is to minimize the former criterion, while keeping the objective values of the latter two criteria to no greater than the given limits. We present two exact methods to solve the problem: (i) A DP-based approach, establishing that the problem is $\mathcal{NP}$-hard in the ordinary sense when the number of machines is fixed. (ii) An enhanced branch-and-price method that includes several features such as execution of the differential evolution algorithm for finding good initial feasible solutions and solving the pricing sub-problem, inclusion of reduced cost fixing during the inner iterations of the algorithm, and use of a heuristic procedure for constructing a good integer feasible solution. To assess the efficiency of the proposed algorithms, we perform extensive computational experiments, the computational results of which demonstrate that the incorporated enhancements greatly improve the performance of the algorithm.

This part is composed of eight sections. In Sect. 3.1 we introduce the problem under study and formulate a mixed integer linear programming model. In Sects. 3.2 and 3.3 we present the properties of the optimal solution and provide a pseudo-polynomial time DP algorithm to solve the problem, respectively, establishing that it is $\mathcal{NP}$-hard in the ordinary sense when the number of machines is fixed. In Sects. 3.4 and 3.5 we present a column generation algorithm, and an exact branch-and-price

D. Wang et al., *Rescheduling Under Disruptions in Manufacturing Systems*,
Uncertainty and Operations Research, https://doi.org/10.1007/978-981-15-3528-4_3

algorithm incorporating several enhancements to improve its efficiency in solving the problem, respectively. In Sect. 3.6 we present computational results to evaluate the performance of the proposed algorithms. We conclude this chapter in Sect. 3.7, and end the chapter in Sect. 3.8 with bibliographic remarks.

3.1 Problem Formulation and Formulation

3.1.1 Problem Formulation

We describe the scheduling problem under study as follows: consider scheduling a set of non-preemptive jobs $J = \{J_1, J_2, \ldots, J_n\}$ to be processed on a set of identical parallel machines $M = \{M_1, M_2, \ldots, M_m\}$ that are all continuously available from time zero onwards on identical parallel machines. Each job J_j is initially available for processing at time zero and needs to be processed by one machine only with a processing requirement of length p_j, and each machine is capable of processing any job but at most one job at a time.

We assume that the jobs have been sequenced in an optimal schedule that minimizes the total completion time of the jobs. It is well known that the jobs should be scheduled in the SPT order with no idle time between them for this purpose, whereby the jobs are sequenced successively on the m machines, i.e., jobs $i, m+i, \ldots, m\lfloor n/m \rfloor + i$ are successively scheduled on machine i without any idle time, $i = 1, \ldots, m$, where $\lfloor x \rfloor$ denotes the largest integer less than or equal to x. Let π^* denote the sequence in which the jobs are scheduled in this SPT order. Based on this optimal schedule, commitments to customers have already been made, and a lot of preparation work, such as ordering raw materials, tooling the equipment, organizing the workforce etc, has been undertaken. However, before the execution of the schedule, the dates at which a subset of the jobs $R \subseteq N$, as a result of an unexpected disruption, will not be available for processing until some integer time $\gamma > 0$. It is assumed that this information becomes available after π^* has been determined, but before processing begins. If the new information becomes available after the start of processing, then the processed and partly processed jobs of N are removed from the problem. If $R = N$, then the problem is equivalent to a processing delay or machine breakdown that makes the machine unavailable during the interval $[0, \gamma]$.

Such unexpected events can disrupt the original SPT schedule and the corresponding resource allocation decisions. This necessitates rescheduling of the jobs in the SPT schedule with a view to not causing excessive schedule disruption with respect to the SPT schedule. We measure the disruption cost as the maximum completion time deviation of the jobs between the SPT and adjusted schedules.

To reduce the negative impact of job unavailability and achieve an acceptable service level, we have the option to reject the processing of some jobs in rescheduling, where each rejected job may either be outsourced or not be processed at all. Naturally, rejecting a job incurs an additional rejection cost due to either the outsourcing cost or the loss in income and customer goodwill. The rejection cost of job J_j is denoted as e_j for $j = 1, \ldots, n$. Denote the sets of accepted jobs and rejected jobs by A and $\overline{A}$, respectively. Since there is no need to schedule the set of rejected jobs, a schedule can be represented by a job sequence (permutation) $\rho = (S, \overline{A})$ in which the first $n_A = |A|$ jobs correspond to set A in the order of S and the last $n - n_A = |\overline{A}|$ jobs correspond to set $\overline{A}$ in any arbitrary sequence.

We focus on addressing the issue of *trade-off* among the total completion time of the scheduled jobs in the adjusted schedule, the disruption cost, and the total rejection cost. That is to say, the quality of a schedule ρ is measured by three criteria. The first is the original scheduling cost, i.e., the total completion time of the accepted jobs, i.e., $\sum_{J_j \in A} C_j$; the second is the total rejection cost representing either the total outsourcing cost or loss in income and customer goodwill, i.e., $\sum_{J_j \in \overline{A}} e_j$; and the third is a measure of the disruption cost of the accepted jobs in terms of the maximum completion time deviation with respect to the original SPT schedule, i.e., $\Delta_{\max} = \max_{J_j \in A} \Delta_j$.

The overall objective of the problem is to determine the rejected job set and the sequences of the accepted jobs on the machines in such a way that $\sum_{J_j \in A} C_j$ is minimized, while keeping $\sum_{J_j \in \overline{A}} e_j \le U$ and $\Delta_{\max} \le Q$, where U and Q are two given non-negative limits.

The constraint $\Delta_{\max} \le Q$ implies that, in a feasible schedule ρ, $C_j(\rho) \ge C_j(\pi^*) - Q$ and $C_j(\rho) \le C_j(\pi^*) + Q$, for $j = 1, \ldots, n$. Accordingly, each job j has an implied release time $\overline{r}_j = \max\{C_j(\pi^*) - Q - p_j, \gamma_j\}$ and an implied deadline $\overline{d}_j = C_j(\pi^*) + Q$.

Using the three-field notation for describing classical scheduling problems introduced by Graham et al. [42], we denote our problem by $P|\gamma_R, rej, \sum_{J_j \in \overline{A}} e_j \le U, \Delta_{\max} \le Q| \sum_{J_j \in A} C_j$, where γ_R denotes that all the jobs in the set R have the same release date γ.

The considered model, whether in its current form or with simple modifications, can also be applied to outpatient appointment scheduling over a planning horizon (a morning or a day). The planning of a doctor for determining the sequence to serve the patients with appointments and to assign a starting time to each patient over a planning horizon is often predefined before the planning horizon. However, some patients may arrive later because of unexpected events, which is a common phenomenon and inevitable in practice and might disrupt the current schedule. In the meantime, due to the over-time hour constraint for the doctor, it may be impossible to serve all patients with appointments during the planning horizon. Thus, an option of rejecting some patients with appointments and assigning them to later planning horizons at additional penalties is necessary.

3.1.2 Mixed Integer Linear Programming

In this subsection we develop a mixed integer linear programming formulation of the problem $P|\gamma_R, rej, \sum_{J_j \in \overline{A}} e_j \leq U, \Delta_{\max} \leq Q| \sum_{J_j \in A} C_j$. Let M be a very large positive number, which can be set as $\overline{d}_{\max}$. The decision variables of the problem are as follows:

C_j: denotes the earliest completion time of job J_j, $j = 1, \ldots, n$, with $C_0 = 0$;
x_{ij}: equals 1 if job J_i is scheduled immediately before job J_j on some machine; 0 otherwise, $i = 0, 1, \ldots, n$, $j = 1, \ldots, n, n+1$, where $x_{0j} = 1$ denotes that job J_j is scheduled first on some machine and $x_{i,n+1} = 1$ denotes that job J_i is scheduled last on some machine;
ζ_{ij}^k: equals 1 if job J_i is scheduled immediately before job J_j on machine M_k; 0 otherwise, $i = 0, 1, \ldots, n$, $j = 1, \ldots, n+1$, $k = 1, \ldots, m$, where $\zeta_{0j}^k = 1$ denotes that job J_j is scheduled first on machine M_k and $\zeta_{i,n+1}^k = 1$ denotes that job J_i is scheduled last on machine M_k;
z_j^k: equals 1 if job J_j is assigned on machine M_k; 0 otherwise, $j = 0, 1, \ldots, n+1$, $k = 1, \ldots, m$, with $z_0^k = z_{n+1}^k = 1$;
y_j: equals 1 if job J_j is rejected, and 0 otherwise, $j = 1, \ldots, n$.

Then we have the following mixed integer linear programming ($MILP$) formulation of the problem.

$MILP$ **Formulation**:

$$\text{Min} \sum_{j=1}^{n} C_j \tag{3.1.1}$$

subject to

$$\sum_{i=0}^{n} x_{ij} + y_j = 1, 1 \leq j \leq n, \tag{3.1.2}$$

$$\sum_{j=1}^{n} x_{0j} \leq m, \tag{3.1.3}$$

$$\sum_{j=1}^{n} e_j y_j \leq U, \tag{3.1.4}$$

$$\sum_{i=0}^{n} x_{ij} = \sum_{l=1}^{n+1} x_{jl}, 1 \leq j \leq n, \tag{3.1.5}$$

$$\sum_{i=0}^{n} x_{ij} = \sum_{k=1}^{m} z_j^k, 1 \leq j \leq n, \tag{3.1.6}$$

$$2\zeta_{ij}^k \leq z_i^k + z_j^k, 0 \leq i \leq n, 1 \leq j \leq n+1, 1 \leq k \leq m, \tag{3.1.7}$$

$$x_{ij} = \sum_{k=1}^{m} \zeta_{ij}^k, 0 \le i \le n, 1 \le j \le n+1, \tag{3.1.8}$$

$$C_i + p_j \le C_j + M(1 - x_{ij}), 0 \le i \le n, 1 \le j \le n, \tag{3.1.9}$$

$$\gamma + p_j \le C_j + My_j, J_j \in R, \tag{3.1.10}$$

$$\overline{r}_j + p_j \le C_j + My_j, 1 \le j \le n, \tag{3.1.11}$$

$$C_j \le \overline{d}_j, 1 \le j \le n, \tag{3.1.12}$$

$$y_j \in \{0, 1\}, 1 \le j \le n, \tag{3.1.13}$$

$$x_{ij} \in \{0, 1\}, 0 \le i \le n, 1 \le j \le n+1,$$

$$\zeta_{ij}^k \in \{0, 1\}, 0 \le i \le n, 1 \le j \le n+1, 1 \le k \le m,$$

$$z_j^k \in \{0, 1\}, 1 \le j \le n, 1 \le k \le m,$$

$$C_j \ge 0, 1 \le j \le n.$$

The objective function (3.1.1) seeks to minimize the total completion time of the accepted jobs. Constraint set (3.1.2) ensures that each job is either assigned to some machine or rejected. Constraint set (3.1.3) states that each machine must be utilized at most once. Constraint set (3.1.4) ensures that the total rejection cost does not exceed the limit U. Constraint set (3.1.5) guarantees that the assignment of jobs to machines is well defined, which plays the same role as the flow conservation constraint in the network flow problem. Constraint set (3.1.6) ensures that there exists a job scheduled immediately before job J_j if and only if job J_j is scheduled on some machine. Constraint set (3.1.7) states that $\zeta_{ij}^k = 1$ implies $z_i^k = 1$ and $z_j^k = 1$, and $z_i^k = 0$ or $z_j^k = 0$ implies $\zeta_{ij}^k = 0$. Constraint set (3.1.8) gives the relationships between the binary variables x_{ij} and ζ_{ij}^k. Constraint set (3.1.9) defines the completion times of the jobs. Constraint set (3.1.10) guarantees that the starting times of the jobs belonging to R are equal to or later than γ. Constraint sets (3.1.11) and (3.1.12) ensure that job J_j is scheduled within the time interval $[\overline{r}_j, \overline{d}_j]$, which ensures that the time disruption Δ_j of J_j does not exceed the limit Q. Constraint sets (3.1.9)–(3.1.12) ensure that the completion time of a rejected job is equal to zero. Finally, constraint set (3.1.13) specifies the non-negativity of C_j and imposes the binary restrictions on y_j, x_{ij}, z_j^k, and ζ_{ij}^k.

3.2 Optimal Properties

In this section we derive some structural properties of the optimal schedules that will be used later in the design of solution algorithms.

The following lemma provides an easy-to-prove property of the SPT schedule for the problem $Pm||\sum C_j$.

Lemma 3.2.1 [176] *For any two jobs j and k in the SPT schedule π^* for the problem $P||\sum_{j=1}^n C_j$, $j < k$ implies $C_j(\pi^*) - p_j \le C_k(\pi^*) - p_k$.*

Lemma 3.2.1 also indicates that $j < k$ implies $\bar{r}_j \leq \bar{r}_k$ and $\bar{d}_j \leq \bar{d}_k$.

After rescheduling, we refer to the partial schedule of the jobs that begin processing before time γ on machine M_i, $i = 1, \ldots, m$, as the earlier schedule on machine M_i, and the partial schedule of the jobs that begin processing at time γ or later as the later schedule. It is evident that all the jobs of R are contained in the later schedule.

Lemma 3.2.2 *For the problem* $P|\gamma_R, rej, \sum_{J_j \in \bar{A}} e_j \leq U, \Delta_{max} \leq Q| \sum_{J_j \in A} C_j$, *there exists an optimal schedule* ρ^* *in which*

(1) *the accepted jobs in the earlier schedule on each machine follow the SPT order;*
(2) *the accepted jobs in the later schedule follow the SPT order.*

Proof It follows from the proof of Lemma 3 in Hall and Potts [55] that both the accepted jobs in the earlier schedule and later schedule on each machine follow the SPT order, and further from the proof of Lemma 3.4 in Yin et al. [176] that the accepted jobs in the later schedule follow the SPT order, as required. □

When there is no job rejection, the following result holds.

Lemma 3.2.3 *For the problem* $P|\gamma_R, \Delta_{max} \leq Q| \sum_{J_j \in N} C_j$, *there exists an optimal schedule* ρ^* *in which there is no idle time between jobs in the later schedule on each machine and* $C_j(\pi^*) \leq C_j(\rho^*)$ *for each job* J_j *in the later schedule.*

Proof It follows from part (2) of Lemma 3.2.2 that the jobs preceding each job J_j in the later schedule in ρ^* also precede it in π^*, so $C_j(\pi^*) \leq C_j(\rho^*)$, which implies that ρ^* has no idle time between the jobs in the later schedule on each machine, as required. □

3.3 A Pseudo-Polynomial Time Algorithm for the Problem with a Fixed Number of Machines

Since even for the case with a single machine without job rejection is $\mathcal{NP}$-hard (Hall and Potts [55]), our problem must be $\mathcal{NP}$-hard, too. In this section we develop a pseudo-polynomial time DP algorithm to solve the problem when m is fixed, establishing that it is NP-hard in the ordinary sense, to which we refer as $Pm|\gamma_R, rej, \sum_{J_j \in \bar{A}} e_j \leq U, \Delta_{\max} \leq Q| \sum_{J_j \in A} C_j$.

Our DP-based solution algorithm $DP\text{-}Pm$ for the problem $Pm|\gamma_R, rej, \sum_{J_j \in \bar{A}} e_j \leq U, \Delta_{\max} \leq Q| \sum_{J_j \in A} C_j$ relies strongly on Lemma 3.2.2. We first fix the following variables:

- $\bar{s} = (s_1, \ldots, s_m)$: s_i, $i = 1, \ldots, m$, denotes the starting time of the later schedule on machine M_i in the final schedule, which extends from γ to $\gamma + p_{\max} - 1$.

For each given $\bar{s}$, the algorithm comprises n phases, where in each phase j, $j = 1, \ldots, n$, a state space $F_j(\bar{s})$ is generated. Any state in $F_j(\bar{s})$ is a vector $(T, \mathcal{T}, V_1, V_2)$ that encodes a feasible partial schedule for the jobs $\{J_1, \ldots, J_j\}$, where

- $T = (t_1, \ldots, t_m)$: $t_i, i = 1, \ldots, m$, denotes that the jobs of the earlier schedule on machine M_i occupy the time interval $[0, t_i]$;
- $\mathcal{T} = (u_1, \ldots, u_m)$: $u_i, i = 1, \ldots, m$, denotes that the jobs of the later schedule on machine M_i occupy the time interval $[s_i, s_i + u_i]$;
- V_1: the total completion time of the partial schedule;
- V_2: the total rejection cost of the partial schedule.

The state spaces $F_j(\overline{s})$, $j = 0, 1, \ldots, n$, are constructed iteratively. The initial space $\mathcal{F}_0(\overline{s})$ contains $(T, \mathcal{T}, 0, 0)$, where $T = \mathcal{T} = \underbrace{(0, \ldots, 0)}_{m}$, as its only element. In the jth phase, $j = 1, \ldots, n$, we build a state by adding a single job J_j to a previous state if it is possible for the given state. That is, for any state $(T, \mathcal{T}, V_1, V_2) \in \mathcal{F}_{j-1}(\overline{s})$, we include $m + 2$ possibly generated states in $\mathcal{F}_j(\overline{s})$ as follows:

Case 1: Assign job J_j in the earlier schedule on machine M_i, $i = 1, \ldots, m$. This is possible only if $J_j \in N \setminus R$, $t_i < \gamma$, and $\max\{t_i, \overline{r}_j\} + p_j \le \min\{s_i, \overline{d}_j\}$. In this case, the contributions of job J_j to the total completion time and total rejection cost are $\max\{t_i, \overline{r}_j\} + p_j$ and zero, respectively. Hence, if $J_j \in N \setminus R$, $t_i < \gamma$ and $\max\{t_i, \overline{r}_j\} + p_j \le \min\{s_i, \overline{d}_j\}$, we include the new state $(T', \mathcal{T}, V_1 + \max\{t_i, \overline{r}_j\} + p_j, V_2)$ in $\mathcal{F}_j(\overline{s})$, where $T' = \{t_1, \ldots, t_{i-1}, \max\{t_i, \overline{r}_j\} + p_j, t_{i+1}, \ldots, t_m\}$.

Case 2: Assign job J_j in the later schedule. By Lemma 3.2.2, it is optimal to place job J_j in the later schedule on some machine M_k at the earliest possible time, where machine M_k is the first machine that becomes available after γ, i.e., $k = \arg\min_{i=1,\ldots,m}\{s_i + u_i\}$. This is possible only if $\overline{r}_j \le s_k$ and $s_k + p_j \le \overline{d}_j$ when $u_k = 0$ since the later schedule on machine M_k starts at time s_k in the final schedule, and $\max\{s_k + u_k, \overline{r}_j\} + p_j \le \overline{d}_j$ when $u_k > 0$. In this case, the contributions of job J_j to the total completion time and total rejection cost are $\max\{s_k + u_k, \overline{r}_j\} + p_j$ and zero, respectively. Thus, if ($u_k = 0$, $\overline{r}_j \le s_k$, and $s_k + p_j \le \overline{d}_j$) or ($u_k > 0$ and $\max\{s_k + u_k, \overline{r}_j\} + p_j \le \overline{d}_j$), we include the new state $(T, \mathcal{T}', V_1 + \max\{s_k + u_k, \overline{r}_j\} + p_j, V_2)$ in $\mathcal{F}_j(\overline{s})$, where $\mathcal{T}' = \{u_1, \ldots, u_{k-1}, \max\{s_k + u_k, \overline{r}_j\} + p_j - s_k, u_{k+1}, \ldots, u_m\}$.

Case 3: Reject job J_j. This is possible only if $V_2 + e_j \le U$. In this case, the contributions of job J_j to the total completion time and total rejection cost are zero and e_j, respectively. Thus, if $V_2 + e_j \le U$, we include the new state $(T, \mathcal{T}, V_1, V_2 + e_j)$ in $\mathcal{F}_j(\overline{s})$.

Naturally, the construction of $\mathcal{F}_j(\overline{s})$ may generate more than a single state that will not lead to a complete optimal schedule. The following result shows how to reduce the state set $\mathcal{F}_j(\overline{s})$.

Lemma 3.3.1 *For any two states $(T, \mathcal{T}, V_1, V_2)$ and $(T', \mathcal{T}', V_1', V_2')$ in $\mathcal{F}_j(\overline{s})$ with $T \le T'$, $\mathcal{T} \le \mathcal{T}'$, $V_1 \le V_1'$, and $V_2 \le V_2'$, we can eliminate the latter one, where $T \le T'$ and $\mathcal{T} \le \mathcal{T}'$ mean $t_i \le t_i'$ and $u_i \le u_i'$ for $i = 1, \ldots, m$, respectively.*

Proof Let π_1 and π_2 be two sub-schedules corresponding to the states $(T, \mathcal{T}, V_1, V_2)$ and $(T', \mathcal{T}', V_1', V_2')$, respectively. And let $\widetilde{\pi}_2$ be a sub-schedule of the jobs $\{J_{j+1}, \ldots, J_n\}$ that is appended to the sub-schedule π_2 so as to create a feasible schedule $\widehat{\pi}_2$ in which the jobs belonging to $A_2 \subseteq \{J_{j+1}, \ldots, J_n\}$ are accepted. In the resulting feasible schedule $\widehat{\pi}_2$, the total completion time $TCT(\widehat{\pi}_2)$ and total rejection cost $TRC(\widehat{\pi}_2)$ are given, respectively, as follows:

$$TCT(\widehat{\pi}_2) = V_1' + \sum_{J_k \in A_2} C_k(\widetilde{\pi}_2)$$

and

$$TRC(\widehat{\pi}_2) = V_2' + \sum_{J_k \in \{J_{j+1},\ldots,J_n\} \setminus A_2} e_k.$$

Since $T \leq T'$, $\mathcal{T} \leq \mathcal{T}'$, and $V_2 \leq V_2'$, set $\{J_{j+1}, \ldots, J_n\}$ can also be added to the sub-schedule π_1 in an analogous way as $\widetilde{\pi}_2$, denoting the resulting sub-schedule as $\widetilde{\pi}_1$, to form a feasible schedule $\widehat{\pi}_1$, we have $C_k(\widetilde{\pi}_1) \leq C_k(\widetilde{\pi}_2)$ for $k \in A_2$. In the resulting feasible schedule $\widehat{\pi}_1$, the total completion time $TCT(\widehat{\pi}_1)$ and total rejection cost $TRC(\widehat{\pi}_1)$ are given, respectively, as follows:

$$TCT(\widehat{\pi}_1) = V_1 + \sum_{J_k \in A_2} C_k(\widetilde{\pi}_1)$$

and

$$TRC(\widehat{\pi}_2) = V_2 + \sum_{J_k \in \{J_{j+1},\ldots,J_n\} \setminus A_2} e_k.$$

It follows from $V_1 \leq V_1'$ and $V_2 \leq V_2'$ that $TCT(\widehat{\pi}_1) \leq TCT(\widehat{\pi}_2)$ and $TRC(\widehat{\pi}_1) \leq TRC(\widehat{\pi}_2)$, respectively. Therefore, sub-schedule π_1 dominates π_2, so the result follows. □

We formally present the procedure for solving the problem $Pm|\gamma_R, rej, \sum_{J_j \in \overline{A}} e_j \leq U, \Delta_{\max} \leq Q| \sum_{J_j \in A} C_j$ as follows.

Algorithm $DP\text{-}Pm$

Step 1. [*Preprocessing*] Re-index the jobs in the SPT order.
Step 2. [*Initialization*] For each $j = 1, \ldots, n$, set $i = j - m\lfloor j/m \rfloor$ and $C_j(\pi^*) = \sum_{k=i,m+i,\ldots,m\lfloor j/m \rfloor + i} p_k$;
set $\mathcal{F}_0(\overline{s}) = \{(\overline{s}, T, \mathcal{T}, 0, 0)\}$, where $T = \mathcal{T} = \underbrace{(0, \ldots, 0)}_{m}$, $\overline{s} = (s_1, \ldots, s_m)$, $s_i = \gamma, \ldots, \gamma + p_{\max} - 1$, $i = 1, \ldots, m$, and set $\overline{r}_j = C_j(\pi^*) - p_j - Q$ and $\bar{d}_j = C_j(\pi^*) + Q$.
Step 3. [*Generation*] Generate $\mathcal{F}_j(\overline{s})$ from $\mathcal{F}_{j-1}(\overline{s})$.
For each $\overline{s} = (s_1, \ldots, s_m)$, where $s_i = \gamma, \ldots, \gamma + p_{\max} - 1$, $i = 1, \ldots, m$, do
  For $j = 1$ to n, do
    Set $\mathcal{F}_j(\overline{s}) = \emptyset$;
    For each $(T, \mathcal{T}, V_1, V_2) \in \mathcal{F}_{j-1}(\overline{s})$, do
      For $i = 1$ to m, do
        /*Alternative 1: Assign job J_j to the earlier schedule on machine M_i:
        If $J_j \in N \setminus R$, $t_i < \gamma$ and $\max\{t_i, \overline{r}_j\} + p_j \leq \min\{s_i, \overline{d}_j\}$, then
          set $\mathcal{F}_j(\overline{s}) \leftarrow \mathcal{F}_j(\overline{s}) \cup \{(X, T', \mathcal{T}, V_1 + \max\{t_i, \overline{r}_j\} + p_j, V_2)\}$,
          where $T' = \{t_1, \ldots, t_{i-1}, \max\{t_i, \overline{r}_j\} + p_j, t_{i+1}, \ldots, t_m\}$;
        Endif
      Endfor

Set $k = \arg\min_{i=1,\dots,m}\{s_i + u_i\}$;
/*Alternative 2: Assign job J_j to the later schedule on machine M_k:
If ($u_k = 0, \overline{r}_j \le s_k$ and $s_k + p_j \le \overline{d}_j$) or ($u_k > 0$ and $\max\{s_k + u_k, \overline{r}_j\} + p_j \le \overline{d}_j$), then
set $\mathcal{F}_j(\overline{s}) \leftarrow \mathcal{F}_j(\overline{s}) \cup \{(T, \mathcal{T}', V_1 + \max\{s_k + u_k, \overline{r}_j\} + p_j, V_2)\}$,
where $\mathcal{T}' = \{u_1, \dots, u_{k-1}, \max\{s_k + u_k, \overline{r}_j\} + p_j - s_k, u_{k+1}, \dots, u_m\}$;
Endif
/*Alternative 3: Reject job J_j:
If $V_2 + e_j \le U$, then
set $\mathcal{F}_j(\overline{s}) \leftarrow \mathcal{F}_j(\overline{s}) \cup \{(T, \mathcal{T}, V_1, V_2 + e_j)\}$,
Endif
Endfor
[*Elimination*] /* Update set $\mathcal{F}_j(\overline{s})$ */
1. For any two states $(T, \mathcal{T}, V_1, V_2)$ and $(T, \mathcal{T}, V_1, V_2')$ in $\mathcal{F}_j(\overline{s})$ with $V_2 \le V_2'$, eliminate the latter state from set $\mathcal{F}_j(\overline{s})$;
2. For any two states $(T, \mathcal{T}, V_1, V_2)$ and $(T, \mathcal{T}, V_1', V_2)$ in $\mathcal{F}_j(\overline{s})$ with $V_1 \le V_1'$, eliminate the latter state from set $\mathcal{F}_j(\overline{s})$;
3. For any two states $(T = (t_1, \dots, t_{i-1}, t_i, t_{i+1}, \dots, t_m), \mathcal{T}, V_1, V_2)$ and $(X, T' = (t_1, \dots, t_{i-1}, t_i', t_{i+1}, \dots, t_m), \mathcal{T}, V_1, V_2)$ in $\mathcal{F}_j(\overline{s})$ with $t_i \le t_i'$, eliminate the latter state from set $\mathcal{F}_j(\overline{s})$;
4. For any two states $(T, \mathcal{T} = (u_1, \dots, u_{i-1}, u_i, u_{i+1}, \dots, u_m), V_1, V_2)$ and $(T, \mathcal{T}' = (u_1, \dots, u_{i-1}, u_i', u_{i+1}, \dots, u_m), V_1, V_2)$ in $\mathcal{F}_j(\overline{s})$ with $u_i \le u_i'$, eliminate the latter state from set $\mathcal{F}_j(\overline{s})$;
5. For any state $(T, \mathcal{T}, V_1, V_2)$ in $\mathcal{F}_j(\overline{s})$ with $u_i > P/m + (m-1)p_{\max}/m$, eliminate the state from set $\mathcal{F}_j(\overline{s})$;
Endfor
Endfor

Step 4. [*Result*] The optimal solution value is given by $V_1^* = \min\{V_1 | (T, \mathcal{T}, V_1, V_2) \in \mathcal{F}_n(\overline{s}), \overline{s} = (s_1, \dots, s_m), s_i = \gamma, \dots, \gamma + p_{\max} - 1, i = 1, \dots, m\}$ and the corresponding optimal schedule can be found by backtracking.

Theorem 3.3.2 *Algorithm* $DP\text{-}Pm$ *solves the problem* $Pm|r_R, rej, \sum_{J_j \in \overline{A}} e_j \le U, \Delta_{max} \le Q| \sum_{J_j \in A} C_j$ *in* $O(nL^m\gamma^m(\gamma + p_{max})^m U)$ *time, where* $L = \min\{P/m + (m-1)p_{max}/m, \overline{d}_{max} - \gamma + 1\}$ *and* $\overline{d}_{max} = \max_{j=1,\dots,n}\{\overline{d}_j\}$.

Proof The optimality of algorithm $DP\text{-}Pm$ is guaranteed by Lemma 3.2.2 and the above analysis. Specifically, the elimination rule 5 in the [Elimination] procedure is valid due to the fact that u_i is upper-bounded by $\min\{P/m + (m-1)p_{\max}/m, \overline{d}_{\max} - \gamma + 1\}$ when there are no rejected jobs by Lemma 3.2.3, and Elmaghraby and Park [37]. We now work out the time complexity of the algorithm. Step 1 implements a sorting procedure that needs $O(n \log n)$ time. In Step 3, before each iteration j, the total number of possible states $(T, \mathcal{T}, V_1, V_2) \in \mathcal{F}_{j-1}(\overline{s})$ can be calculated in the following way: there are at most $\gamma - 1$ and $\min\{P/m + (m-1)p_{\max}/m, \overline{d}_{\max} - \gamma + 1\}$ possible values for t_i and u_i, $i = 1, \dots, m$, respectively, and at most U possible values for V_2. Because of the elimination rule, the total number of different states at the beginning of each iteration is equal to the number of different pairs of $\{T, \mathcal{T}, V_1, V_2\}$, which is upper-bounded by $O(L^m\gamma^m U)$. In each iteration j, there are at most $m + 2$ new states generated from each state in $\mathcal{F}_{j-1}(\overline{s})$ for each candidate job. Thus, the number of new states generated is at most $(m+2)O(L^m\gamma^m U)$. However, due to the elimination rules, the number of new states generated in $\mathcal{F}_j(\overline{s})$ is upper-bounded by $O(L^m\gamma^m U)$ after the elimination step. Thus, after $n(\gamma + p_{\max} - 1)^m$ iterations, Step 3 can be executed in $O(nL^m\gamma^m(\gamma + p_{\max})^m U)$ time, which is also the overall time complexity of the algorithm. □

3.4 Column Generation Algorithm

Solving large instances of the problem $P|\gamma_R, rej, \sum_{J_j \in \overline{A}} e_j \leq U, \Delta_{\max} \leq Q| \sum_{J_j \in A} C_j$ via $MILP$ is impractical because it involves a huge number of variables and provides weak linear relaxations. Column generation is an effective method to cope with a huge number of variables. The idea behind column generation is to use the linear relaxation of a smaller core problem in order to efficiently compute good lower bounds on the optimal solution value. It works by repeatedly executing two phases. In the first phase, instead of solving a linear relaxation of the whole problem in which all the columns are required, we quickly solve a smaller problem, called the *restricted master problem*, that deals only with a subset of the original columns. Upon solving the smaller problem, we proceed to the second phase where we identify one or more not yet considered variables (columns) with negative reduced costs based on the dual solution of the restricted master problem. This sub-problem is called the *pricing sub-problem*. If we fail, i.e., we are unable to find at least one negative reduced cost column, it has been proven that the optimal solution has been found. Otherwise, we add a number of columns with negative reduced costs to the restricted master problem and return to the first phase to repeat the whole solution process.

3.4.1 The Master Problem

In this subsection we show how to decompose $MILP$ into a master problem using the Dantzig-Wolfe decomposition paradigm and then solve it by column generation.

Define a *feasible partial schedule* as a schedule on a single machine formed by a subset of all the jobs possessing the properties stated in Lemma 3.2.2. Accordingly, a feasible schedule for the problems under consideration associated with m machines is simply m partial schedules with no intersecting jobs while keeping the total rejection cost and the disruption cost to no greater than the limits U and Q, respectively. To develop the master problem, we re-formulate $MILP$ in a different way. Let P denote the set of all the feasible partial schedules and $\hat{c}_p$ be the total completion time of the jobs covered in the partial schedule $p \in P$. For each job $J_j \in N$, let $a_{jp} = 1$ if the partial schedule $p \in P$ covers job J_j; 0 otherwise.

Define the variables $\lambda_p = 1$ if the feasible partial schedule p is selected for some machine and $\lambda_p = 0$ otherwise, $p \in P$, which are referred to as the master variables.

Consider the following integer master problem:

$$\text{Min} \sum_{p \in P} \hat{c}_p \lambda_p \tag{3.4.1}$$

subject to constraint (3.1.4) and

$$\sum_{p \in P} a_{pj} \lambda_p + y_j = 1, 1 \leq j \leq n, \tag{3.4.2}$$

$$\sum_{p \in P} \lambda_p \leq m, \tag{3.4.3}$$

$$y_j \in \{0, 1\}, 1 \leq j \leq n, \tag{3.4.4}$$

$$\lambda_p \in \{0, 1\}, p \in P.$$

Constraint sets (3.4.2) and (3.4.3) correspond to the original constraint sets (3.1.2) and (3.1.3), and guarantee that each job is covered by exactly one feasible partial schedule and at most m feasible partial schedule are occupied by the m machines, respectively.

The above decomposed problem with linear relaxation of constraint set (3.4.4) is called the *master problem* (MP). The *restricted master problem* (RMP) is a relaxation of MP that contains only a subset $\overline{P} \subset P$ of the master variables. To convert the master variables in MP back to the original variables in $MILP$, we make use of the following relationship

$$x_{ij} = \sum_{p \in P} e_{ij}^p \lambda_p, \quad i = 0, 1, \ldots, n, j = 1, \ldots, n, \tag{3.4.5}$$

where $e_{ij}^p = 1$ if jobs J_i and J_j are covered in the feasible partial schedule p, and J_i is scheduled immediately before J_j; 0 otherwise. It is evident that the original variable x is integral if and only if the corresponding master variable λ is integral.

3.4.2 DE-Based Algorithm for the Master Problem Initialization

The column generation procedure calls for an initial set of columns to start with. For this purpose, we use the differential evolution (DE) algorithm to generate some feasible schedules, which we then translate to the initial columns of MP. The DE algorithm is a powerful search engine for solving multi-objective and constrained optimization problems (Ali et al. [6]). The most important issues during the procedure are to maintain diversity of the population and to generate potential candidate solutions from the beginning of the algorithm. Thus, we use the structural property based encoding scheme to design the corresponding differential mutation, binary

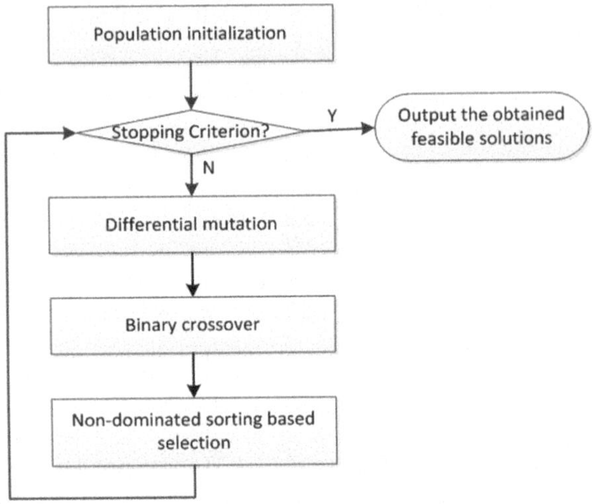

Fig. 3.1 Flowchart of DE-based solution initialization procedure

crossover, and non-dominated sorting based selection to deal with the problem to prevent the search from becoming a purely random search and to strike a good balance between exploration and exploitation. Let *pop* be the population size and P_T be the population in the Tth iteration. Figure 3.1 outlines the DE algorithm ($DE\text{-}INI$), which we formally describe as follows:

Algorithm $DE\text{-}INI$

Step 1. Let $T = 1$, randomly sample *pop* solutions to form the initial population P_T, and compute the objective and constraint values of each individual.
Step 2. If the problem-related stopping criterion is met, output the obtained feasible solutions; otherwise go to Step 3.
Step 3. Apply differential mutation and binary crossover on each individual in P_T to generate new individuals, followed by computing their objective and constraint values.
Step 4. Apply non-dominated sorting based selection on the original individuals and the newly generated individuals to construct the next population P_{T+1}. Set $T = T + 1$ and go back to Step 2.

We present the implementation details of Algorithm DE to address the main issues as follows:

(i) **Encoding scheme**

We represent a solution to the problem by a $(n + \iota)$-dimensional vector $\overline{\psi}_{il}$ as follows:

$$\overline{\psi}_{il} = \left(\underbrace{\psi_{i1l}, \ldots, \psi_{inl}}_{a\text{-part}}, \underbrace{\psi_{i,n+1,l}, \ldots, \psi_{i,n+\iota,l}}_{s\text{-part}} \right), \quad i = 1, \ldots, pop, l = 1, \ldots, L, \tag{3.4.6}$$

where $\psi_{ijl} \in \{1, \ldots, m+1\}$ for $j = 1, \ldots, n$
and $\psi_{i,n+j,l} \in \{1, 2\}$ for $j = 1, \ldots, \iota$,

where ι denotes the number of jobs in $N \setminus R$, l denotes the evolutionary generation number, and L denotes the maximum evolutionary generation number. Specifically, vector $\overline{\psi}_{il}$ represents the ith individual in the lth generation and ψ_{ijl} stands for the jth entry of $\overline{\psi}_{il}$, $1 \leq j \leq n + \iota$. The solution consists of two parts: machine assignment flags (a-part for short) and schedule assignment flags (s-part for short). Then for each entry in the a-part, $\psi_{ipl} = k$, $k = 1, \ldots, m$, denotes that the pth job in N arranged in the SPT order is assigned to machine M_k for processing, while $\psi_{ipl} = m + 1$ indicates that the pth job is rejected. For each entry in the s-part, $\psi_{i,n+q,l} = 1$ means that the qth job in $N \setminus R$ arranged in the SPT order is assigned in the early schedule and $\psi_{i,n+q,l} = 2$ indicates that it is assigned in the later schedule.

Given a solution expressed in Eq. (3.4.6), we can obtain from the entries in the a-part the assigned machine for each job, and for each machine, we can obtain from the entries in the s-part the jobs assigned to this machine that are scheduled in the early schedule and that are scheduled in the later schedule. The jobs assigned to the early schedule and later schedule are both sequenced in the SPT order by Lemma 3.2.2. The resulting schedule may be infeasible due to the constraints of the problem. To make it feasible, the jobs starting later than γ in the early schedule should be moved to the later schedule, and the job J_j whose starting time does not fall into the time interval $\left[\overline{r}_j, \overline{d}_j - p_j\right]$ is removed from the schedule and added to the rejected job set.

For the evaluation of the individual, the objective value corresponds to the total completion time of the scheduled jobs and the constraint value corresponds to the total rejection cost.

(ii) **Differential mutation**

Before we discuss differential mutation, we explain several terms from the current DE literature, including the target vector, donor vector and trial vector [1, 2]. The target is a mutant obtained from DE mutation, the donor vector is the one to be mutated, and the trial vector is an offspring formed by recombining the target and donor. According to the characteristics of the encoding scheme, we apply the $DE\,|rand\,|1\,|bin$ strategy developed by Wang and Cai [154] on the chromosomes of individuals.

To begin with, for the ith donor individual of the lth generation represented as $\overline{\alpha}_{il}$, two other distinct individuals $\overline{\psi}_{i_1,l}$ and $\overline{\psi}_{i_2,l}$ are randomly sampled from the current population, where i_1 and i_2 are randomly chosen from the range $[1, pop]$. Then the target vector $\overline{\beta}_{il}$ can be obtained by Eq. (3.4.7), where F represents the scaling between $\overline{\psi}_{i_1,l}$ and $\overline{\psi}_{i_2,l}$, which is commonly set at 0.5 or 0.9 according to Das and Suganthan [31].

$$\overline{\beta}_{il} = \overline{\psi}_{i_1,l} + F \times (\overline{\psi}_{i_2,l} - \overline{\psi}_{i_1,l}). \tag{3.4.7}$$

In this paper, if the jth component β_{ijl} of the target vector $\overline{\beta}_{il}$ violates the boundary constraint, we repair the component as follows:

$$\beta_{ijl} = \begin{cases} \min\{U_j, 2L_j - \beta_{ijl}\}, \beta_{ijl} < L_j, \\ \max\{L_j, 2U_j - \beta_{ijl}\}, \beta_{ijl} \geq U_j, \end{cases} \tag{3.4.8}$$

where $[L_j, U_j]$ stands for the feasible interval for β_{ijk}.

(iii) **Binary crossover**

In order to preserve the good structure from the obtained individuals and to enhance the ability of local search, a binary crossover is embedded after generating the target vector, which $\overline{\beta}_{il}$ exchanges its chromosome with the donor vector $\overline{\alpha}_{il}$ at a crossover rate $cr \in (0, 1)$, which is described as follows:

$$u_{ijl} = \begin{cases} \beta_{ijl}, \; rand_j(0, 1) \leq cr \; or \; j = j_{rand}, \\ \alpha_{ijl}, \text{ otherwise}, \quad i = 1, \ldots, pop, j = 1, \ldots, n + \iota, l = 1, \ldots, L, \end{cases} \tag{3.4.9}$$

where u_{ijl} is the jth component of the trial vector $\overline{u}_{i\iota}$, $rand_j$ (0, 1) is a number randomly generated from a uniform distribution and $j_{rand} \in [1, n + \iota]$ is a randomly chosen index to ensure that $\overline{u}_{i\iota}$ has at least one component from $\overline{\beta}_{i\iota}$.

(iv) **Non-dominated sorting based selection**

In order to determine the better individual between the trial vector $\overline{u}_{il}$ and the donor vector $\overline{\alpha}_{il}$ after the binary crossover operation, we use non-dominated sorting based selection to deal with this constrained optimization problem. We describe the strategy as follows:

- The feasible solution is better than the infeasible solution;
- If both the two solutions are feasible, then the one with optimal objective value is selected;
- If both solutions are infeasible and one is non-dominated by the other, then the non-dominated solution is optimal;
- If both solutions are infeasible and they are non-dominated solutions, then the one with fewer constraint violations is selected.

Combining the above strategy with the differential evolution algorithm, we involve the infeasible solutions in the population, which improves its diversity.

To perform the computational experiments, we set the values of the parameters of the DE-based algorithm as follows: population size $(pop) = 40$, maximum generations $(L) = 60$, scaling factor $(F) = 0.5$, and crossover probability $(cr) = 0.5$.

We chose these values (and the other parameter values presented in the following subsections) based on preliminary computational tests.

3.4.3 The Pricing Sub-problem

Denote by π_j, $j = 1, \ldots, n$, and ρ the dual variables associated with constraint sets (3.4.2) and (3.4.3) in RMP, respectively. The reduced cost r_p of the column corresponding to $p \in \overline{P}$ is given as

$$r_p = \hat{c}_p - \sum_{j=1}^{n} \pi_j a_{pj} - \rho \tag{3.4.10}$$

So we formulate the pricing sub-problem as follows:

$$c^* = \min\{0; \hat{c}_p - \sum_{j=1}^{n} \pi_j a_{pj} - \rho | p \in P\}. \tag{3.4.11}$$

If its optimal value is non-negative, then the column generation algorithm terminates. Otherwise, at least one negative reduced cost column is identified.

In implementing the branch-and-price algorithm (Sect. 3.5), we choose the original variables from which to branch. This imposes additional job-ordering restrictions on the jobs for the pricing sub-problem resulting from the branching constraints. We use $B_j = \{J_i \in N |$ job J_i can precede job J_j on a single machine$\}$ to denote the job-ordering restriction on job J_j for the pricing sub-problem for RMP, which is initiated as $B_j = \{0, 1, \ldots, n, n+1\}$, where $B_j = \{n+1\}$ denotes that job J_j is rejected. Then the pricing sub-problem is concerned with a search for a subset of all the jobs and a schedule for these jobs on a machine that satisfies the job-ordering restrictions such that the total completion time of the scheduled jobs minus the total dual variable value of these jobs is minimized.

By the duality of linear programming, $\bar{z} = \sum_{j=1}^{n} \pi_j + m\rho + \lambda U$ is the optimal objective value of RMP, where $\lambda \geq 0$ is the dual variable associated with constraint (3.1.4) in RMP, and we obtain in each iteration the following bounds.

Lemma 3.4.1 [40] *Let z^*_{LRMP} be the optimal objective value of the linear programming relaxation of MP. Then $\bar{z} + mc^* \leq z^*_{LRMP} \leq \bar{z}$.*

Since $z^*_{LRMP1} \leq z^*$, where z^* is the optimal objective value of MP, $\bar{z} + \sum_{i=1}^{m} c^{i*}$ is also a lower bound on z^*.

In the following we first show that the pricing sub-problem is NP-hard. We then develop a pseudo-polynomial time dynamic programming algorithm to solve the problem, establishing that it is NP-hard in the ordinary sense. We also show that the DE-based algorithm can price out the columns with negative reduced costs quickly, and present two strategies for solving the pricing sub-problem and adding columns with negative reduced costs to RMP.

Theorem 3.4.2 *The pricing sub-problem is $\mathcal{NP}$-hard even if Q is sufficiently large and there are no job-ordering restrictions.*

Proof For a sufficiently large Q, the constraint $\Delta_{\max} \leq Q$ becomes redundant. In addition, if π_j and ρ are made sufficiently small, e.g., $\pi_j = \rho = 0$, $j = 1, \ldots, n$, our problem reduces to the problem $1|r_R|\min \sum_{j=1}^{n} C_j$. Given that the problem $1|r_j|\min \sum_{j=1}^{n} C_j$ is NP-hard (Rinnooy Kan [122]) even for the case of a single non-zero release date, our problem is NP-hard, too. □

3.4.3.1 Dynamic Programming Algorithm for the Pricing Sub-problem

We present in this section a forward dynamic programming algorithm for the pricing sub-problem. As before, we refer to a partial schedule of jobs that begin processing at time before time γ on a machine as the earlier schedule and a partial schedule of jobs that begin processing at time γ or later on a machine as the later schedule. Note also that the property that there exists an optimal schedule for the sub-problem in which the jobs in the earlier schedule and the later schedule both follow the SPT order still holds.

The dynamic programming algorithm $DP\text{-}PRI$ is similar to that of $DP\text{-}Pm$. We first renumber the jobs in the SPT order and fix a variable s, which denotes the starting time of the later schedule in the final partial schedule and extends from γ to $\gamma + p_{\max} - 1$. For each given s, the algorithm comprises n phases and in each phase j, $j = 1, \ldots, n$, a state space $S_j(s)$ is generated. Any state in $S_j(s)$ is a vector (j_e, j_l, j_f, t, u, V) encoding a partial schedule for the jobs $\{J_1, \ldots, J_j\}$, where

- j_e denotes that job J_{j_e} is the last job in the current earlier schedule, where $j_e = 0$ implies that there is no job in the current earlier schedule;
- j_l denotes that job J_{j_l} is the last job in the current later schedule, where $j_l = 0$ implies that there is no job in the current later schedule;
- j_f denotes that job J_{j_f} is the first job in the later schedule, where $j_f = 0$ implies $j_l = 0$;
- t denotes that the jobs in the current earlier schedule occupy the time interval $[0, t]$;
- u denotes that the jobs in the current later schedule occupy the time interval $[s, s + u]$;
- V measures the objective value of the current partial schedule.

The state spaces $S_j(s)$, $j = 0, 1, \ldots, n$, are constructed iteratively with $S_0(s) = \{(0, 0, 0, 0, 0, -\rho)\}$. In the jth phase, $j = 1, \ldots, n$, we build a state by adding a single job J_j to a previous state if it is possible for the given state. That is, for any state $(j_e, j_l, j_f, t, u, V) \in S_{j-1}(s)$, we include three possibly generated states as follows:

Case 1: Assign job J_j in the earlier schedule. In this case, there must be $J_j \in N \setminus R$, $j_e \in B_j$, $t < \gamma$, and $\max\{t, \overline{r}_j\} + p_j \leq \min\{s, \overline{d}_j\}$ to ensure feasibility of this decision. The contribution of job J_j to the objective value is $\max\{t, \overline{r}_j\} + p_j - \pi_j$. Hence, if $J_j \in N \setminus R$, $j_e \in B_j$, $t < \gamma$, and $\max\{t, \overline{r}_j\} + p_j \leq \min\{s, \overline{d}_j\}$, we include the new state $(j, j_l, j_f, \max\{t, \overline{r}_j\} + p_j, u, V + \max\{t, \overline{r}_j\} + p_j - \pi_j)$ in $S_j(s)$.

Case 2: Assign job J_j in the later schedule. This is possible only if $\overline{r}_j \leq s$ and $s + p_j \leq \overline{d}_j$ when $j_f = 0$, and $j_l \in B_j$ and $\max\{s + u, \overline{r}_j\} + p_j \leq \overline{d}_j$ when $j_f \neq 0$. In this case, the contribution of job J_j to the objective value is $\max\{s + u, \overline{r}_j\} + p_j - \pi_j$. Thus, we include the new state $(j_e, j, j, t, p_j, V + s + p_j - \pi_j)$ in $S_j(s)$ if $j_f = 0, \overline{r}_j \leq s$ and $s + p_j \leq \overline{d}_j$, and $(j_e, j, j_f, t, \max\{s + u, \overline{r}_j\} + p_j - s, V + \max\{s + u, \overline{r}_j\} + p_j - \pi_j)$ if $j_f \neq 0$, $j_l \in B_j$, and $\max\{s + u, \overline{r}_j\} + p_j \leq \overline{d}_j$.

Case 3: Do not assign job J_j to the partial schedule. In this case, job J_j does not incur any cost. Thus, we include the state (j_e, j_l, j_f, t, u, V) in $S_j(s)$.

The following result shows how the state set $S_j(s)$ can be reduced.

Lemma 3.4.3 *For any two states (j_e, j_l, j_f, t, u, V) and $(j_e, j_l, j_f, t', u', V')$ in $S_j(s)$ with $t \leq t'$, $u \leq u'$, and $V \leq V'$, we can eliminate the latter state.*

Proof The proof is analogous to that of Lemma 3.3.1. □

We provide a formal description of algorithm *DP-PRI* as follows:

Algorithm *DP-PRI*

Step 1. [*Preprocessing*] Re-index the jobs in the SPT order.

Step 2. [*Initialization*] For each $j = 1, \ldots, n$, set $i = j - m\lfloor j/m \rfloor$ and $C_j(\pi^*) = \sum_{k=i,m+i,\ldots,m\lfloor j/m\rfloor+i} p_k$; set $S_0(s) = \{(0, 0, 0, 0, 0, -\rho)\}$ for $s = \gamma, \ldots, \gamma + p_{\max} - 1$, $\overline{r}_j = C_j(\pi^*) - p_j - Q$, $\bar{d}_j = C_j(\pi^*) + Q$.

Step 3. [*Generation*] Generate $S_j(s)$ from $S_{j-1}(s)$.
For $s = \gamma$ to $\gamma + p_{\max} - 1$, do
  For $j = 1$ to n, do
    Set $S_j(s) = \emptyset$;
    For each $(j_e, j_l, j_f, t, u, V) \in S_{j-1}(s)$, do
      /* Alternative 1: Assign job J_j to the earlier schedule:
      If $J_j \in N \setminus R$, $j_e \in B_j$, $t < \gamma$, and $\max\{t, \overline{r}_j\} + p_j \leq \min\{s, \overline{d}_j\}$, then
        set $S_j(s) \leftarrow S_j(s) \cup \{(j, j_l, j_f, \max\{t, \overline{r}_j\} + p_j, u, V + \max\{t, \overline{r}_j\} + p_j - \pi_j)\}$;
      Endif
      /* Alternative 2: Assign job J_j to the later schedule:
      If $j_f = 0, \overline{r}_j \leq s$ and $s + p_j \leq \overline{d}_j$, then
        set $\mathcal{S}_j(s) \leftarrow \mathcal{S}_j(s) \cup \{(j_e, j, j, t, p_j, V + s + p_j - \pi_j)\}$;
      Endif
      If $j_f \neq 0$, $j_l \in B_j$ and $\max\{s + u, \overline{r}_j\} + p_j \leq \overline{d}_j$, then
        set $\mathcal{S}_j(s) \leftarrow \mathcal{S}_j(s) \cup \{(j_e, j, j_f, t, \max\{s + u, \overline{r}_j\} + p_j - s, V + \max\{s + u, \overline{r}_j\}$
        $+ p_j - \pi_j)\}$;
      Endif
      /* Alternative 3: Do not assign job J_j to the partial schedule:
      set $\mathcal{S}_j(s) \leftarrow \mathcal{S}_j(s) \cup \{(j_e, j_l, j_f, t, u, V)\}$;
    Endfor
    [*Elimination*] /* Update set $\mathcal{S}_j(s)$ */
    1. For any state (j_e, j_l, j_f, t, u, V) in $\mathcal{S}_j(s)$ with $j_e \notin B_{j_f}$ and $j = n$, eliminate the state from set $\mathcal{S}_j(s)$;
    2. For any two states (j_e, j_l, j_f, t, u, V) and $(j_e, j_l, j_f, t', u, V)$ in $\mathcal{S}_j(s)$ with $t \leq t'$, eliminate the latter state from set $\mathcal{S}_j(s)$;
    3. For any two states (j_e, j_l, j_f, t, u, V) and $(j_e, j_l, j_f, t, u', V)$ in $\mathcal{S}_j(s)$ with $u \leq u'$,

eliminate the latter state from set $\mathcal{S}_j(s)$;
4. For any two states (j_e, j_l, j_f, t, u, V) and $(j_e, j_l, j_f, t, u, V')$ in $\mathcal{S}_j(s)$ with $V \le V'$, eliminate the latter state from set $\mathcal{S}_j(s)$;
Endfor
Endfor
Step 4. [*Result*] The optimal solution value is given by $V^* = \min\{V|((j_e, j_l, j_f, t, u, V) \in \mathcal{S}_n(s), s = \gamma, \ldots, \gamma + p_{\max} - 1\}$ and the corresponding optimal schedule can be found by backtracking.

Theorem 3.4.4 *Algorithm DP-PRI solves the pricing sub-problem in $O(n^4\gamma(\gamma + p_{max})(\overline{d}_{max} - \gamma))$ time.*

Proof The proof is analogous to that of Theorem 3.3.2 where the only difference is that the number of different combinations of $\{j_e, j_l, j_f, t, u\}$ is upper-bounded by $n^3\gamma P$ because there are at most n possible values for j_e, j_l, and j_f, respectively, at most δ possible values for t, and at most $\overline{d}_{\max} - \gamma + 1$ values for u. □

It is worth noting that when applying DP-PRI to solve the pricing sub-problem at the root node, we can drop the variables j_e, j_l, and j_f because in this case there are no restrictions imposed on the jobs.

3.4.3.2 Strategy for Solving the Pricing Sub-problem

Preliminary tests indicate that the optimal solution is found in $\mathcal{S}_n(s)$ with smaller values of s in most cases when applying DP-PRI for solving the pricing sub-problem. Based on this observation, we adopt the following strategy for solving the pricing sub-problem using DP-PRI. We iteratively fix s extending from γ to $\gamma + p_{\max} - 1$. Initially, we set $s = \gamma$. When the state set $\mathcal{S}_n(s)$ is obtained, we select among all the columns in $\mathcal{S}_n(s)$ those columns with the most negative reduced costs, if any exist (especially if the number of columns in $\mathcal{S}_n(s)$ with a negative reduced cost is larger than φ (a pre-defined parameter, which is set at 10 in our computational experiments), we select those φ columns with the most negative reduced costs; otherwise, all the columns with a negative reduced cost are selected). If there is at least one column with a negative reduced cost in $\mathcal{S}_n(s)$, we stop. Otherwise, we set $s = s + 1$ and continue the process.

3.5 Branch-and-Price Algorithm

As the optimal solution to RMP may not be an integer, it is necessary to embed a branch-and-bound tree in the solution process for RMP, giving rise the so-called *branch-and-price* algorithm. The basic idea of the branch-and-price algorithm is to solve RMP to optimality at each node. If the current RMP, with all the possible columns, becomes infeasible, or an integral solution is obtained, the node is fathomed and it continues the search with the remaining active nodes. In the latter case, the optimal solution is also compared with the best available integral solution, and if the current solution is better, it is declared to be the best available solution for the problem. Otherwise, this solution is discarded. If the optimal solution for the current RMP is fractional, then a partition of the solution space is refined by further branching. The algorithm stops after it finds the first solution that is shown to be optimal. In the following we present the implementation details of the algorithm, covering the reduced cost fixing strategy, the branching strategy, the upper bounding technique, and the node search strategy.

3.5.1 Fixing and Setting of Variables

Reduced cost fixing is a well-known and important idea in the literature of integer programming. Given an optimal solution to the current RMP, the reduced costs r_p, $p \in \overline{P}$, are non-negative for all the non-basic variables at 0, and non-positive for all the non-basic variables at 1. Let $\widetilde{\kappa} = (\widetilde{\lambda}, \widetilde{y})$ be an optimal solution to the current RMP having objective value z_{LL}, z_U be the current best upper bound, and $\widetilde{\lambda}_p$ (resp., $\widetilde{y}_j$) be a non-basic variable in $\widetilde{\kappa}$. We have following results.

- If $\widetilde{\lambda}_p = 0$ (resp., $\widetilde{y}_j$) in $\widetilde{\kappa}$ and $z_{LL} + r_p \geq z_U$ (resp., $z_{LL} + r_j \geq z_U$), then there exists an optimal solution to the master problem with $\widetilde{\lambda}_p = 0$ (resp., $\widetilde{y}_j = 0$).
- If $\widetilde{\lambda}_p = 1$ (resp., $\widetilde{y}_j$) in $\widetilde{\kappa}$ and $z_{LL} - r_p \geq z_U$ (resp., $z_{LL} - r_j \geq z_U$), then there exists an optimal solution to the master problem with $\widetilde{\lambda}_p = 1$ (resp., $\widetilde{y}_j = 1$).

In the branch-and-price algorithm, before branching, global reduced cost fixing (i.e., permanently fixing the variables at their respective upper and lower bounds) is performed at the root node when RMP is solved to optimality. Local fixing is performed at each node of the search tree using the optimal solution value to the current RMP and the current best upper bound.

When some variables in $\widetilde{\kappa}$ are fixed, we need to update the job-ordering restrictions accordingly. Specifically, we consider the following four cases.

- Variable $\widetilde{\lambda}_p$ is fixed at 1. This means that the partial schedule p is covered in the final schedule. Let $J_1 = \{j | a_{pj} = 1, J_j \in N\}$. Then for each $j \in J_1$, we determine $i \in J_1 \cup \{0\}$ such that $x_{ij} = 1$, update B_j such that $B_j = \{i\}$ and $B_{j'}$, $j' \neq j$ such that $B_{j'} = B_{j'} \setminus \{i\}$, and delete the columns from the coefficient matrix of this node in which J_i is not scheduled immediately before J_j.
- Variable $\widetilde{\lambda}_p$ is fixed at 0. In this case, we do not update B_j but delete the corresponding column from the coefficient matrix of this node.
- Variable $\widetilde{y}_j$ is fixed at 1. In this case, we update B_j such that $B_j = \{n + 1\}$ and delete the columns from the coefficient matrix of this node in which job J_j is scheduled on some machines.
- Variable $\widetilde{y}_j$ is fixed at 0. In this case, we update B_j such that $B_j = B_j \setminus \{n + 1\}$.

3.5.2 Branching Strategy

Once we have explored a branch-and-bound node (i.e., a RMP), if the solution $\widetilde{\kappa} = (\widetilde{\lambda}, \widetilde{y})$ is fractional and the integer part of its solution value is less than the current upper bound of the branch-and-bound tree minus one, then the corresponding x-variable solution is computed by Eq. (3.4.5), which must be fractional. Based on this x-variable solution, an appropriate fractional x-variable is then selected to branch next.

For notational convenience, we let $x_{n+1,j} = y_j$, $j = 1, \ldots, n$, and implement branching on the most doubtful fractional x-variable. This means that we branch on x_{kh} such that $x_{kh} = \arg\min\{|x_{ij} - 1/2| : 0 < x_{ij} < 1\}$. Two branches are then created that set x_{kh} to 1 or 0. If a variable x_{kh}, $k, h = 1, \ldots, n$, is fixed at 0 at a node, then the initial RMP of the corresponding son node consists of all the columns of its father node except the ones in which job J_k is scheduled immediately before job J_h. At the same time, the job-ordering restriction is updated such that $B_h = B_h \setminus \{k\}$, which guarantees that no feasible partial schedule will be generated where job J_k is scheduled immediately before job J_h. On the other hand, if a variable $x_{kh}, k, h = 1, \ldots, n$, is fixed at 1 at a node, then job J_k must be scheduled immediately before job J_h. However, this leads to a restriction that cannot be enforced in an efficient way in the pricing sub-problem. Instead, we modify the sub-problem by imposing the restrictions $x_{k'h} = 0$ $(k' \neq k)$ and $x_{kh'} = 0$ $(h' \neq h)$. In this case, the initial RMP of the corresponding son node consists of all the columns of its father node except the ones in which job J_k is not scheduled immediately before job J_h. At the same time, the job-ordering restrictions are updated such that $B_h = \{k\}$ and $B_{h'} = B_{h'} \setminus \{k\}$ $(k' \neq k)$, which guarantees that no feasible partial schedule will be generated where job J_k is not scheduled immediately before job J_h.

In addition, if a variable y_h, i.e., $x_{n+1,h}$, $h = 1, \ldots, n$, is fixed at 0 at a node, then the initial RMP of the corresponding son node consists of all the columns of its father node except the ones in which job J_h is rejected. At the same time, the job-ordering restriction is updated such that $B_h = B_h \setminus \{n+1\}$. On the other hand, if a variable y_h is fixed at 1 at a node, then the initial RMP of the corresponding son node consists of all the columns of its father node except the ones in which job J_h is scheduled on some machine. At the same time, the job-ordering restrictions are updated such that $B_h = \{n+1\}$ and $B_{h'} = B_{h'} \setminus \{h\}$ $(h' \neq h)$.

3.5.3 Constructing a Feasible Integral Solution

The use of quick heuristic methods is crucial in the branch-and-bound method, especially for identifying integer feasible solutions, which are used to prune the nodes. When exploring a branch-and-bound tree, two solutions are typically at our disposal. One is the best available integral solution $\overline{\kappa} = (\overline{\lambda}, \overline{y})$, and the other is the solution to the current RMP, say, $\widetilde{\kappa} = (\widetilde{\lambda}, \widetilde{y})$, which in general is not integral. We develop in this section two heuristic methods to construct a "good" feasible integral solution based on the aforementioned solutions.

The main idea of the first heuristic is to collect all the columns corresponding to the master variables in $\overline{\kappa}$ whose values are equal to 1, in addition to those in the current RMP. The resulting RMP with integrity constraints is referred to as the *sub-ILP* and solved by an MIP solver without any further column generation. Note that the resulting sub-ILP may also be potentially large and difficult to solve, so its exploration must often be truncated. We do so by setting a node limit nl.

The second heuristic relies on a simple residual rounding heuristic (Munari and Gondzio [102]), which we briefly describe as follows: Assume that we have a fractional solution $\widetilde{\kappa} = (\widetilde{\lambda}, \widetilde{y})$. The first step is to fix at 1 all the components that are already at 1. Then we select one non-zero component of $\widetilde{\kappa}$ that has the largest value and fix it at 1 and update the job-ordering restrictions accordingly as done in Sect. 3.5.1. The resulting problem is solved again and the process is repeated until an integer solution is obtained or noting that no feasible integer solution can be found by the heuristic. It may happen that the resulting problem is infeasible, so column generation must be invoked again until a feasible solution is obtained or infeasibility is again identified by the column generation procedure. All the columns associated with the fixed components are stored to eventually create an integer feasible solution.

We formally describe the procedure for constructing a near-optimal solution at the tree node as follows:

Algorithm CFS

Step 1. Construct the sub-ILP from the restricted master problem by collecting all the columns corresponding to the master variables in $\overline{\kappa}$ whose values are equal to 1, in addition to those in the restricted master problem at the current node, and imposing the integrity constraints on the variables;

Step 2. Apply an MIP solver to the resulting sub-ILP with node limit nl and set an objective value cutoff equal to the objective value provided by $\overline{\kappa}$;
If a new solution κ_{new} is found, then set $\overline{\kappa} \leftarrow \kappa_{new}$. Otherwise, go to Step 3.
Endif

Step 3. Apply the second heuristic;
If a better feasible solution κ_{new} is found, then set $\overline{\kappa} \leftarrow \kappa_{new}$.

3.5.4 Node Selection Strategy

We explore the search-tree according to the strategy that combines the depth-first rule and the best-bound rule. If the current branch-and-bound node is not fathomed, then the depth-first rule is applied such that one of the two son nodes of the current branch-and-bound node in which the binary variable is fixed to the value of the best available integral solution is selected as the next node to be explored. If the current branch-and-bound node is fathomed, then the best-bound rule is applied such that an active node in the fathomed tree with the smallest local lower bound generated during the column generation phase is selected as the next node to be explored.

3.5.5 Branch-and-Price Example

We solve an instance with ten jobs, two machines, $U = 141$, $\gamma = 19$, and $Q = 9$ to illustrate the working of the branch-and-price algorithm. Table 3.1 provides the other input data, where $x_j = 1$ if and only if job J_j is not available for processing until time $\gamma = 19$, $j = 1, \ldots, 10$.

The branch-and-price algorithm starts by solving RMP with an initial set of columns provided by Algorithm *DE-INI*. Specifically, the initial solution generated by applying Algorithm *DE-INI* is to reject the processing of the job set $\{J_2, J_4, J_6, J_7, J_8, J_9\}$, and schedule jobs J_1 and J_5 on machine 1 in the order $J_5 \to J_1$ and J_3 and J_{10} on machine 2 in the order $J_3 \to J_{10}$. These results give $z_U = 71$.

In the first iteration, at node 1 (root), a solution to MP is found after 23 more columns are added. The optimal solution is fractional and the objective function value of MP is $z_{ll}^1 = 64.6852$. During the solution process, Algorithm CFS does not provide an improved feasible solution, and no mast variables are fixed through reduced cost fixing. Variable x_{76} is chosen as the branching variable and two son nodes are created. The left son node, indexed as node 2, has the branching restriction $x_{76} = 0$ and the right son node, indexed as node 3, has the branching restriction $x_{76} = 1$. Both nodes 2 and 3 are put in the active pool P.

In the second iteration, examining the active pool $P = \{2, 3\}$, the node selection procedure arbitrarily selects node 2. The current RMP is then constructed and solved to optimality after adding one more column with the objective function value $z_{ll}^2 = 64.6852$. Some of the variables in the solution are fractional, and variable x_{56} is chosen as the branching variable and two son nodes are created. The left son node, indexed as node 4, has the branching restriction $x_{56} = 0$ and the right son node, indexed as node 5, has the branching restriction $x_{56} = 1$. Both nodes 4 and 5 are put in the active pool P.

In the third iteration, examining the active pool $P = \{3, 4, 5\}$, the node selection procedure selects node 4 according to the depth-first rule. The current RMP is then constructed and solved to optimality after adding four more columns with the objective function value $z_{ll}^4 = 64.7222$. Variable x_{05} is chosen as the branching

Table 3.1 Data of the problem set

J_j	J_1	J_2	J_3	J_4	J_5	J_6	J_7	J_8	J_9	J_{10}
p_j	9	12	5	6	7	18	16	10	2	12
e_j	36	12	20	18	28	54	32	20	2	60
x_j	1	1	0	1	0	1	0	1	1	1

variable and two son nodes are created. The left son node, indexed as node 6, has the branching restriction $x_{05} = 0$ and the right son node, indexed as node 7, has the branching restriction $x_{05} = 1$. Both nodes 6 and 7 are put in the active pool P.

In the fourth iteration, examining the active pool $P = \{3, 5, 6, 7\}$, the node selection procedure selects node 7 according to the depth-first rule. The current RMP is then constructed and solved to optimality after adding eight more columns with the objective function value $z_{ll}^7 = 65.6111$. Variable $x_{11,6}$ is chosen as the branching variable and two son nodes are created. The left son node, indexed as node 8, has the branching restriction $x_{11,6} = 0$ and the right son node, indexed as node 9, has the branching restriction $x_{11,6} = 1$. Both nodes 8 and 9 are put in the active pool P.

In the fifth iteration, examining the active pool $P = \{3, 5, 6, 8, 9\}$, the node selection procedure selects node 9 according to the depth-first rule. The current RMP is then constructed and solved to optimality after adding eight more columns with the objective function value $z_{ll}^9 = 135 > z_U = 71$. As a consequence, node 9 is fathomed.

In the sixth iteration, examining the active pool $P = 3, 5, 6, 8$, we see that $z_{ll}^3 = z_{ll}^5 = 64.6852$, $z_{ll}^6 = 64.7222$, and $z_{ll}^8 = 65.6111$, and the node selection procedure selects node 5 according to the best-bound rule. The current RMP is then constructed and solved to optimality after adding no more than one column. The objective function value $z_{ll}^5 = 77 > z_U = 71$, so node 5 is fathomed.

In the seventh iteration, examining the active pool $P = \{3, 6, 8\}$, we see that $z_{ll}^3 = 64.6852$, $z_{ll}^6 = 64.7222$, and $z_{ll}^8 = 65.6111$, and the node selection procedure selects node 3 according to the best-bound rule. The current RMP is then constructed and solved to optimality after adding no more than one column. The objective function value $z_{ll}^3 = 73 > z_U = 71$, so node 3 is fathomed.

In the eighth iteration, examining the active pool $P = \{6, 8\}$, we see that $z_{ll}^6 = 64.7222$, and $z_{ll}^8 = 65.6111$, and the node selection procedure selects node 6 according to the best-bound rule. The current RMP is then constructed and solved to optimality after adding three more columns. The objective function value $z_{ll}^6 = 77 > z_U = 71$, so node 6 is fathomed.

In the ninth iteration, examining the active pool $P = \{8\}$, node 8 is chosen. The current RMP is then constructed and solved to optimality after adding six more columns. The objective function value $z_{ll}^8 = 85 > z_U = 71$, so node 8 is fathomed.

The full problem is solved in 10.25 s and the optimal solution is the initial solution determined by Algorithm *DE-INI*.

3.6 Computational Experiments

We performed extensive computational experiments to assess the efficacy and efficiency of the proposed algorithms in solving randomly generated problem instances. We constructed two branch-and-price algorithms: one (denoted by DP-BP) is based on the first strategy for solving the pricing sub-problem and the other (denoted by DE&DP-BP) is based on the second strategy for solving the pricing sub-problem.

We embedded the linear programming models into the branch-and-bound algorithm in the YALMIP/CPLEX 12.6 optimization solver and the DP algorithms in MATLAB. We performed all the computational experiments on a personal computer with a 3.40 GHz CPU and 4 GB memory. We generated the data for the computational experiments according to the following scheme.

3.6.1 Data Sets

- The number of jobs was $n \in \{20, 30, \ldots, 50\}$, and the number of jobs in R was randomly chosen from the set $\{0.1n, 0.2n, 0.5n\}$;
- The number of machines was $m \in \{2, 4, 6, 8\}$;
- The job processing times were randomly generated from the discrete uniform distribution $[1, 30]$;
- For the rejected cost, we followed the model used in Thevenin et al. [140], where the rejected cost e_j of job J_j is related to its processing time p_j because normally a longer job is more valuable, which brings more benefit to the manufacturer, so we set $e_j = k_j p_j$, where k_j is an integer chosen at random between 1 and 10;
- U was randomly chosen from the set $\{\lfloor\sum_{j=1}^n e_j/3\rfloor, \lfloor\sum_{j=1}^n e_j/2\rfloor, \lfloor 2\sum_{j=1}^n e_j/3\rfloor\}$;
- γ was randomly chosen from the set $\{\lfloor\sum_{j=1}^n p_j/3\rfloor, \lfloor\sum_{j=1}^n p_j/2\rfloor, \lfloor 2\sum_{j=1}^n p_j/3\rfloor\}$;
- $Q = \gamma + 0.25(\sum_{j=1}^n p_j - \gamma)$.

For each problem characterized by given numbers of jobs and machines, we randomly generated 20 test instances.

3.6.2 Analysis of Computational Results

The aim of the first part of the computational experiments is to assess the value of the proposed enhancements, i.e., reduced cost fixing and the CFS heuristic, over the standard branch-and-price procedure. We focus on analyzing the benefits of the two enhancements.

We summarize the results in Table 3.2, in which we only provide the results for the 20-job problem instances. The first column records different combinations of numbers of machines and jobs. The three columns under the heading ANN give the average number of nodes in the branch-and-bound tree generated by each of the considered algorithms, i.e., the branch-and-price procedure without reduced cost fixing (B#P-RF), the branch-and-price procedure without the CFS heuristic (B#P-H), and the branch-and-price procedure with both enhancements. The next three columns provide the average numbers of columns generated (ANC) by the three algorithms.

Table 3.2 Effectiveness of the computational enhancements

(m, n)	ANN			ANC			AT(s)		
	B#P-RF	B#P-H	B#P	B#P-RF	B#P-H	B#P	B#P-RF	B#P-H	B#P
(2, 20)	29.25	45.45	21.60	88.65	97.65	77.80	91.19	102.59	72.22
(3, 20)	68.50	109.25	54.50	95.30	109.80	82.25	161.63	176.47	135.14
(4, 20)	121.65	229.60	84.65	77.15	126.65	69.15	171.45	277.28	136.84
(6, 20)	35.45	86.05	13.50	69.25	112.15	59.15	111.16	186.30	42.29
(8, 20)	13.20	39.85	12.45	44.25	84.75	44.45	47.18	128.64	45.41

The last three columns report the average CPU times (in seconds) consumed for solving the problem (AT) by the three algorithms.

The results in Table 3.2 confirm the efficiency of the two enhancements. The results clearly show the benefits of using the reduced cost fixing strategy and the CFS heuristic. Specifically, from the computational results presented in Table 3.2, we draw the following conclusions:

- The numbers of nodes and columns generated by B#P-RF are 54.69 and 11.70% more than those generated by B#P, respectively, and the numbers of nodes and columns generated by B#P-H are 227.92 and 64.49% more than those generated by B#P, respectively, indicating that the two enhancements significantly help improve the convergence of the branch-and-price algorithm.
- In terms of CPU time, B#P is 47.67% faster than B#P-RF and 139.81% faster than B#P-H on average.

3.6.3 Comparison with Alternative Solution Methods

We now present comparisons of our branch-and-price algorithm against the methods of solving $MILP$ using the state-of-the-art MIP solver CPLEX and using Algorithm DP-Pm. Table 3.3 provides the detailed results. Whenever a solution method cannot optimally solve an instance within two hours of CPU time, we put "time" in the corresponding entry of the table. Similarly, if an algorithm runs out of memory, we put "memory" in the corresponding entry. The results in Table 3.3 clearly demonstrate that CPLEX is unable to solve instances with $n > 12$ in most cases due to the large increase in the number of variables in $MILP$ and the intrinsic complexity of the problem, although the solution time of CPLEX is less than that of our branch-and-price algorithm when it can solve an instance. We can also see that Algorithm DP-Pm is unable to solve instances within the two-hour of CPU time limit when $n > 6$. These observations clearly confirm the superiority of our branch-and-price algorithm, and expose the limitations of using a general-purpose solver or a DP-based solution method to solve our problem.

Table 3.3 Performance of CPLEX, and algorithms DP-INI and B#P

m	2				3					
n	6	8	13	14	4	6	12	13		
Time of CPLEX	0.11	0.13	3.25	Memory	0.14	0.09	0.61	Memory		
Time of DP-INI	383.19	Time	Time	Time	706.64	Time	Time	Time		
Time of B#P	15.84	20.78	49.04	54.41	7.65	10.50	22.08	123.77		
m	4				6				8	
n	4	6	11	12	4	6	10	11	4	10
Time of CPLEX	0.06	0.10	0.41	Memory	0.08	0.09	0.13	Memory	0.07	Memory
Time of DP-INI	2460.48	Time	Time	Time	5680.26	Time	Time	Time	Time	Time
Time of B#P	8.90	17.32	41.12	229.06	7.60	8.06	6.19	21.91	8.05	9.82

3.6.4 Detailed Performance of the Branch-and-Price Algorithm

The purpose of this section is to evaluate the performance of the branch-and-price algorithm. We report on the number of problems solved at the root node (NO_{root}), the average number of nodes in the branch-and-bound tree (ANN), the average percentage gap between the linear programming objective value at the root node and optimal objective value (ALB_{root}), the average number of columns generated (ANC), the average CPU time (in seconds) consumed for solving the problem (AT), the average CPU time (in seconds) consumed for solving the pricing sub-problem (AT_{price}), and the average percentage gap between the objective value obtained by Algorithm DE and the optimal objective value (NG_{DE}).

We make the following observations from the results in Table 3.4.

- The lower bound given by the solution value of MP at the root node using the column generation algorithm is extremely close to the optimal solution value, which confirms the efficacy of the column generation algorithm for our problem. For each set of 20 test instances with the same size, the average gap between the lower bound and the optimal solution value is less than 7.5%, which decreases as m and n increase in most cases.
- For fixed n, the instances become easier to solve with increasing m for most tested instances. The reason behind this phenomenon may be as follows: The more machines are involved, fewer jobs are expected to appear in the optimal partial schedules and, consequently, the smaller is the relevance of the solution space.
- Our branch-and-price algorithm is able to solve instances with $n > 50$ within one hour as long as there are not too few machines.
- The pricing time is responsible for more than 73.91% of the total execution time, on average, over all the instances.

Table 3.4 Performance of the branch-and-price algorithm

(m, n)	NO_{root}	ANN	$ALB_{root}(\%)$	ANC	AT(s)	$AT_{price}(s)$	$NG_{DE}(\%)$
(2, 10)	0	12.20	7.50	23.20	14.05	8.90	0.00
(2, 20)	1	53.25	5.05	107.25	179.47	141.19	2.17
(2, 30)	0	96.60	1.28	200.45	1276.97	577.06	11.08
(2, 40)	1	195.65	2.63	388.25	2731.68	1632.81	15.95
(3, 10)	0	14.50	7.10	15.25	30.38	24.11	0.00
(3, 20)	1	72.50	3.57	73.75	116.61	69.09	2.88
(3, 30)	0	223.25	2.50	268.65	971.20	777.51	17.39
(3, 40)	0	359.20	2.59	371.60	1851.55	1427.49	25.06
(3, 50)	0	412.05	1.28	357.45	2664.70	2094.60	33.27
(4, 10)	2	15.45	6.81	14.25	21.25	15.58	0.00
(4, 20)	0	196.70	6.91	102.15	231.35	197.77	6.45
(4, 30)	0	467.50	2.63	158.75	903.50	524.32	18.05
(4, 40)	1	494.00	1.59	224.45	1731.60	1532.72	15.46
(4, 50)	0	648.25	1.60	282.25	2158.00	1647.75	48.38
(6, 10)	1	7.25	7.12	13.30	10.64	6.53	0.36
(6, 20)	1	6.50	4.19	91.25	95.67	66.44	7.51
(6, 30)	0	297.00	3.06	229.35	801.70	725.30	22.70
(6, 40)	0	349.00	5.57	192.75	1526.70	1284.92	42.50
(6, 50)	1	465.50	0.65	374.05	2007.90	1820.41	55.13
(8, 10)	0	16.05	1.53	22.45	21.59	15.32	0.61
(8, 20)	3	143.00	3.68	364.00	109.47	89.87	7.74
(8, 30)	4	197.50	2.90	460.65	460.24	303.18	22.53
(8, 40)	3	217.00	1.45	418.50	915.72	767.48	45.30
(8, 50)	1	220.40	2.27	414.55	1542.50	1307.40	64.24

- Algorithm $DE\text{-}INI$ performs relatively well, where the average gap NG_{DE} is no more than 64.24%. As expected, the performance of Algorithm $DE\text{-}INI$ deteriorates as m and n increase.

3.7 Summary

In this chapter we focus on the issue of rescheduling on identical parallel machines in the presence of unexpected delays causing unavailability to some jobs where job rejection is allowed. The degree of disruption is measured by the maximum time deviation of the scheduled jobs relative to the planned schedule. We consider the classical objective of minimizing the total completion time as the scheduling cost, and model the maximum completion time deviation and total rejection cost as constraints. We develop two exact algorithms to solve the problem. One is a DP-based algorithm, which helps establish that the problem is $\mathcal{NP}$-hard in the ordinary sense when the number of machines is fixed. The other is a branch-and-price method incorporating a range of computational enhancements, including the use of the differential evolution algorithm for finding good initial feasible solutions and solving the pricing sub-problem, the inclusion of reduced cost fixing during the inner iterations of the algorithm, and the use of a heuristic for constructing a good integer feasible solution. The computational results demonstrate that our algorithms are very effective and efficient in solving small- to medium-sized instances of the problem.

Our research findings have several managerial implications for industrial, health care, manufacturing, and process management. First, our branch-and-price algorithm is very effective and efficient, which performs better than using a general-purpose solver or a dynamic programming-based solution method. Second, the lower bound given by the solution value of MP at the root node using the column generation algorithm is extremely close to the optimal solution value, which enables the decision-maker to obtain high-quality solutions quickly. Finally, since job unavailability often arises in practice, we hope that our work will highlight the importance of addressing the issues associated with job unavailability and job rejection option in real-life production.

3.8 Bibliographic Remarks

Scheduling has been extensively studied in the literature often under the assumption that all the jobs have to be processed. However, rejecting the processing of some jobs by either outsourcing them or just rejecting them may reduce the inventory and tardiness costs in a highly loaded make-to-order manufacturing system at the expense of the outsourcing cost or penalty. A higher level of decision concerning the splitting of the jobs into accepted and rejected portions should be made prior to the scheduling decision. Scheduling problems with rejection are quite interesting from practical and theoretical points of view, and researchers have over the last decade paid a great deal of attention to such problems (Shabtay et al. [131]). The idea of scheduling with rejection was first introduced by Bartal et al. [13], who studied the problem of minimizing the makespan of scheduling the accepted jobs plus the sum of the penalties of the rejected jobs on identical parallel machines. Other studies on scheduling with rejection concerning the total (weighted) completion time criterion in various scheduling environments include Cheng and Sun [23], Li and Lu [83], Manavizadeh et al. [95], Ou and Zhong [111], Shabtay [128], Yin et al. [175], and Zhang et al. [182], among others. Shabtay et al. [130] provided a robust approach to scheduling with rejection by performing a bicriterion analysis of a large set of scheduling problems that can all be represented by (or reduced to) the same mathematical formulation. For the other scheduling criteria and more comprehensive surveys on scheduling with rejection, we refer the reader to Nobibon and Leus [108], Shabtay et al. [129], Slotnick [134], and Thevenin et al. [140]. However, compared with the problem considered in this chapter, all the above papers and the references therein focus only on the deterministic case, neglecting the effect of unexpected disruption.

Table 3.5 Summary of the literature on rescheduling problems

Reference	Machine setting	Disruption type	Job rejection option	Solution methods
Hall and Potts [55]	Single machine	Job unavailability	Without	Complexity analysis, DP, approximation method
Hall and Potts [54]	Single machine	Arrival of new jobs	Without	Complexity analysis, DP
Liu and Ro [88]	Single machine	Machine unavailability	Without	DP, approximation method
Qi et al. [120]	Single machine, parallel machines	Machine unavailability	Without	DP, approximation method
Yin et al. [176]	Parallel machines	Machine unavailability	Without	Complexity analysis, DP, approximation method
Wang et al. [146]	Single machine	Arrival of new jobs	With	Genetic algorithm

Although scheduling with job rejection has attracted more and more attention, the study on rescheduling with job rejection is relative few. Table 3.5 summarizes the literature on rescheduling problems by the machine setting, disruption type, job rejection option, and solution methods.

As shown in Table 3.5, most of the existing literature mainly focuses on analyzing the computational complexity of the problems, and designing dynamic programming-based polynomial or pseudo-polynomial solution algorithms or approximation algorithms. Comparing our research with the above papers, there are two main differences as follows: (i) In the problem considered in this chapter we consider the option of rejecting the processing of some jobs at an additional cost so as to reduce the negative impact of job unavailability and achieve an acceptable service level, whereas in all the above papers, it is assumed that all the jobs have to be processed. (ii) We design an exact branch-and-price algorithm by incorporating several features that make it more efficient so that large instances can be solved within a reasonable computational time.

It is worth noting that the main results of this chapter come from Wang et al. [149].

Chapter 4
Rescheduling with Controllable Processing Times and Job Rejection in the Presence of New Arrival Jobs and Deterioration Effect

This chapter considers a dynamic multi-objective machine scheduling problem in response to continuous arrival of new jobs with deterioration effect, under the assumption that jobs can be rejected and job processing time is controllable by allocating extra resources. By deterioration effect, we mean that each job's processing time may be subject to change due to the capability deterioration with machine's usage, i.e., the actual processing time of a job becomes longer if the job starts processing later. The operational cost and the disruption cost need to be optimized simultaneously. To solve these dynamic scheduling problems, a directed search strategy (DSS) is introduced into the elitist non-dominated sorting genetic algorithm (NSGA-II) to enhance its capability of tracking changing optimums while maintaining fast convergence. The DSS consists of a population re-initialization mechanism (PRM) to be adopted upon the arrival of new jobs and an offspring generation mechanism (OGM) during evolutionary optimization. PRM re-initializes the population by repairing the non-dominated solutions obtained before the disturbances occur, modifying randomly generated solutions according to the structural properties, as well as randomly generating solutions. OGM generates offspring individuals by fine-tuning a few randomly selected individuals in the parent population, employing intermediate crossover in combination with Gaussian mutations to generate offspring, and using intermediate crossover together with differential evolution based mutation operator. Both PRM and OGM aim to strike a good balance between exploration and exploitation in solving the dynamic multi-objective scheduling problem. Comparative studies are performed on a variety of problem instances of different sizes and with different changing dynamics. Experimental results demonstrate that the proposed DSS is effective in handling the dynamic scheduling problems under investigation.

This part is composed of six sections. In Sect. 4.1 we describe the problem. In Sect. 4.2 we derive some structural properties. In Sect. 4.3 we propose the directed search strategy embedded in NSGA-II for the dynamic multi-objective machine scheduling problem. Empirical studies are performed in Sect. 4.4 to verify the

D. Wang et al., *Rescheduling Under Disruptions in Manufacturing Systems*,
Uncertainty and Operations Research, https://doi.org/10.1007/978-981-15-3528-4_4

effectiveness of the evolutionary dynamic multi-objective optimization algorithm using directed search strategy. We conclude this chapter in Sect. 4.5, and end the chapter in Sect. 4.6 with bibliographic remarks.

4.1 Problem Formulation

We describe the scheduling problem under study as follows: Assume that a set of non-preemptive jobs $N = \{J_1, J_2, \ldots, J_{n_o}\}$ to be processed without interruption on a common machine. All the jobs and the machine are available for processing at time zero. Each job J_j has a basic processing time $\bar{p}_j$. In this chapter, we focus on one type of common issues existing in practical manufacturing: the continuous usage and accompanying aging of the processing machine would incur deterioration and weariness to industrial systems, which would increase the probability of machine breakdown, increase production cost and decrease product quality. From an operational point of view, the impact of machine deterioration is directly reflected by that the actual processing of a job depends on its scheduled position or starting time in a given schedule. Since the processing condition deteriorates as time evolves, later starting of the processing of a job usually requires longer duration. One effective reaction to deal with this issue is to control job processing times by allocating extra amount of continuous resource, such as gas, fuel and electricity power to the operation. As a result, the actual processing time of a job can be modeled as a linear function of its starting time and the amount of resource allocated to it. Specially, the actual processing time of a job can be defined as $p_j = \bar{p}_j + \alpha t_j - b_j u_j, 0 \le u_j \le \bar{u}_j < \bar{p}_j / b_j$ if it starts its processing at time t_j, where α is a common deteriorating rate shared by all jobs, b_j is the positive compression rate of job J_j, u_j is the amount of resource allocated to job J_j, and $\bar{u}_j$ is the upper bound on u_j.

Due to the limited machine capacity and customers' expectation of short-term delivery, the decision maker reserves the option to reject the processing of some jobs in order to achieve an acceptable service quality at additional penalties. Here, the service quality is measured by the total completion times of all jobs.

The original goal of this machine scheduling problem without considering the arrival of new jobs is to determine the accepted job set A, accepted job sequence and resource allocation strategy to generate the baseline schedule that minimizes the following operational costs: $q \sum_{J_j \in A} C_j + \sum_{J_j \in A} c_j u_j + \sum_{J_j \in \bar{A}} e_j$, where C_j denotes the completion time of job J_j in the accepted job sequence, c_j is the unit resource cost of job J_j, $\bar{A}$ denotes the rejected job set, e_j is the rejection cost of job J_j, and q is the scalar coefficient for the aggregation of time and cost. Using the three-field notation $\alpha|\beta|\gamma$ introduced by Graham et al. [42], we can formulate the original operational cost minimization problem, denoted by problem (**P**), as follows

$$1 \left| rej, \bar{p}_j + \alpha t_j - b_j u_j \right| q \sum_{J_j \in A} C_j + \sum_{J_j \in A} c_j u_j + \sum_{J_j \in \bar{A}} e_j \tag{4.1.1}$$

where "*rej*" in the β field indicates that job rejection is allowed.

It is assumed that the jobs in A have been scheduled optimally to minimize the original operational cost objective $q\sum_{J_j\in A}C_j+\sum_{J_j\in A}c_ju_j+\sum_{J_j\in\bar{A}}e_j$, and that S^* is the obtained optimal baseline schedule. However, S^* can hardly be executed as planned due to the continuous arrival of new jobs. The new jobs together with jobs that have not been finished processing when disruption occurs should be rescheduled. We assume that this information becomes available after π^* has been determined, but before processing begins. If the updated information becomes available after the processing starts, then the processed jobs in A will be removed, and any partly processed jobs in A will be processed to completion. Let Ω denote the set of originally scheduled jobs that have not been finished processing and $\bar{\Omega}$ denote the set of the new arrived jobs.

To efficiently reduce the impact of arrival of new jobs, the flexible strategies of allocation extra resources and job rejection are adopted here. For jobs in $\Omega\cup\bar{\Omega}$, let Λ denote the set of jobs that would be accepted, and $\bar{\Lambda}$ denote the set of jobs that would be rejected. The quality of a schedule π of the jobs in $\Omega\cup\bar{\Omega}$ is measured by two criteria. The first is the operational cost, i.e., $q\sum_{J_j\in\Lambda}C_j+\sum_{J_j\in\Lambda}c_ju_j+\sum_{J_j\in\bar{\Lambda}}e_j$, and the second is the total virtual tardiness $\sum_{J_j\in\Lambda\cap\Omega}T_j$, where $T_j=\max\{C_j-\bar{C}_j,0\}$, C_j is the completion time of job J_j in S, and $\bar{C}_j$ is the completion time of job J_j in S^*.

It is obviously that the two criteria are conflicting with each other. First, as pointed out by Minella et al. [97], the total completion time and the total tardiness are not correlated. In other words, optimizing costs $\sum_{J_j\in A}C_j$ does not necessarily mean the optimization of $\sum_{J_j\in A\cap B}T_j$. Therefore in scheduling, there have been several studies concentrating on examining the relationship between the total completion time and the total tardiness [35, 92, 121]. Second, if we reject more original jobs and allocate more resources to the accepted jobs, the operational cost may be increased due to additional rejection and resource cost. Meanwhile the completion times of the accepted jobs will decrease as fewer jobs are involved in scheduling, so does the deviation cost. To summarize, the above two criteria are in-conflict with each other.

Thus, the above scheduling problem can be formulated as the following bi-criterion optimization problem: Given two criteria $V_1=\sum_{J_j\in\Lambda}C_j+\sum_{J_j\in\Lambda}c_ju_j+\sum_{J_j\in\bar{\Lambda}}e_j$ and $V_2=\sum_{J_j\in\Lambda\cap\Omega}T_j$, determine the set of all Pareto optimal solutions (V_1, V_2), that is, the Pareto front, *PF* for short. Again by using the three-field notation $\alpha|\beta|\gamma$, we formulate the above problem (denoted by **P1**) as follows.

$$1\left|rej,\bar{p}_j+\alpha t_j-b_ju_j\right|(q\sum_{J_j\in A}C_j+\sum_{J_j\in A}c_ju_j+\sum_{J_j\in\bar{A}}e_j,\ \sum_{J_j\in A\cap B}T_j)\qquad(4.1.2)$$

Note that even without considering the deterioration effect, controllable processing time and job rejection, the problem is already $\mathcal{NP}$-hard [54], hence problem (**P1**) is $\mathcal{NP}$-hard too.

4.2 Problem Analysis

In this section we derive some structural properties of the optimal schedules and useful results that will be used later in the design of solution algorithms.

Lemma 4.2.1 *Problem (P) can be solved in $O(n_O^4)$ time.*

Proof An optimal solution of the problem (**P**) can be determined by solving the following three sub-problems:

- *Sub-problem* 1: determine the optimal resource allocation strategy $u^* = (u^*_{[1]}, u^*_{[2]}, \ldots, u^*_{[n_O-h]})$ for a given accepted job sequence $S = (J_{[1]}, J_{[2]}, \ldots, J_{[n_O-h]})$, where $J_{[j]}$ denotes the j-th job scheduled in S and h is the number of rejected jobs;
- *Sub-problem* 2: determine the optimal rejected job set and accepted job sequence under the optimal resource allocation strategy for given h;
- *Sub-problem* 3: enumerate all the possible values of h to determine the optimal solution.

(1) Solving *Sub-problem* 1

For given h and job sequence $S = (J_{[1]}, J_{[2]}, \ldots, J_{[n_O-h]})$, the operational cost can be formulated as follows:

$$
\begin{aligned}
& q\sum_{J_j\in A} C_j + \sum_{J_j\in A} c_j u_j + \sum_{J_j\in \bar{A}} e_j \\
&= q\sum_{j=1}^{n_O-h} C_{[j]} + \sum_{j=1}^{n_O-h} c_{[j]}u_{[j]} + \sum_{j=n_O-h+1}^{n_O} e_{[j]} \\
&= q\left(C_{[1]} + C_{[2]} + \cdots + C_{[n_O-h]}\right) + \sum_{j=1}^{n_O-h} c_{[j]}u_{[j]} + \sum_{j=n_O-h+1}^{n_O} e_{[j]} \\
&= q\sum_{j=1}^{n_O-h} (n_O - h + 1 - j)\, p_{[j]} + \sum_{j=1}^{n_O-h} c_{[j]}u_{[j]} + \sum_{j=n_O-h+1}^{n_O} e_{[j]} \\
&= q\sum_{j=1}^{n_O-h} \tilde{w}_j p_{[j]} + \sum_{j=1}^{n_O-h} c_{[j]}u_{[j]} + \sum_{j=n_O-h+1}^{n_O} e_{[j]}
\end{aligned}
$$

Now substituting $p_j = \bar{p}_j + \alpha t_j - b_j u_j$ into the above equation, we have

$$
\begin{aligned}
& q\sum_{j=1}^{n_O-h} \tilde{w}_j p_{[j]} + \sum_{j=1}^{n_O-h} c_{[j]}u_{[j]} + \sum_{j=n_O-h+1}^{n_O} e_{[j]} \\
&= q\sum_{j=1}^{n_O-h} W_j \left(\bar{p}_{[j]} - b_{[j]}u_{[j]}\right) + \sum_{j=1}^{n_O-h} c_{[j]}u_{[j]} + \sum_{j=n_O-h+1}^{n_O} e_{[j]}
\end{aligned}
$$

$$= q\sum_{j=1}^{n_O-h} W_j\bar{p}_{[j]} + \sum_{j=1}^{n_O-h}\left(c_{[j]} - qW_jb_{[j]}\right)u_{[j]} + \sum_{j=n_O-h+1}^{n_O} e_{[j]}$$

where $W_j = \sum_{i=j}^{n_O-h}\sum_{k=0}^{i-j}\mathbf{M}_{i-j+1,k+1}\alpha^k\tilde{w}_i$, and $\mathbf{M}_{i,j}$ can be iteratively calculated as $\mathbf{M}_{i,j} = \mathbf{M}_{i-1,j-1} + \mathbf{M}_{i-1,j}$ with $\mathbf{M}_{1,1} = 1$, $\mathbf{M}_{1,j} = 0$, $\mathbf{M}_{i,1} = 0$ for $i, j = 2, 3, \ldots, n_O - h$.

Therefore, for the j-th accepted job in given schedule, when $c_{[j]} \geq W_jb_{[j]}$ its optimal resource allocation amount should be $u_{[j]} = 0$; otherwise, its optimal resource allocation amount should be $u_{[j]} = \bar{u}_{[j]}$.

Since the first and third terms in the above equation are constant, it is easy to see that for each $j = 1, 2, \ldots, n_O - h$, if $c_{[j]} \geq W_jb_{[j]}$, the optimal resource allocation is $u^*_{[j]} = 0$; otherwise, the optimal resource allocation is $u^*_{[j]} = \bar{u}_{[j]}$.

(2) Solving *Sub-problem* 2

For $1 \leq j, r \leq n_O$, let us define

$$C_{jr} = \begin{cases} W_r\bar{p}_j, & r = 1, 2, \ldots, n_O - h;\ c_j \geq W_rb_j \\ W_r\bar{p}_j + \left(c_j - W_rb_j\right)\bar{u}_j, & r = 1, 2, \ldots, n_O - h;\ c_j < W_rb_j \\ e_j, & r = n_O - h + 1, \ldots, n_O \end{cases}$$

where C_{jr} denotes the minimum possible cost resulting from assigning job J_j to position r in the sequence.

Now let us introduce binary variable x_{jr}, where $x_{jr} = 1$ if job J_j is assigned at position r and $x_{jr} = 0$ otherwise. Then *Sub-problem* 2 can be transferred into the following assignment problem:

$$\begin{aligned} \min & \sum_{r=1}^{n_O}\sum_{j=1}^{n_O} C_{jr}x_{jr} \\ \text{s.t.} & \sum_{r=1}^{n_O} x_{jr} = 1,\ j = 1, 2, \ldots, n_O \\ & \sum_{j=1}^{n_O} x_{jr} = 1,\ r = 1, 2, \ldots, n_O \\ & x_{jr} \in \{0, 1\},\ r, j = 1, 2, \ldots, n_O \end{aligned}$$

It is well known that the linear assignment problem can be solved in $O(n_O^3)$ time.

(3) Solving *Sub-problem* 3

Since the optimal h value is unknown, we have to enumerate all the possible h values and solve the corresponding series of assignment problems to determine the optimal solution. Thus, the overall time complexity is indeed $O(n_O^4)$. □

Lemma 4.2.2 *For given accepted jobs and resource allocation strategy, there exists an optimal schedule for problem* (**P**) *in which the accepted jobs are processed according to the non-decreasing order of* $\bar{p}_j - b_j u_j$.

Proof We prove the result by pairwise job interchange argument. For a given accepted job set Ω and a corresponding resource allocation strategy, assume there exists an optimal accepted job sequence $\delta = (S_1, J_j, J_k, S_2)$ with $\bar{p}_j - b_j u_j > \bar{p}_k - b_k u_k$, where S_1 and S_2 are partial job sequences and the completion time of the last job scheduled in S_1 is t_0. Construct a new scheduling $\tilde{\delta}$ from δ by swapping jobs J_j and J_k while leaving the other jobs unchanged, i.e., $\tilde{\delta} = (S_1, J_k, J_j, S_2)$. Then the completion times of jobs J_j and J_k in δ and jobs J_k and J_j in $\tilde{\delta}$ are given, respectively, by $C_j(\delta) = t_0 + \bar{p}_j - b_j u_j + \alpha t_0$, $C_k(\delta) = \bar{p}_k - b_k u_k + (1+\alpha)(t_0 + \bar{p}_j - b_j u_j + \alpha t_0)$, $C_k(\tilde{\delta}) = \bar{p}_k - b_k u_k + (1+\alpha)t_0$ and $C_j(\tilde{\delta}) = \bar{p}_j - b_j u_j + (1+\alpha)(\bar{p}_k - b_k u_k + (1+\alpha)t_0)$.

From $\bar{p}_j - b_j u_j > \bar{p}_k - b_k u_k$, it is easy to see that $C_k(\tilde{\delta}) < C_j(\delta)$ and $C_j(\tilde{\delta}) < C_k(\delta)$, and hence $C_k(\tilde{\delta}) + C_j(\tilde{\delta}) < C_j(\delta) + C_k(\delta)$. It follows that $\tilde{\delta}$ is better than δ, which contradicts the optimality of δ. Thus, Lemma 4.2.2 holds. □

An important structural property of problem (**P1**) is given below, which will be used in Sect. 4.3 to help speed up the convergence in tracking the moving *PF* in dynamic environments.

Theorem 4.2.3 *For given accepted jobs and resource allocation strategy, there exists an optimal schedule for the problem* (***P1***) *in which both the jobs in* $A \cap B$ *and jobs in* $A \cap \bar{B}$ *are processed according to the non-decreasing order of* $\bar{p}_j - b_j u_j$, *respectively.*

Proof The idea is similar to the proof of Lemma 4.2.2. For a given accepted job set A and the corresponding resource allocation strategy, assume that there exists an optimal accepted job sequence $\delta = (S_1, J_j, S_2, J_k, S_3)$ with $J_j, J_k \in A \cap B$ and $\bar{p}_j - b_j u_j > \bar{p}_k - b_k u_k$, where S_1, S_2 and S_3 are partial job sequences. Construct a new scheduling $\tilde{\delta}$ from δ by swapping jobs J_j and J_k while leaving the other jobs unchanged, i.e., $\tilde{\delta} = (S_1, J_k, S_2, J_j, S_3)$. We now analyze the impact of the exchanging on the operational cost and deviation cost as follows.

(1) For the operational cost

By the proof of Lemma 4.2.2, the completion time of J_k in $\tilde{\delta}$ is less than that of job J_j in δ. It follows that the completion time of any job belonging to S_2 in $\tilde{\delta}$ is less than that of the corresponding job in δ. Hence, the completion time of J_j in $\tilde{\delta}$ is less than that of job J_k in δ. Therefore, the total completion time of sequence $\tilde{\delta}$ is less than that of δ.

(2) For the disruption cost

By Lemma 4.2.2, $\bar{p}_j - b_j u_j > \bar{p}_k - b_k u_k$ implies that $\bar{C}_k < \bar{C}_j$. By the above proof, we have $C_k(\tilde{\delta}) < C_j(\delta) < C_j(\tilde{\delta}) < C_k(\delta)$. Hence, it is easy to see that $T_k(\tilde{\delta}) +$

$T_j(\tilde{\delta}) = \max\{C_k(\tilde{\delta}) - \bar{C}_k, 0\} + \max\{C_j(\tilde{\delta}) - \bar{C}_j, 0\} \leq \max\{C_j(\delta) - \bar{C}_j, 0\} + \max\{C_k(\delta) - \bar{C}_k, 0\} = T_j(\delta) + T_k(\delta)$. It follows that the total deviation cost of sequence $\tilde{\delta}$ is less than that of δ.

Summing up the above observations, $\tilde{\delta}$ is better than δ, which contradicts the optimality of δ. Thus, the result for the jobs in $A \cap B$ holds. The case for the jobs in $A \cap \bar{B}$ can be proved in a similar manner. Therefore Theorem 4.2.3 holds. □

Theorem 4.2.3 describes certain patterns that the original and new arrived jobs follow in the Pareto optimal schedule of problem (**P1**). This can be used to predict the location of the Pareto front after new jobs arrive, thereby speeding up the convergence.

4.3 A Directed Search Strategy for Dynamic Multi-objective Scheduling

In Sect. 4.3 we have introduced a dynamic scheduling problem in response to arrival of new jobs during the production process. For such a problem, the new arrival jobs will make the planned schedule no longer optimal, and rescheduling will give rise to a deviation of the completion time of the original jobs from the planned schedule. In order to effectively respond to the disruption caused by the arrival of new jobs, a directed search strategy (DSS) is proposed to be embedded in NSGA-II [33], termed as NSGA-II/PRM + OGM, to minimize the operational cost and the deviation cost. Here, NSGA-II is selected as the basic search engine for its demonstrated robust search performance in solving multi-objective optimization problems. DSS is composed of a population re-initialization mechanism (PRM) when a change occurs (arrival of new jobs), and an offspring generation mechanism (OGM) in reproduction, in an attempt to strike a good balance between exploration and exploitation in solve dynamic multi-objective machine scheduling problem. Intermediate crossover, Gaussian mutation as well as differential evolution based mutation are the most usually used operators in Evolutionary Algorithms, and they are redesigned in OGM according to the dynamic scheduling problem for their effectiveness in dealing with scheduling problems [137, 148].

In the following subsections, we introduce the solution representation first of all, then describe the population re-initialization mechanism (PRM) to be employed upon arrival of new jobs, following by a presentation of the offspring generation mechanism (OGM). Finally, a brief account of the selection method is given. The overall framework of NSGA-II/PRM + OGM is shown in Fig. 4.1.

4.3.1 Solution Representation

We represent a solution to problem (**P1**) by a $3(\tilde{n}_O + n_N)$-dimensional vector $\vec{x}_{i,t}$ as shown in Eq. (4.3.1), where $\tilde{n}_O$ is the number of originally accepted jobs satisfying $\tilde{n}_O \leq n_O$, and n_N is the number of newly arrived jobs. Let *pop* represent the

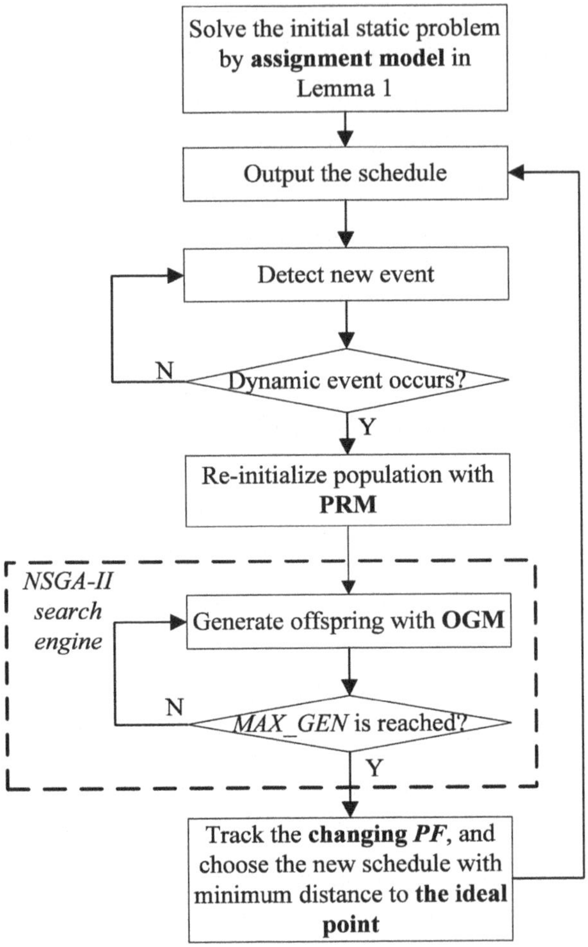

Fig. 4.1 The overall framework of NSGA-II/PRM + OGM

population size, t the generation number, and GEN_MAX the maximum number of generations. The solution contains three chromosomes. The first chromosome, chromosome r for short, indicates whether a job is to be accepted or rejected. The processing sequence is represented in the second chromosome, denoted as chromosome π. The third chromosome, denoted as the chromosome y, describes the resource allocation. Vector $\vec{x}_{i,t}$ represents the i-th individual in the t-th generation, and $x_{i,j,t}$ stands for the j-th entry of $\vec{x}_{i,t}$, $1 \le j \le 3(\tilde{n}_O + n_N)$.

$$\begin{aligned}\vec{x}_{i,t} = (&x_{i,1,t}, x_{i,2,t}, \ldots, x_{i,\tilde{n}_O+n_N,t},\\ &x_{i,\tilde{n}_O+n_N+1,t}, x_{i,\tilde{n}_O+n_N+2,t}, \ldots, x_{i,2(\tilde{n}_O+n_N),t},\\ &x_{i,2(\tilde{n}_O+n_N)+1,t}, \ldots, x_{i,3(\tilde{n}_O+n_N),t})\end{aligned} \quad (4.3.1)$$

where $i = 1, 2, \ldots, pop$; $t = 1, 2, \ldots, Gen\_max$.

An element of '0' or '1' in the first $(\tilde{n}_O + n_N)$ entries in chromosome r means the rejection or acceptance of a job. The $(\tilde{n}_O + n_N)$ entries in chromosome π contain the sequence of accepted jobs and a set of rejected jobs. Each entry in chromosome π takes a unique job index from the set $\{1, \ldots, \tilde{n}_O + n_N\}$. For each entry in chromosome π, if the entry of the same position in chromosome r is 1, the corresponding job is accepted, otherwise it is rejected. The $(\tilde{n}_O + n_N)$ entries in chromosome y indicate the fraction of resource allocation to the job represented in the corresponding position of chromosome π. The entities in y chromosome take a value between [0, 1]. Therefore, a feasible schedule can be fully described by the three chromosomes in the representation in Eq. (4.3.1).

$$\begin{aligned}\vec{x}_{1,1} = &(1, 0, 0, 1, 1, 1, 0, 1, 1, 1,\\ &4, 2, 6, 1, 9, 10, 8, 3, 5, 7,\\ &0.3, 0.1, 0.5, 1.0, 0, 0.9, 0.3, 0.1, 0, 0.2)\end{aligned} \tag{4.3.2}$$

Equation (4.3.2) gives a sample chromosome for $i = 1, t = 1, \tilde{n}_O + n_N = 10$ where jobs 4, 1, 9, 10, 3, 5, 7 are accepted and processed in the corresponding order. The resource allocated to them are 0.3, 1.0, 0, 0.9, 0.1, 0, 0.2 of their maximum amount of resource allocation.

4.3.2 Population Re-initialization Mechanism (PRM)

Once a new environment (arrival of new jobs) is detected, the population is re-initialized using the PRM consisting of the following three population initialization strategies.

- A fraction of λ_1 $(0 \leq \lambda_1 \leq 1)$ individuals of the initial population are generated by taking over a subset of the non-dominated solutions obtained in the previous environment, i.e., before the new jobs arrive. For those individuals, the processing sequence and resource allocation of the originally accepted jobs $J_j \in A \cap B$ are kept unchanged. A subset of new jobs are randomly accepted or rejected, and random feasible resource amount is allocated to each accepted new job. Then, the accepted new jobs $J_j \in A \cup \bar{B}$ are scheduled in a non-decreasing order of $\bar{p}_j - b_j u_j$, and inserted into the existing schedules (the non-dominated solutions before the new jobs arrive) to serve as one part of the initial individuals.
- To enhance diversity of the initial population, a fraction of $\lambda_2 + \lambda_3 = 1 - \lambda_1$ $(\lambda_2, \lambda_3 \geq 0)$ individuals of the initial population are randomly generated, including the decision on job rejection/acceptance, processing sequence, and resource allocation of original and new jobs.
- Of the randomly generated individuals, a fraction of $\lambda_2/(\lambda_2 + \lambda_3)$ individuals are further fine-tuned using the structural property stated in Theorem 4.2.3. In other words, the sequences of original and newly accepted jobs are re-arranged separately in a non-decreasing order of $\bar{p}_j - b_j u_j$ according to Theorem 4.2.3.

The above three population reinitialization strategies aim to achieve a good balance between making use of information of the solutions in the previous environment and maintaining adequate degree of diversity. This balance is controlled by the three fractions, λ_1, λ_2, and λ_3 of the individuals generated using each of the three strategies. The influence of parameter setting on the performance will be discussed in the experiments.

4.3.3 *Offspring Generation Mechanism (OGM)*

While PRM is proposed for population re-initialization in the beginning of each new optimization environment, OGM is designed to enhance population diversity by creating offspring individuals by using a combination of Gaussian mutation and differential evolution based mutation to enhance exploration. The convergence has also been sped up by partly generating individuals from the previous generation through adjusting the processing sequence of original and new jobs according to Theorem 4.2.3.

- A fraction of δ_1 $(0 \leq \delta_1 \leq 1)$ individuals of the offspring population are generated by arranging the processing sequence of original and newly accepted jobs according to Theorem 4.2.3 on the basis of individuals randomly chosen from the previous generation. This is meant to speed up the convergence.
- A fraction of δ_2 $(0 \leq \delta_2 \leq 1 - \delta_1)$ individuals of the offspring population are generated by performing intermediate crossover on two randomly selected parent individuals followed by Gaussian mutation.
- A fraction of δ_3 $(\delta_3 = 1 - \delta_1 - \delta_2)$ offspring individuals are created by performing intermediate crossover on two parent individuals randomly selected followed by a DE-based mutation.

In the following, we provide some details on the intermediate crossover, Gaussian mutation as well as the DE-based mutation. These details are important for understanding the proposed algorithm, as they need to be re-designed according to the needs of the machine scheduling problems.

4.3.3.1 Intermediate Crossover

The intermediate crossover is performed at a probability $CrossFraction$ $(0 < CrossFraction < 1)$ on two randomly chosen individuals, which are indicated using a subscript $r1$ and $r2$, respectively. The intermediate crossover operation is applied on the three chromosomes of the individuals, respectively. Let $o_{i,j,t}$ denote the j-th entry of the i-th offspring individual in the t-th generation, $p_{r1,j,t}$ and $p_{r2,j,t}$ represent the j-th entries of the two individuals in the t-th generation. More specifically, the intermediate crossover can be described by:

$$o_{i,j,t} = p_{r1,j,t} + rand \cdot Ratio \cdot \left(p_{r2,j,t} - p_{r1,j,t}\right) \tag{4.3.3}$$

where $rand$ is a decimal randomly generated from [0, 1], $Ratio$ is the parameter to control the crossover process, $i = 1, 2, \ldots, pop$, $j = 1, 2, \ldots, 3(\tilde{n}_O + n_N)$ and $t = 1, 2, \ldots, Gen\_max$.

After the intermediate crossover operation, chromosome π of $o_{i,j,t}$ may need to be repaired by removing duplicated jobs and inserting missing jobs in case the created offspring is infeasible. Similar repair needs also to be done to chromosome r and chromosome y to fix infeasible solutions.

4.3.3.2 Gaussian Mutation

The following Gaussian mutation is applied on the three chromosomes of the offspring individuals created by intermediate crossover at a probability of $MutateFraction$ $(0 < MutateFraction < 1)$.

$$\tilde{o}_{i,j,t} = o_{i,j,t} + gaussian(\delta) \cdot \left(\text{Scale} - Shrink \cdot Scale \cdot \frac{t}{Gen\_max}\right) \times \left(u_{limit,j} - l_{limit,j}\right) \tag{4.3.4}$$

where $i = 1, 2, \ldots, pop$, $j = 1, 2, \ldots, 3(\tilde{n}_O + n_N)$, $t = 1, 2, \ldots, Gen\_max$, $gaussian(\delta)$ is a number randomly generated from Gaussian distribution, it can be calculated from $\delta = 0.1 \times Length\,of\,search\,space$. $Scale$ is used to control the mutation scale, $Shrink$ represents the mutation shrink coefficient, and $u_{limit,j}$ and $l_{limit,j}$ are the upper and lower bound of $o_{i,j,t}$. Similarly, individuals created by the Gaussian mutation may need to be repaired in case they are infeasible.

4.3.3.3 DE-Based Mutation

The DE-based mutation is composed of the following three steps, by which a fraction of δ_3 $(\delta_3 = 1 - \delta_1 - \delta_2)$ offspring individuals are created.

- **Step 1: Mutation with different individuals**
  Before describing the details, we first define a number of terms taken from the DE literature, including target individual, donor individual and trial individual [31]. The target individual is the solution to be mutated, the donor is a mutant created using the DE mutation, and the trial individual is an offspring generated by recombining the target and donor. Different DE mutation operations can be applied on different chromosomes of the individuals. For example, $DE|rand|1|bin$ strategy [31] can be applied on chromosome r and chromosome y, while the permutation-based DE mutation [154] can be applied on chromosome π.
  To begin with, let $\vec{x}_{i,t}$ be the i-th target individual of the t-th generation, $\vec{x}_{r_1,t}$ and $\vec{x}_{r_2,t}$ represent two randomly sampled individuals from the parent population,

where r_1 and r_2 are mutually exclusive integers randomly chosen from the range $[1, pop]$. Then, chromosome r and y of the trial individual $\vec{v}_{i,t}$ can be obtained as follows, where the number F is used to scale the difference between $\vec{x}_{r_1,t}$ and $\vec{x}_{r_2,t}$.

$$\vec{v}_{i,t} = \vec{x}_{i,t} + F \cdot \left(\vec{x}_{r_1,t} - \vec{x}_{r_2,t}\right) \tag{4.3.5}$$

In this paper, if the j-th component $v_{i,j,t}$ of the donor individual $\vec{v}_{i,t}$ violates the boundary constraint, this component is repaired as follows:

$$v_{i,j,t} = \begin{cases} \min\left\{U_j, 2L_j - v_{i,j,t}\right\}, v_{i,j,t} < L_j \\ \max\left\{L_j, 2U_j - v_{i,j,t}\right\}, v_{i,j,t} \geq U_j \end{cases} \tag{4.3.6}$$

where $[L_j, U_j]$ stands for the feasible interval for $v_{i,j,t}$.
In addition, chromosome π of the trial individual $\vec{v}_{i,t}$ can be obtained through a permutation-based DE mutation proposed by Wang et al. [150], which has been shown to be effective for permutation-based mutations. Here we use $\otimes$ operation to calculate the location difference for the same index in two permutations as P_1 and P_2, and the result of $P_1 \otimes P_2$ is a location offset vector L with the same dimension as P_1 and P_2. With the help of the $\oplus$ operation, any permutation with the same dimension can be transferred into a new one using the location offset vector L. The common issue of repairing infeasible solutions faced by other mutation operations can be avoided, thereby enhancing the global search capability. We can express the permutation-based DE mutation as follows:

$$\vec{v}_{i,t} = \vec{x}_{i,t} \oplus (\vec{x}_{r_1,t} \otimes \vec{x}_{r_2,t}) \tag{4.3.7}$$

Then, the trial individual $\vec{v}_{i,t}$ can be obtained by combining the three chromosomes obtained in the above-mentioned mutation processes.

- **Step 2: Crossover operation in DE-based mutation**
  In order to preserve good structures from the obtained individuals and to accelerate convergence of the algorithm, a crossover operation is embedded after generating the donor individual, where $\vec{v}_{i,t}$ exchanges its chromosome r and y with that of individual $\overrightarrow{best}_{i,t}$, which is selected randomly from the parent population or from the best individuals in the current non-dominated front at a probability of 50%. The binomial crossover is used for exchanging the components at a crossover rate $C_r \in (0, 1)$, which can be described using the following expression:

$$u_{i,j,t} = \begin{cases} v_{i,j,t}, \ rand_j(0,1) \leq C_r \ or \ j = j_{rand} \\ best_{i,j,t}, \ \text{otherwise} \end{cases} \tag{4.3.8}$$

where $i = 1, 2, \ldots, pop$, $j = 1, 2, \ldots, \tilde{n}_O + n_N$, $rand_j(0, 1)$ is a number randomly generated according to a uniform distribution, and $j_{rand} \in [1, \tilde{n}_O + n_N]$ is a randomly chosen position to ensure that $\vec{u}_{i,t}$ gets at least one component from $v_{i,t}$. Thus, chromosome r and y of the trial individual $\vec{u}_{i,t}$ can be obtained.

In order to obtain chromosome π of $\vec{u}_{i,t}$, one-point crossover is performed on the corresponding part of $v_{i,t}$ and $\overrightarrow{best}_{i,t}$, by which good structures from the current individuals can be inherited. After this operation is applied, the obtained chromosome π should be repaired by replacing the repeated components with missing ones. Then, the trial individual $\vec{u}_{i,t}$ can be constructed by combining the three chromosomes generated in the above crossover processes.

- **Step 3: Selection in DE-based mutation**
  After the crossover operation, the better individual of the obtained trial individual $\vec{u}_{i,t}$ and the target individual $\vec{x}_{i,t}$ is selected as the offspring.

4.3.4 *Non-dominated Sorting Based Selection*

After filling up the offspring population using the three different types of operators in OGM, we evaluate the two optimality criteria of all offspring individuals, where the first criterion accounts for the sum of total completion time, resource allocation cost and rejection cost, and the second is the disruption cost that can be calculated. Once the values of the optimality criteria are calculated, the offspring population is combined with the parent population. Non-dominated sorting is then performed and crowding distance is calculated for all individuals in the combined population and then selection is carried out, as proposed in [33].

4.4 Comparative Studies

In this section we conduct numerical experiments to compare the performance of NSGA-II/PRM + OGM with the existing methods, mostly designed for solving stationary optimization problems, to demonstrate the effectiveness of the proposed algorithm for dynamic scheduling in the presence of continuous arrival of new jobs. All the compared algorithms are implemented in MATLAB, and executed on a PC with 4G RAM, Intel Core i5 CPU 2.5 GHz.

4.4.1 *Numerical Test Instances*

The performance of the proposed NSGA-II/PRM + OGM is evaluated on seven randomly generated cases. Those cases are categorized by the problem size, i.e., the number of original and new jobs. For problem cases 1–7, the number of original jobs n_O is 30, 50, 80, 100, 130, 200 and 300, respectively, and the number of new jobs n_N is a randomly sampled integer from the following uniform distributions: $U[1, 5]$, $U[6, 10]$, $U[11, 20]$, $U[21, 35]$, $U[36, 55]$, $U[56, 85]$ and $U[86, 100]$. For each problem case, the basic processing time $\bar{p}_j$ of job J_j is generated from $U[1, 100]$, the positive compression rate b_j of job J_j is generated from $U(0, 1]$, the maximum amount of resource $\bar{u}_j$ that can be allocated to job J_j is generated from $U[0.6\bar{p}_j/b_j, 0.9\bar{p}_j/b_j]$, the rejection cost e_j of job J_j is generated from $U[200, 400]$ and the unit resource cost c_j of job J_j is generated from $U[2, 9]$. The deteriorating rate shared by all jobs is set to $\alpha = 0.01$. The scalar coefficient for the aggregation of time and cost is set to $q = 1$.

For each problem case, 30 independent test instances of dynamic scheduling are generated, and the number of dynamic environments (events) in each test instance is set to $I = 20$. Therefore we have performed a total number of $20 \times 30 \times 7 = 4200$ times of dynamic optimization runs for each problem case.

4.4.2 Performance Indicators

The performance of multi-objective evolutionary algorithms is mainly reflected by the diversity and convergence of the achieved Pareto front, which can be quantitatively assessed by two widely used performance indicators, i.e., inverse generational distance (IGD) [183] and hypervolume (HV) [193]. To take into account the dynamic nature of the scheduling problems studied in this work, we use the slightly modified version of IGD and HV metrics described in the following. Let PF and PF^* be the non-dominated front approximated by an evolutionary algorithm and a reference non-dominated front, respectively, we have

$$IGD\left(PF^*, PF\right) = \frac{\sum_{v \in PF^*} d\left(v, PF\right)}{\left|PF^*\right|} \tag{4.4.1}$$

where v is a non-dominated optimal solution in PF^*, $d(v, PF)$ represents the distance between v and PF, and $|PF^*|$ returns the number of non-dominated solutions in PF^*, which is either a representative set chosen from a known theoretic Pareto optimal front, or a set of non-dominated solutions selected from a combination of all non-dominated solutions obtained by all algorithms to be compared. Here, PF^* is generated using the latter approach.

In this chapter, the target of the evolutionary algorithm is to track a moving *PF* of the dynamic multi-objective scheduling problem when different new jobs arrive. Considering all the *PF*s, we use the mean IGD denoted by $MIGD$ over different events to measure PF_i's proximity to PF_i^*, where $1 \leq i \leq I$, I is the number of events in total.

$$MIGD = \frac{1}{I}\sum_{i=1}^{I} IGD\left(PF_i^*, PF_i\right) \tag{4.4.2}$$

where I is set to 20 in the experiment. A smaller $MIGD$ value means better tracking performance of the algorithm.

Performance indicator *HV* calculates the area dominated by the obtained *PF*, measuring both convergence and diversity of the obtained solution set. Similar to *MIGD*, the mean *HV* denoted by *MHV* over different environments $1 \leq i \leq I$ is adopted. The larger the *MHV* value, the better the performance.

4.4.3 Parameters Setting for Compared Algorithms

To examine the influence of the different mechanisms in the proposed DSS, three variants are considered.

- NSGA-II: The original NSGA-II using randomly re-initialized population, and intermediate crossover and Gaussian mutation for offspring generation.
- NSGA-II/PRM: NSGA-II using PRM for population re-initialization.
- NSGA-II/PRM + OGM: The proposed algorithm.

In the proposed algorithm, there are two types of parameters. The first set of parameters are related to the algorithm itself, including the population size (*pop*), *CrossFraction* and *Ratio* used in the crossover operation, *MutateFraction*, *Shrink*, and *Scale* used in the Gaussian mutation, F and C_r used in the DE-based mutation. The second set of parameters are used in DSS for controlling the balance between exploration and exploitation, including λ_1, λ_2 and λ_3 for PRM, and δ_1, δ_2 and δ_3 for OGM. We tune the parameters in NSGA-II/PRM + OGM by running a number of pilot experiments on solving test instances of problem case 3 with $n_O = 80$ and $n_N \in U[1, 5]$. By default, NSGA-II and NSGA-II/PRM use the same setting for their parameters wherever applicable. The nearest distance to the ideal point is chosen as the criterion for tuning parameters, and the ideal point is constructed by the minimum operational cost which can be obtained by solving the assignment model provided in Lemma 4.2.1 and the minimum deviation cost which is obviously zero. For the sake of convenience, the relative distance fraction (RDP) to the smallest distance value is adopted. The results of the pilot studies are presented in Table 4.1, in which the parameters resulting in the best performance are highlighted.

In the pilot experiments, it is also found out that the algorithms under comparison converges within 100 generations. Therefore the predetermined maximum number of generations, *Max_Gen* is set to 100 for all runs.

4.4.4 Results

Using the fine-tuned parameters identified in the pilot studies shown in Table 4.1, we now examine the performance of the compared algorithms on all the instances of seven problem cases. For problem case 3, the average *IGD* and *HV* values over 30 instances versus event index for three algorithms are shown in Figs. 4.2 and 4.3,

Table 4.1 Pilot experimental results for parameter tuning

Parameters	Values	RDP	Parameters	Values	RDP
pop	50	0.16	$(\lambda_1, \lambda_2, \lambda_3)$	(0.2, 0.3, 0.5)	0.08
	100	0.02		(0.2, 0.5, 0.3)	0.07
	150	**0.00**		**(0.3, 0.2, 0.5)**	**0.00**
CrossFraction	$2/(\tilde{n}_O + n_N)$	**0.00**		(0.3, 0.5, 0.2)	0.05
	$4/(\tilde{n}_O + n_N)$	0.04		(0.5, 0.2, 0.3)	0.00
	$6/(\tilde{n}_O + n_N)$	0.06		(0.5, 0.3, 0.2)	0.24
	$8/(\tilde{n}_O + n_N)$	0.02	$(\delta_1, \delta_2, \delta_3)$	(0.2, 0.3, 0.5)	0.08
Ratio	0.4	0.05		(0.2, 0.5, 0.3)	0.21
	0.8	0.02		**(0.3, 0.2, 0.5)**	**0.00**
	1.2	**0.00**		(0.3, 0.5, 0.2)	0.09
	1.6	0.03		(0.5, 0.2, 0.3)	0.07
MutateFraction	$2/(\tilde{n}_O + n_N)$	0.11		(0.5, 0.3, 0.2)	0.09
	$4/(\tilde{n}_O + n_N)$	0.02	F	0.1	0.07
	$6/(\tilde{n}_O + n_N)$	**0.00**		0.5	0.12
	$8/(\tilde{n}_O + n_N)$	0.05		0.7	0.07
$(Shrink, Scale)$	(0.1, 0.1)	0.01		**0.9**	**0.00**
	(0.1, 0.5)	0.02	C_r	0.1	0.59
	(0.1, 0.9)	0.04		**0.5**	**0.00**
	(0.5, 0.1)	0.01		0.7	0.38
	(0.5, 0.5)	0.01		0.9	0.38
	(0.5, 0.9)	0.03			
	(0.9, 0.1)	0.02			
	(0.9, 0.5)	**0.00**			
	(0.9, 0.9)	0.01			

respectively. The final PFs obtained by the three compared algorithms in the first six events are plotted in Fig. 4.4, and the corresponding convergence curves are given in Fig. 4.5. Similar results have been obtained for other problem cases and the rest events, which are not reported here. From these results, it can be clearly seen that after a dynamic event occurs, NSGA-II/PRM + OGM converges mostly faster than or similar to NSGA-II/PRM and NSGA-II. In addition, diversity of the PF obtained by NSGA-II/PRM + OGM is the highest and their distance to the ideal point is the shortest, indicating better performance in terms of both diversity and convergence.

To quantitatively measure the diversity and convergence of the PF's obtained in different events, the mean and standard deviation of $MIGD$ and MHV for the compared algorithms over 30 instances of seven problem cases are reported in Tables 4.2 and 4.3, respectively. In each table that summarize the statistical results, the first line presents the mean values and the second line presents the standard deviations. In order to verify the significance in performance differences between NSGA-II/PRM

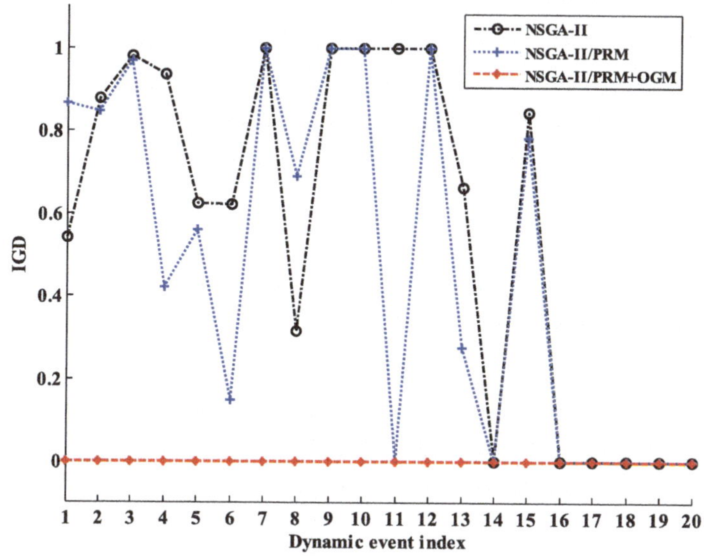

Fig. 4.2 Average *IGD* values over 30 instances versus event index for NSGA-II/PRM + OGM, NSGA-II/PRM, and NSGA-II for problem case 3

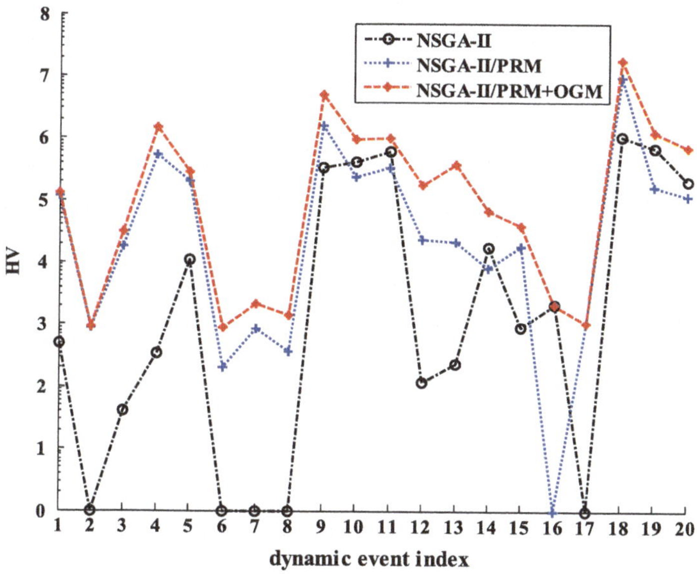

Fig. 4.3 Average *HV* values over 30 instances versus event index for NSGA-II/PRM + OGM, NSGA-II/PRM, and NSGA-II for problem case 3. Note that the y-axis uses the logarithm scale to clearly show differences in the values

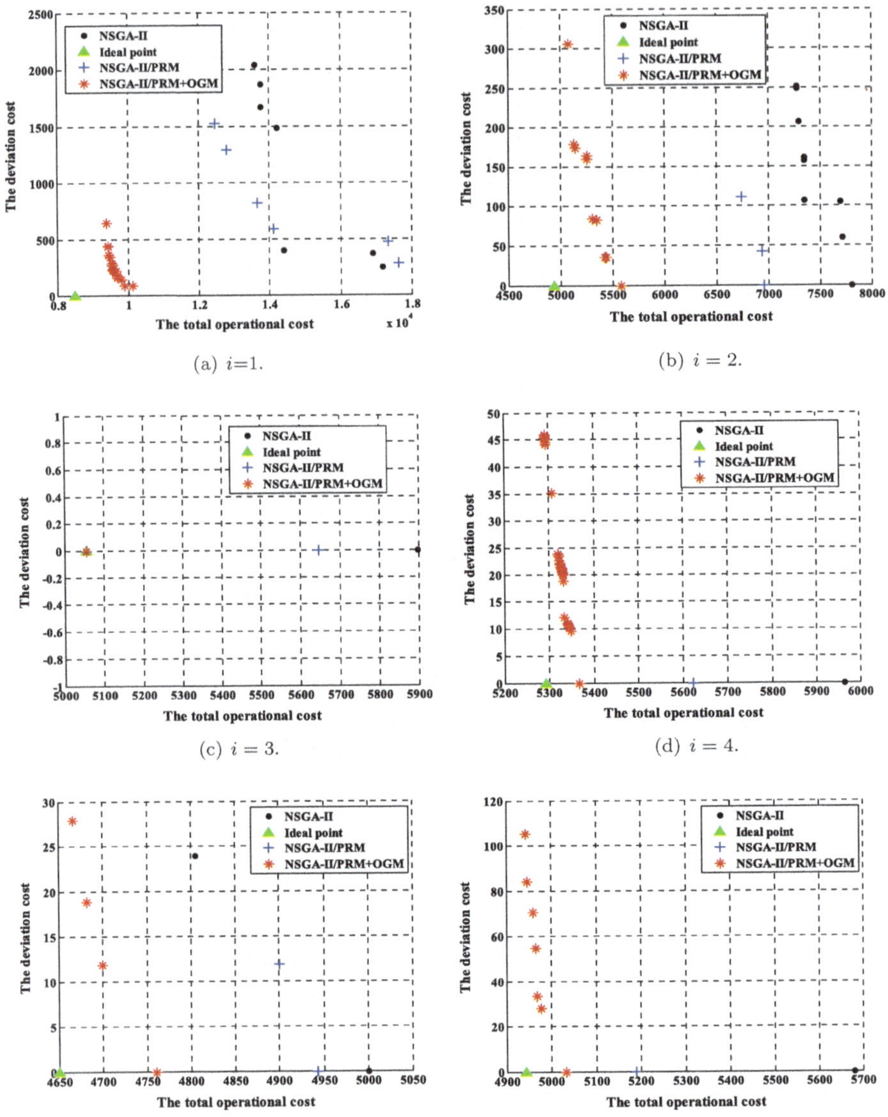

(a) i=1. (b) $i = 2$.

(c) $i = 3$. (d) $i = 4$.

(e) $i = 5$. (f) $i = 6$.

Fig. 4.4 Final *PF* obtained by NSGA-II/PRM + OGM, NSGA-II/PRM, and NSGA-II at six event indexes

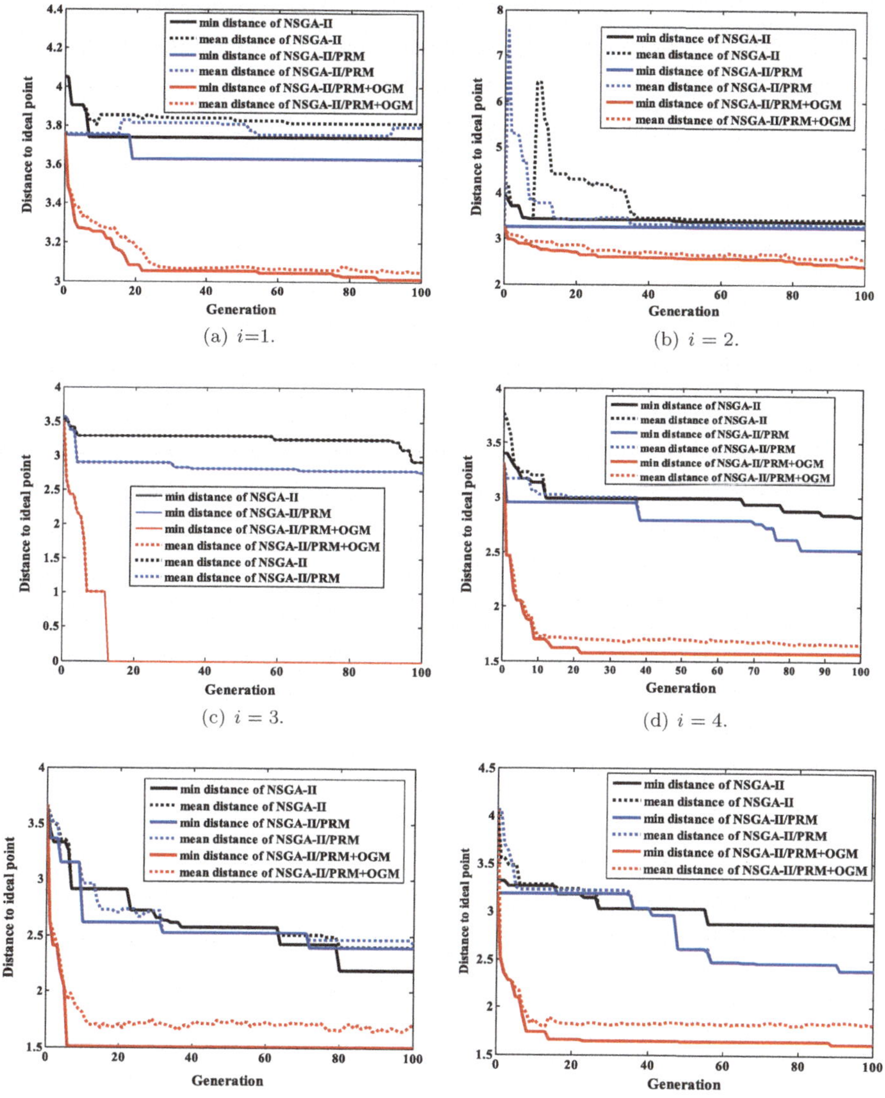

(a) i=1. (b) $i = 2$.

(c) $i = 3$. (d) $i = 4$.

(e) $i = 5$. (f) $i = 6$.

Fig. 4.5 Convergence curves of NSGA-II/PRM + OGM, NSGA-II/PRM, and NSGA-II at six event indexes. Note that y-axis uses the logarithm scale

Table 4.2 Statistical results of *MIGD* values obtained by NSGA-II/PRM + OGM and each algorithm in comparison over 30 instances of seven problem cases

Test instances	NSGA-II/PRM + OGM		NSGA-II/PRM		NSGA-II
Case 1	**0.00** 0.00	+	0.50 0.19	+	0.56 0.19
Case 2	**0.00** 0.00	+	0.69 0.18	+	0.69 0.19
Case 3	**0.00** 0.00	+	0.78 0.16	+	0.77 0.13
Case 4	**0.00** 0.00	+	0.86 0.10	+	0.85 0.11
Case 5	**0.00** 0.00	+	0.88 0.07	+	0.89 0.06
Case 6	**0.00** 0.00	+	0.86 0.09	+	0.89 0.07
Case 7	**0.00** 0.00	+	0.90 0.04	+	0.90 0.04

Table 4.3 Statistical results of *MHV* values obtained by NSGA-II/PRM + OGM and each algorithm in comparison over 30 instances of seven problem cases

Test instances	NSGA-II/PRM + OGM		NSGA-II/PRM		NSGA-II
Case 1	$\mathbf{7.99} \times 10^4$ 7.27×10^4	+	3.17×10^4 4.65×10^4	+	2.78×10^4 4.50×10^4
Case 2	$\mathbf{3.19} \times 10^5$ 3.18×10^5	+	1.55×10^5 1.75×10^5	+	1.54×10^5 1.91×10^5
Case 3	$\mathbf{1.21} \times 10^6$ 1.50×10^6	$\approx$	6.99×10^5 1.10×10^6	$\approx$	5.24×10^5 6.70×10^5
Case 4	$\mathbf{7.55} \times 10^6$ 1.68×10^7	+	2.99×10^6 6.61×10^6	+	1.73×10^6 2.39×10^6
Case 5	$\mathbf{2.34} \times 10^7$ 2.17×10^7	+	1.00×10^7 1.61×10^7	+	7.55×10^6 1.68×10^7
Case 6	$\mathbf{1.17} \times 10^8$ 1.02×10^8	+	4.46×10^7 4.73×10^7	+	2.15×10^7 2.24×10^7
Case 7	$\mathbf{9.49} \times 10^8$ 9.88×10^8	+	4.90×10^8 5.95×10^8	+	3.06×10^7 1.50×10^7

+ OGM and the compared algorithms in terms of $MIGD$ and MHV, we perform Wilcoxon rank sum test at a significance level of 0.05. As a result of the Wilcoxon rank sum test, a + labeled in front of a result indicates that the compared algorithm is outperformed by NSGA-II/PRM + OGM; by contrast, a − means that NSGA-II/PRM + OGM is outperformed by the compared algorithms; while a $\approx$ means that there is no statistically significant difference between the results obtained by NSGA-II/PRM + OGM and the compared algorithms. To examine the computational efficiency, the

Table 4.4 Mean running time in second for NSGA-II/PRM + OGM, NSGA-II/PRM, and NSGA-II over 30 instances of seven problem cases

	Case 1	Case 2	Case 3	Case 4	Case 5	Case 6	Case 7
NSGA-II	**11.14**	12.38	**13.55**	**15.53**	**17.05**	**19.90**	**23.49**
NSGA-II/PRM	11.15	**12.37**	**13.55**	15.61	17.14	20.09	23.77
NSGA-II/PRM + OGM	13.57	15.36	16.49	18.94	22.12	27.55	28.18

runtime of the compared algorithms over 30 instances of the seven problem cases are shown in Table 4.4. From the results, we can make the following observations.

- Without the proposed DSS, NSGA-II performs the worst on the considered scheduling problems in terms of *IGD* and *HV* over 20 events, especially in the early and middle stages of the optimization, as shown in Figs. 4.2 and 4.3, respectively. By re-initializing the population using historical information and the problem structural properties, PRM is able to improve the performance of NSGA-II, but is not capable enough for handling dynamic events. With the help of OGM, the population diversity is further enhanced and convergence is accelerated, as clearly demonstrated by the better diversity and convergence of the non-dominated solutions obtained by NSGA-II/PRM + OGM.
- From the various *PF*s in different events as shown in Fig. 4.4, the diversity of *PF* obtained by NSGA-II and NSGA-II/PRM are gradually lost over time. Only very few solutions are found in the final *PF* from event 3 to event 6. To a certain extent, this explains the inferior performance of the average *IGD* and *HV* metrics of these two algorithms. As the population tends to converge and lose its diversity over time, it becomes increasingly difficult for NSGA-II to track the moving *PF* in dynamic environments. The issue is partly resolved by PRM that re-initializes the population using information of the previous *PF* and the problem structural properties. The performance is improved further by OGM.
- From the statistical results in terms of *MIGD* and *MHV* values summarized in Tables 4.2 and 4.3, we can see that NSGA-II/PRM + OGM shows the best over all performance. The best results on case 1-case 7 are obtained by NSGA-II/PRM + OGM. And NSGA-II/PRM + OGM significantly outperforms NSGA-II/PRM and NSGA-II in terms of *MIGD* and *MHV*. As the problem size increases, the advantage of NSGA-II/PRM + OGM over NSGA-II/PRM and NSGA-II in *MIGD* and *MHV* becomes even more obvious.
- From the results listed in Table 4.4, we can conclude that the runtime of NSGA-II/PRM + OGM is the highest among the three algorithms as it involves more operations in each generation. However, we can see that the runtime of NSGA-II/PRM + OGM remains acceptable even for large problem instances.

4.5 Summary

In this chapter we consider a dynamic scheduling problem in the presence of continuous arrival of new jobs, in which job rejection is allowed, job processing times are controllable, and processing capability of the machine may deteriorate over time. In response to dynamic events, the unfinished and new arrived jobs should be scheduled to minimize the operational cost and disruption cost. To address this dynamic scheduling problem, a directed search strategy (DSS) is introduced into the widely used elitist non-dominated sorting genetic algorithm (NSGA-II) for tracking the moving Pareto front. DSS is designed to speed up the evolutionary search in changing environments by making use of historical information as well as structural properties, complemented by various strategies that help enhance the diversity of the population. Empirical comparative studies demonstrate that the proposed algorithm is effective and efficient in solving the dynamic scheduling problem, including those considering continuous arrival of new jobs addressed in this chapter as well as our previous work [176]. Such problems are commonly seen in the real-world, e.g., in the container manufacturing process. Therefore, developing algorithms capable of quickly reacting to unexpected disruptions and rescheduling the affected jobs with a view to reducing the scheduling cost while not causing excessive schedule disruption is of great importance in practice.

4.6 Bibliographic Remarks

Most existing work on scheduling with arrival of new jobs assumed that all jobs must be accepted upon request. Unfortunately, many real-world manufacturing systems are characterized by limited production capacity and tight delivery requirements [112, 173]. Consequently, the manufacturer usually has to reject certain number of jobs that require long processing time but contribute little to firm revenue [21]. This is particularly true for make-to-order manufacturers. Such scheduling problems are known as machine scheduling with job rejection [129]. Another common assumption in the literature is that the processing time of the jobs is constant and cannot be changed. However, in practice, it is likely that the processing time becomes longer when the processing is started later, which is known as the *deterioration effect*, often observed in steel-making and fire-fighting processes [186]. Meanwhile, the processing time is controllable by allocating extra non-renewable resources [51, 167, 168, 174]. The deteriorating effect eventually makes the manufacturing environment more complicated, while allowing resource allocation adds one more decision to be made besides job rejection and sequencing. Thus, allowing resource allocation together with job rejection and deterioration effect will greatly enhance the decision flexibility, which, to the best of our knowledge, has not yet been widely studied in handling dynamic scheduling problems.

Evolutionary algorithms (EAs) have shown to be very successful in tackling both single and multi-objective machine scheduling problems [11]. Increasing attention has also been paid to solving dynamic scheduling problems [66, 107, 118, 137]. It has been recognized, however, that conventional EAs are inefficient for solving dynamic optimization problems and consequently many interesting ideas have been developed for dynamic single and multi-objective optimization [68, 106, 180]. One key issue in evolutionary dynamic optimization is to achieve a good balance between preventing an EA from a full convergence and taking full use of historical information of the moving optimums of the dynamic optimization problem. Methods for maintaining population diversity to prevent full convergence include using hyper-mutation [32, 181] and random immigrants [7, 9, 32], or setting a lower bound to self-adaptation parameters [69]. On the other hand, convergence acceleration in a new environment is equally important for evolutionary dynamic optimization. To this end, memory mechanisms for re-using information of previous optimums have been developed [162]. A more general idea is to predict the location of the new optimum [56, 60, 180]. In the feed-forward prediction strategy [57], an individual's new position was predicted by considering the positions of several previous optimums relevant to this individual. In the population prediction strategy for dynamic multi-objective optimization [180], an entire population was re-initialized based on the prediction of the center point and manifold of a moving Pareto front. Most recently, a directed search strategy has been reported in [156], where the population was re-initialized based on the prediction of the moving direction of the Pareto front as well as the direction that is orthogonal to the moving front, once an environmental change is detected. Meanwhile, convergence is accelerated by generating solutions along the moving direction of the Pareto fronts between consecutive generations. It has been shown that the directed search strategy outperforms the feed-forward prediction strategy and population prediction strategy in solving dynamic continuous multi-objective optimization problems [156]. Deb and his colleagues modify the commonly-used NSGA-II procedure in tracking a new Pareto optimal front, as soon as there is a change in the problem. Strategies introduced are introduction of a few random solutions or a few mutated solutions [32]. They also propose a direction-based search method for solving dynamic multi-objective optimization problems [39], which encourage researchers to develop more efficient algorithms for dynamic optimization problems. But they also indicate that the algorithm developed in their paper is for real-value variables, and the inclusion of integer-value variables would require the inclusion of an additional algorithm which is out of the range of their paper. While the dynamic scheduling problem investigated in our paper is a discrete dynamic multi-objective optimization problem, and its decision variables involve both real variables and integer variables. Therefore, we do not compare their algorithm with the proposed algorithm in this chapter. It is of course a very meaningful research work to improve their algorithm to solve our dynamic scheduling problem and we will take it as our further research work.

It is worth noting that the main results of this chapter come from Wang et al. [146].

Chapter 5
Rescheduling with Controllable Processing Times and Preventive Maintenance in the Presence of New Arrival Jobs and Deterioration Effect

This chapter considers the rescheduling problem analogous to that investigated in Chap. 4. However, to alleviate the inherent deteriorating effect in manufacturing system and reduce the negative impact of new arrival jobs, the strategies of preventive maintenance together with controllable processing times are adopted here, where the machine could be totally recovered after being maintained, i.e., deteriorating effect for jobs arranged after the maintenance activity should be restarted from zero. The processing sequences of original and new arrival jobs, resource allocation strategy, and position of the maintenance activity should be optimized simultaneously to minimize the total operational cost consisting of the total completion times of all jobs, maintenance cost and resource allocation cost, and total completion time deviation. An improved NSGA-II has been proposed to solve the rescheduling problem. In order to address the key problem of balancing between exploration and exploitation, we hybridize differential evolution mutation operation with NSGA-II to enhance diversity, constitute high-quality initial solution based on assignment model for exploitation, and incorporate analytic property of non-dominated solutions for exploration. Computational study is designed by randomly generating various instances with regards to the problem size from given distributions. By use of existing performance indicators for convergence and diversity of Pareto fronts, we illustrate the effectiveness of the hybrid algorithm and the incorporation of domain knowledge into evolutionary optimization in rescheduling.

This part is composed of six sections. In Sect. 5.1 we describe the problem. In Sect. 5.2 we derive the properties of non-dominated solution as problem domain knowledge for reuse in evolutionary optimization. In Sect. 5.3 we improve NSGA-II in two aspects. A mechanism is designed based on differential evolution mutation operation similar with that of Pan et al. [116], and the extracted knowledge introduced in Chap. 3 is used to guide the evolutionary search. In Sect. 5.4 we assess the effectiveness of the algorithm for solving the rescheduling problem. We conclude this chapter in Sect. 5.5, and end the chapter in Sect. 5.6 with bibliographic remarks.

D. Wang et al., *Rescheduling Under Disruptions in Manufacturing Systems*,
Uncertainty and Operations Research, https://doi.org/10.1007/978-981-15-3528-4_5

5.1 Problem Formulation

Analogous to the problem investigated in Chap. 4, the scheduler should determine the optimal plan for a set of jobs $\{J_1, J_2, \ldots, J_{n_o}\}$ in a single machine layout. The processing time of each job, which is subject to deterioration effect and could be compressed by allocating more resources, is denoted by $p_j = \overline{p}_j + \alpha t_j - b_j u_j$. However, different from the problem investigated in Chap. 4, to alleviate the deterioration effect, the preventive maintenance strategy is adopted. To be precise, one maintenance activity should be performed during the planning horizon, performing which may completely restore the state of the machine. In addition, we further assume that:

- The machine cannot process any job when the maintenance activity is being carried out.
- The maintenance activity is performed immediately after the completion of some job.
- The duration of the maintenance activity is also subject to deterioration effect, which is a linear function of its start time t, i.e., $D_m = M + \gamma t$, where $M > 0$ is the basic duration, $\gamma \geq 0$ is the deterioration rate, and t is the actual starting time of the maintenance activity.
- Performing machine maintenance may completely restore the state of the machine. Thus, the actual processing time of a job $J_{[r]}$ that is sequenced in the rth position in a sequence is given by $p_{[r]} = \overline{p}_{[r]} + \alpha t_{[r]} - b_{[r]} u_{[r]}$ for $1 \leq j \leq m$, and $p_{[r]} = \overline{p}_{[r]} + \alpha[t_{[r]} - C_{[m]} - (M + \gamma C_{[m]})] - b_{[r]} u_{[r]}$ for $m + 1 \leq r \leq n_O$, where the maintenance activity is performed immediately after the completion of the mth job, and $C_{[m]}$ is the completion time of the mth job in the schedule.

Performing maintenance activity would also incur certain cost positively related to the maintenance duration. Let q be the cost rate and the cost of maintenance could be calculated as $q \cdot D_m$. To summarize, the processing sequence, resource allocation strategy, and the position of the maintenance activity should be determined simultaneously in order to generate the optimal baseline schedule which optimizes the sum of schedule performance, resource allocation cost and maintenance cost.

By use of the classic the three-field notation, the above problem denoted by (**P**) could be expressed as follows.

$$1 \left| p_j = \overline{p}_j + \alpha t_j - b_j u_j, ma \right| \sum_{j=1}^{n_o} c_j + \sum_{j=1}^{n_o} c_{j u_j} + q D_m$$

where ma stands for the maintenance activity.

As a response to new arrival jobs $J_{n_o+1}, J_{n_o+2}, \ldots, J_{n_o+n_N}$, rescheduling of the $n_O + n_N$ jobs is triggered to simultaneously optimize the total operational cost of $n_O + n_N$ jobs, and the disruption of the original n_O jobs. The disruption cost is modeled as the total virtual tardiness $\sum_{J_j \in \Lambda \cap \Omega} T_j \sum_{j=1}^{n_o} T_j$. By use of the three-field notation again, the rescheduling problem denoted by (**P1**) could be formulated as follow.

$$1|p_j = \overline{p}_j + \alpha t_j - b_j u_j, ma|\left(\sum_{j=1}^{n_o+n_N} c_j + \sum_{j=1}^{n_o+n_N} c_j u_j + qD_m, \sum_{j=1}^{n_o} T_j\right)$$

5.2 Problem Analysis

We derive in this subsection some structural properties of the optimal schedules of problems **P** and **P1** and useful results that will be used later in the design of solution algorithms.

Lemma 5.2.1 indicates the underlying complexity of problem (**P**), and Lemma 5.2.2 gives the structural properties of the optimal schedules of problem **P**.

Lemma 5.2.1 *Problem* **P** *can be solved is* $O(n_0^4)$ *time.*

Proof The total operational cost $\sum C_j + \sum c_j u_j + qM$ could be formulated as follows:

$$\begin{aligned}\sum C_j + \sum c_j u_j + qM &= \sum_{j=1}^{m} [(n_o - j + 1) + \gamma(n_o - m + 1)] p_{[j]} \\ &\quad + \sum_{j=m+1}^{n_o} (n_o - j + 1) p_{[j]} + \sum_{j=1}^{n_o} c_{[j]} u_{[j]} \\ &= \sum_{j=1}^{n_o} \tilde{w}_j p_{[j]} + \sum_{j=1}^{n_o} c_{[j]} u_{[j]}\end{aligned}$$

where the weight for the jth position is

$$\tilde{w}_j = \begin{cases} (n_o - j + 1) + \gamma(n_o - m + q), & 1 \le j \le m \\ n_o - j + 1, & m + 1 \le j \le n_o \end{cases}$$

(1) **For the optimal resource allocation strategy**.

$$\begin{aligned}\sum_{j=1}^{m} \tilde{w}_j p_{[j]} + \sum_{j=m+1}^{n_o} \tilde{w}_j p_{[j]} + \sum_{j=1}^{n_o} c_{[j]} u_{[j]} &= \sum_{j=1}^{n_o} W_j (\bar{p}_{[j]} - b_{[j]} u_{[j]}) + \sum_{j=1}^{n_o} c_{[j]} u_{[j]} \\ &= \sum_{j=1}^{n_o} W_j \bar{p}_{[j]} + \sum_{j=1}^{n_o} (c_{[j]} - W_j b_{[j]}) u_{[j]}\end{aligned}$$

where $W_j = \begin{cases} \sum_{i=j}^{m} \sum_{k=0}^{i-j} R_{i-j+1,k+1}\alpha^k \tilde{w}_i, & 1 \le j \le m \\ \sum_{i=j}^{n_o} \sum_{k=0}^{i-j} R_{i-j+1,k+1}\alpha^k \tilde{w}_i, & m+1 \le j \le n_o \end{cases}$, and R is a matrix of size $n_o \times n_o$. We have $R_{1,1} = 1$ and $R_{1,j} = 0$, $R_{i,1} = 0$, $R_{i,j} = R_{i-1,j-1} + R_{i-1,j}$ for $i, j = 2, 3, \ldots, n_o$.

From the above formulation, we could easily conclude that for the schedule where maintenance takes place after the completion of the mth job, if $c_{[j]} \ge W_j b_{[j]}$, the optimal resource allocation is $u_{[j]} = 0$; and if $c_{[j]} < W_j b_{[j]}$, the optimal resource allocation is $u_{[j]} = \bar{u}_{[j]}$.

(2) **For the optimal maintenance position and job sequence**.

Let

$$C_{jr} = \begin{cases} W_r \overline{p}_{j,}, & r = 1, 2, \ldots, n_o;\ c_j \ge W_r b_j \\ W_r \overline{p}_j + \left(c_j - W_r b_j\right) \overline{u}_j, & r = 1, 2, \ldots, n_o;\ c_j < W_r b_j \end{cases}$$

where $W_r = \begin{cases} \sum_{i=r}^{m} \sum_{k=0}^{i-r} R_{i-r+1,k+1}\alpha^k \tilde{w}_i, & 1 \le r \le m \\ \sum_{i=r}^{n_o} \sum_{k=0}^{i-r} R_{i-r+1,k+1}\alpha^k \tilde{w}_i, & m+1 \le r \le n_o \end{cases}$, and the weight for position i is $\tilde{w}_i = \begin{cases} (n_o - i + 1) + \gamma\,(n_o - m + q)\,, & 1 \le i \le m \\ n_o - i + 1, & m+1 \le i \le n_o \end{cases}$.

Here we introduce binary variable x_{jr} to denote whether job J_j is arranged at the rth position: $x_{jr} = 1$ means "yes" and $x_{jr} = 0$ means "no", $j, r = 1, 2, \ldots, n_o$. Then the problem could be transferred into the following assignment problem $A(m)$:

$$\min \sum_{r=1}^{n_o} \sum_{j=1}^{n_o} C_{jr} x_{jr}$$

$$\text{s.t.} \sum_{r=1}^{n_o} x_{jr} = 1, \qquad j = 1, 2, \ldots, n_o$$

$$\sum_{j=1}^{n_o} x_{jr} = 1, \qquad r = 1, 2, \ldots, n_o$$

$$x_{jr} \in \{0, 1\}, \quad r, j = 1, 2, \ldots, n_o$$

The time complexity of solving the above model is $O(n_o^3)$. Note that the obtained optimal objective value is based on fixing m. Let m take the value of $1, 2, \ldots, n_o$ and solve n_o assignment respectively, then pick out the optimal objective value. The corresponding maintenance position, job sequence, and resource allocation strategy could be integrated to form the optimal baseline schedule. The time complexity of the entire procedure would be $O(n_o^4)$, therefore Lemma 5.2.1 holds. □

Lemma 5.2.2 *For a given resource allocation strategy $u = (u_1, u_2, \ldots, u_{n_o})$, there exists an optimal schedule for problem (**P**) in which the jobs are processed according to non-decreasing order of $\overline{p}_j - b_j u_j$.*

Proof Given a resource allocation strategy and an optimal schedule σ of problem (P), let $J_{[j]}$ denote the job with minimum position that does not satisfy the above SPT rule, and let $J_{[i]}$ denote the job which immediately precedes $J_{[j]}$ in σ. We have $j > i$ but $\bar{p}_{[j]} - b_{[j]}u_{[j]} < \bar{p}_{[i]} - b_{[i]}u_{[i]}$. Let the starting time of $J_{[i]}$ be t_0. By exchanging the processing order of these two jobs, we could obtain a new schedule $\tilde{\sigma}$, and we have $C_{[j]}(\tilde{\sigma}) = t_0 + \bar{p}_{[j]} - b_{[j]}u_{[j]} < C_{[i]}(\sigma)$. We also have $t_{[i]}(\tilde{\sigma}) < t_{[j]}(\sigma)$, where $t_{[i]}(\tilde{\sigma})$ is the starting time of job $J_{[i]}$ in $\tilde{\sigma}$, and $t_{[j]}(\sigma)$ is the starting time of job $J_{[i]}$ in σ. Then it holds that $t_0 + \bar{p}_{[j]} - \alpha t_0 b_{[j]}u_{[j]} + \bar{p}_{[i]} + \alpha t_{[i]}(\tilde{\sigma}) - b_{[i]}u_{[i]}$, meaning $C_{[i]}(\tilde{\sigma}) < C_{[j]}(\sigma)$. Therefore we could conclude that after the exchanging, both of the completion times of the two jobs have been reduced, which is contradictory to the optimality of schedule σ. Lemma 5.2.2 holds. □

Theorems 5.2.3 and 5.2.4 give the structural properties of the optimal schedules of problem **P1**, which would limit the specific characteristics of solution representation, and direct the searching towards promising areas in the solution space.

Theorem 5.2.3 *Given the resource allocation strategy and maintenance position in the non-dominated solution to problem (***P1***), the original jobs and new jobs scheduled before and after the maintenance activity are scheduled according to non-decreasing order of* $\overline{p}_j - b_j u_j$.

Proof In the Pareto optimal solution denoted by σ with given resource allocation strategy and maintenance position m, let $J_{[j]}(j < m)$ be the original job with minimum position that violates SPT rule, and let $J_{[i]}$ be the last original job that is scheduled before $J_{[j]}$. We have $j > i$ and $\overline{p}_{[j]} - b_{[j]}u_{[j]} < \overline{p}_{[i]} - b_{[i]}u_{[i]}$. Denote by t_0 the starting time of $J_{[i]}$ in σ, and let $\tilde{J}_1, \tilde{J}_2, \ldots, \tilde{J}_h$ be the new jobs scheduled between $J_{[i]}$ and $J_{[j]}$ in σ. By exchanging the positions of $J_{[i]}$ and $J_{[j]}$, we could obtain a new schedule $\tilde{\sigma}$, and analyze the change of total operational cost and disruption cost after exchanging as follows.

(1) **For the change of total operational cost**.

Firstly we have $C_{[j]}(\tilde{\sigma}) = t_0 + \overline{p}_{[j]} + \alpha t_0 - b_{[j]}u_{[j]} < C_{[i]}(\sigma)$, and thus the completion times of the jobs $\tilde{J}_1, \tilde{J}_2, \ldots, \tilde{J}_h$ in $\tilde{\sigma}$ are earlier than those in σ. Let $t_{[i]}(\tilde{\sigma})$ and $t_{[j]}(\sigma)$ be the starting times of job $J_{[i]}$ in $\tilde{\sigma}$ and $J_{[j]}$ in σ respectively, and we have $t_{[i]}(\tilde{\sigma}) < t_{[j]}(\sigma)$. Then it holds that $t_0 + \overline{p}_{[j]} + \alpha t_0 - b_{[j]}u_{[j]} + \overline{p}_{[i]} + \alpha t_{[i]}(\tilde{\sigma}) - b_{[i]}u_{[i]} < t_0 + \overline{p}_{[i]} + \alpha t_0 - b_{[i]}u_{[i]} + \overline{p}_{[j]} + \alpha t_{[j]}(\sigma) - b_{[j]}u_{[j]}$. Therefore $C_{[i]}(\tilde{\sigma}) < C_{[j]}(\sigma)$. As for the optimal maintenance position, the duration of the maintenance activity in $\tilde{\sigma}$ is no larger than that in σ since $C_{[m]}(\tilde{\sigma}) \leq C_{[m]}(\sigma)$. It follows that the maintenance cost in $\tilde{\sigma}$ is no larger than that in σ. To summarize, the total operational cost in $\tilde{\sigma}$ is no larger than that in σ.

(2) **For the change of disruption cost**.

By definition, we have $T_{[i]}(\tilde{\sigma}) = \max\left\{C_{[i]}(\tilde{\sigma}) - \overline{C}_{[i]}, 0\right\}$, $T_{[j]}(\tilde{\sigma}) = \max\left\{C_{[j]}(\tilde{\sigma}) - \overline{C}_{[j]}, 0\right\}$, $T_{[i]}(\sigma) = \max\left\{C_{[i]}(\sigma) - \overline{C}_{[i]}, 0\right\}$, $T_{[j]}(\sigma) = \max\left\{C_{[j]}(\sigma) - \overline{C}_{[j]}, 0\right\}$. Hence $T_{[i]}(\tilde{\sigma}) + T_{[j]}(\tilde{\sigma}) - \left(T_{[i]}(\sigma) + T_{[j]}(\sigma)\right) = \max\left\{C_{[i]}(\tilde{\sigma}) - \overline{C}_{[i]}, 0\right\} - \max$

$\{C_{[j]}(\sigma) - \overline{C}_{[j]}, 0\} + \max\{C_{[j]}(\tilde{\sigma}) - \overline{C}_{[j]}, 0 - \max\{C_{[i]}(\sigma) - \overline{C}_{[i]}, 0\}\}$. Combining $C_{[j]}(\tilde{\sigma}) < C_{[i]}(\sigma) < C_{[i]}(\tilde{\sigma}) < C_{[j]}(\sigma)$ with $\overline{C}_{[j]} < \overline{C}_{[i]}$ derived from $\overline{p}_{[j]} - b_{[j]}u_{[j]} < \overline{p}_{[i]} - b_{[i]}u_{[i]}$ (Lemma 5.2.2), we could easily conclude that $T_{[i]}(\tilde{\sigma}) + T_{[j]}(\tilde{\sigma}) - \left(T_{[i]}(\sigma) + T_{[j]}(\sigma)\right) \le 0$. As for jobs between $J_{[i]}$ and $J_{[j]}$ and after position m, their virtual tardiness would not be increased since they are all completed earlier after exchanging.

To summarize, by repeating the above procedures, we could finally obtain a partial SPT schedule for the original jobs before the maintenance activity. The two optimality criteria would not be increased during this procedure. By use of similar analysis, we could obtain similar conclusions for the new jobs before the maintenance activity, original and new jobs after the maintenance activity, respectively. Therefore Theorem 5.2.3 holds. □

Theorem 5.2.4 *For the linear weighted combination problem variant of* (**P1**)*:* $1|p_j = \overline{p}_j + \alpha t_j - b_j u_j, ma|(1-a)(\sum_{j=1}^{n_o+n_N} c_j + \sum_{j=1}^{n_o+n_N} c_j u_j + qD_m) + a(\sum_{j=1}^{n_o} T_j), 0 < a < 1$, *there exists an optimal solution in which each job is either compressed to its upper bound or not compressed at all.*

Proof Assume in the optimal solution, the resource allocation for the job in the kth position is $u_{[k]} \in \left[0, \overline{u}_{[k]}\right]$. Given a small resource allocation deviation $\delta \in \left[-u_{[k]}, \overline{u}_{[k]} - u_{[k]}\right]$, we would analyze the change of two optimality criteria from $u_{[k]}$ to $u_{[k]} + \delta$. Denote the optimal maintenance position as m, and for the purpose of convenience, denote $\overline{C}_j = +\infty$ for $J_j \in \left\{J_{n_o+1}, J_{n_o+2}, \ldots, J_{n_o+n_N}\right\}$.

(1) To show the change of $\sum_{j=1}^{n_o+n_N} C_j + \sum_{j=1}^{n_o+n_N} c_j u_j + qM$ from $u_{[k]}$ to $u_{[k]} + \delta$, there are two cases to consider:

Case 1: $m < k$. In this case, we have

$$
\begin{aligned}
&- b_{[k]}\delta + \left[-(\alpha+1)b_{[k]}\delta\right] + \left[-(\alpha+1)^2 b_{[k]}\delta\right] + \cdots + \left[-(\alpha+1)^{n_o+n_N-k} b_{[k]}\delta\right] + c_{[k]}\delta \\
&= \left(c_{[k]} - \sum_{j=k}^{n_o+n_N} (\alpha+1)^{j-k} b_{[k]}\right)\delta
\end{aligned}
$$

Case 2: $m \ge k$. In this case, we have

$$
\begin{aligned}
&- b_{[k]}\delta + \left[-(\alpha+1)b_{[k]}\delta\right] + \left[-(\alpha+1)^2 b_{[k]}\delta\right] + \cdots + \left[-(\alpha+1)^{m-k} b_{[k]}\delta\right] \\
&+ \left[-(1+\gamma)(\alpha+1)^{m+1-k} b_{[k]}\delta\right] + \cdots + \left[-(1+\gamma)(\alpha+1)^{n_o+n_N-k} b_{[k]}\delta\right] \\
&+ c_{[k]}\delta - q\gamma(\alpha+1)^{m-k} b_{[k]}\delta \\
&= \left(c_{[k]} - \sum_{j=k}^{m} (\alpha+1)^{j-k} b_{[k]} - \sum_{j=m+1}^{n_o+n_N} (1+\gamma)(\alpha+1)^{j-k} b_{[k]} - q\gamma(\alpha+1)^{m-k} b_{[k]}\right)\delta
\end{aligned}
$$

(2) To show the change of $\sum_{j=1}^{n_o} T_j$. There are 4 cases to consider:

Case 1: $m < k$ and $\delta \geq 0$. In this case, we have

$$\max\left\{\min\left\{\overline{C}_{[k]} - C_{[k]}, 0\right\}, -b_{[k]}\delta\right\} + \max\left\{\min\left\{\overline{C}_{[k+1]} - C_{[k+1]}, 0\right\}, -(\alpha+1)b_{[k]}\delta\right\} + \cdots$$
$$+ \max\left\{\min\left\{\overline{C}_{[n_o+n_N]} - C_{[n_o+n_N,0\}}, -(\alpha+1)^{n_o+n_N-k}b_{[k]}\delta\right\}$$
$$= \sum_{j=k}^{n_o+n_N} \max\left\{\min\left\{\overline{C}_{[j]} - C_{[j]}, 0\right\}, -(\alpha+1)^{j-k}b_{[k]}\delta\right\}$$

Case 2: $m < k$ and $\delta < 0$. In this case, we have

$$\max\left\{\min\left\{\overline{C}_{[k]} - C_{[k]}, 0\right\}, -b_{[k]}\delta\right\} + \max\left\{\min\left\{\overline{C}_{[k+1]} - C_{[k+1]}, 0\right\} - (\alpha+1)b_{[k]}\delta, 0\right\} + \cdots$$
$$+ \max\left\{\min\left\{\overline{C}_{[n_o+n_N]} - C_{[n_o+n_N,0\}} - (\alpha+1)^{n_o+n_N-k}b_{[k]}\delta, 0\right\}$$
$$= \sum_{j=k}^{n_o+n_N} \max\left\{\min\left\{\overline{C}_{[j]} - C_{[j]}, 0\right\} - (\alpha+1)^{j-k}b_{[k]}\delta, 0\right\}$$

Case 3: $m \geq k$ and $\delta \geq 0$. In this case, we have

$$\max\left\{\min\left\{\overline{C}_{[k]} - C_{[k]}, 0\right\}, -b_{[k]}\delta\right\} + \max\left\{\min\left\{\overline{C}_{[k+1]} - C_{[k+1]}, 0\right\}, -(\alpha+1)b_{[k]}\delta\right\} + \cdots$$
$$+ \max\left\{\min\left\{\overline{C}_{[m]} - C_{[m]}, 0\right\}, -(\alpha+1)^{m-k}b_{[k]}\delta\right\}$$
$$+ \max\left\{\min\left\{\overline{C}_{[m+1]} - C_{[m+1]}, 0\right\}, -(1+\gamma)(\alpha+1)^{m+1-k}b_{[k]}\delta\right\} + \cdots$$
$$+ \max\left\{\min\left\{\overline{C}_{[n_o+n_N]} - C_{[n_o+n_N]}, 0\right\}, -(1+\gamma)(\alpha+1)^{n_o+n_N-k}b_{[k]}\delta\right\}$$
$$= \sum_{j=k}^{m} \max\left\{\min\left\{\overline{C}_{[j]} - C_{[j]}, 0\right\}, -(\alpha+1)^{j-k}b_{[k]}\delta\right\}$$
$$+ \sum_{j=m+1}^{n_o+n_N} \max\left\{\min\left\{\overline{C}_{[j]} - C_{[j]}, 0\right\}, -(1+\gamma)(\alpha+1)^{j-k}b_{[k]}\delta\right\}$$

Case 4: $m \geq k$ and $\delta < 0$. In this case, we have

$$\max\left\{\min\left\{\overline{C}_{[k]} - C_{[k]}, 0\right\} - b_{[k]}\delta, 0\right\} + \max\left\{\min\left\{\overline{C}_{[k+1]} - C_{[k+1]}, 0\right\} - (\alpha+1)b_{[k]}\delta, 0\right\} + \cdots$$
$$+ \max\left\{\min\left\{\overline{C}_{[m]} - C_{[m]}, 0\right\} - (\alpha+1)^{m-k}b_{[k]}\delta, 0\right\}$$
$$+ \max\left\{\min\left\{\overline{C}_{[m+1]} - C_{[m+1]}, 0\right\} - (1+\gamma)(\alpha+1)^{m+1-k}b_{[k]}\delta, 0\right\} + \cdots$$
$$+ \max\left\{\min\left\{\overline{C}_{[n_o+n_N]} - C_{[n_o+n_N]}, 0\right\} - (1+\gamma)(\alpha+1)^{n_o+n_N-k}b_{[k]}\delta, 0\right\}$$
$$= \sum_{j=k}^{m} \max\left\{\min\left\{\overline{C}_{[j]} - C_{[j]}, 0\right\} - (\alpha+1)^{j-k}b_{[k]}\delta, 0\right\}$$
$$+ \sum_{j=m+1}^{n_o+n_N} \max\left\{\min\left\{\overline{C}_{[j]} - C_{[j]}, 0\right\} - (1+\gamma)(\alpha+1)^{j-k}b_{[k]}\delta, 0\right\}$$

To summarize, the change of $(1-\alpha)(\sum_{j=1}^{n_o+n_N} C_j + \sum_{j=1}^{n_o+n_N} c_j u_j + qM) + \alpha(\sum_{j=1}^{n_o} T_j)$ would be a linear function of δ. Thus, The optimal objective value would be taken at two extreme points $\delta = -u_{[k]}$ or $\delta = \overline{u}_{[k]} - u_{[k]}$, i.e., job $J_{[k]}$ is either compressed to its upper bound or not compressed at all. Therefore Theorem 5.2.4 holds. □

It should be noted that the optimal solution to the linear weighted problem would be in the optimal Pareto front. Theorem 5.2.4 does not necessarily hold for every solution in optimal Pareto front, the shape of which is not guaranteed to be convex. However Theorem 5.2.4 could be used as an approximation heuristic strategy guiding the searching procedure, and the effectiveness would be verified in the computational study section.

5.3 An Improved NSGA-II for Integrating Preventive Maintenance and Rescheduling

It is quite difficult to find the non-dominated solutions to this $\mathcal{NP}$-hard problem (**P1**) in polynomial time [54]. We improve NSGA-II by hybridization with differential evolution mutation operation to effectively solve the problem. Based on the hybrid algorithm framework similar with the idea from Pan et al. [116]. We make use of knowledge extracted from analytic properties to improve the convergence and diversity of Pareto fronts obtained during evolution. The main ideas of improving NSGA-II are summarized in Table 5.1.

Firstly, differential evolution mutation operation is introduced to speed up the convergence and enhance global searching ability of NSGA-II to obtain elitist Non-dominated Sorting Genetic Algorithm with Differential Evolutionary (NSGA-II/DE for short). DE evolves from a randomly generated population of individual vectors, each of which corresponds to a candidate solution to the optimization problem. It uses mutation process to update the population. Several variants of DE have emerged and are formulated by "$DE/x/y/z$" [31], where "DE" stands for "differential evolution", "x" represents the base vector to be perturbed, "y" is the number of difference vectors considered for perturbation of "x", and "z" stands for the crossover with

Table 5.1 Algorithm improvement approach

Algorithm	Improvement measure
NSGA-II/DE	Introduce differential mutation process into mutation operation
NSGA-II/DE + POSQ	Introduce Pareto optimal solution property into NSGA-II/DE
NSGA-II/DE + POSQ + AHS	Introduce approximation heuristic strategy into NSGA-II/DE + POSQ

"*bin*" for "*binomial*" and "*exp*" for "*exponential*". In this chapter, the mostly-often used DE strategy "$DE|rand|1|bin$" is utilized for its competitive performance in quality and robustness.

Then, we introduce the non-dominated solution property stated in Theorem 5.2.3 and approximation heuristic strategy in Theorem 5.2.4 respectively into the algorithm to further improve its convergence speed and quality of Pareto front and get elitist Non-dominated Sorting Genetic Algorithm with Differential Evolutionary and Pareto Optimal Solution Quality (NSGA-II/DE + POSQ for short) algorithm and elitist Non-dominated Sorting Genetic Algorithm with Differential Evolutionary, Pareto Optimal Solution Quality and Approximation Heuristic Strategy (NSGA-II/DE + POSQ + AHS for short) algorithm. Note that in NSGA-II/DE + POSQ + AHS, we constitute high-quality initial solution by optimizing total operational cost and total deviation respectively according to Lemma 5.2.1.

5.3.1 NSGA-II/DE Algorithm

According to the improvement approach given in Sect. 5.3, we will design an algorithm entitled elitist Non-dominated Sorting Genetic Algorithm with Differential Evolutionary (NSGA-II/DE for short) as follow. Here, we will provide the solution representation, the initial population constitution, fitness value calculation, crossover operation and mutation operation corresponding to NSGA-II/DE.

Algorithm $NSGA\text{-}II/DE$
Input: pop, Max_{gen}, P_c, $ratio$, P_m, $scale$, $shrink$, C_r and F.
Output: E the Pareto front to problem (P1).

Step 1. [*Initialization*]
Step 1.1 Randomly generate an initial population P_t with size pop and evaluate each individual's fitness value.
Step 1.2 Sort all individuals of P_t using non-dominated sorting algorithm and crowding distance procedure.
Step 1.3 Set $E = \varnothing$. /* E denotes the current non-dominated individual collection */
Step 1.4 $t = 1$. /* t denotes the generation number */

Step 2. [*Population evolution*]
Step 2.1 Get the parents from P_t through tournament selection, apply crossover operation proposed in Sect. 5.3.1.4 and mutation operation proposed in Sect. 5.3.1.5 on the parent, and get an offspring population P_O with size pop.
Step 2.2 Combine P_t with P_O to create a combined population R_t, and select the best individual of size pop according to their rank and crowded distance as the next population P_{t+1}

Step 2.3 Compare each new generated non-dominated solution in P_{t+1} with previously archived solution in E, and add the non-dominated solution into the archive.

Step 3. Set $t = t + 1$.

Step 4. [*Stopping Criterion*] If $t \geq Max_{gen}$ or the result tends /* The stability is judged by the fixed to be stable,then stop and output the individual in E within a certain number of solution in E, otherwise go to step 2 iterations */

5.3.1.1 Solution Representation

For solution representation, a $2(n_o + n_N) + 1$ dimensional vector $\vec{x}_{i,t}$ as shown in formula (5.3.1) is used.

$$\vec{x}_{i,t} = (\overbrace{x_{i,1,t}, x_{i,2,t}, \ldots, x_{i,n_o+n_N,t}}^{\pi-part}, \underbrace{x_{i,n_o+n_N+1,t}, x_{i,n_o+n_N+2,t}, \ldots, x_{i,2(n_o+n_N),t}}_{y-part}, \overbrace{x_{i,2(n_o+n_N)+1,t}}^{m-part}) \tag{5.3.1}$$

$$i = 1, 2, \ldots, pop;\ t = 1, 2, \ldots, Max_{gen}$$

where n_o is the number of original jobs, n_N is the number of new jobs, pop represents population size, t represents evolutional generation, and Max_{gen} represents maximum evolutional generation.

In order to constitute a solution, we would add the $\pi - part$ of permutation of $n_o + n_N$ jobs for processing sequence, the $y - part$ of the resource allocation percentage of the corresponding jobs in $\pi - part$, and the $m - part$ of preventive maintenance position together.

5.3.1.2 Initial Solution

For NSGA-II/DE, an initial population having pop individuals is randomly generated. For each individual in the initial population, its $\pi - part$ components are randomly generated job processing sequence, its $y - part$ components are decimals randomly taken from the interval [0, 1] and its $m - part$ component is taken from the set $\{1, 2, \ldots, n_o + n_N\}$.

5.3.1.3 Calculation of Fitness Value

In order to evaluate each individual, we could jointly determine the resource allocation percentage of each job based on the solution's $\pi - part$ and $y - part$, and then obtain the maintenance position based on the solution's $m - part$. We can calculate each job's completion time, starting time and duration of the maintenance activity. Based on these, each solution's original operational cost and disruption cost can be gained according to their formula described in Sect. 5.2. For all the individuals in population, perform non-dominated sorting and crowding distance procedures based on their objective values in order to achieve fitness assignment [33].

5.3.1.4 Crossover Operation

We perform crossover operation on each selected pair of parents, and produce two children. Here each component of the pair of parents like $\pi - part$, $y - part$ and $m - part$ will do Intermediate crossover separately with P_c as its crossover probability. Intermediate crossover is shown in formula (5.3.2).

$$o_{i,j,t} = p_{r1,j,t} + rand \cdot ratio \cdot (p_{r2,j,t} - p_{r1,j,t}) \tag{5.3.2}$$

$$i = 1, 2, \ldots, pop, \; j = 1, 2, \ldots, 2(n_o + n_N) + 1, \; t = 1, 2, \ldots, Max_{gen}$$

where $o_{i,j,t}$ is the jth component of the ith individual in the tth generation offspring, $p_{r1,j,t}$ and $p_{r2,j,t}$ indicate the jth component of the r_1th and r_2th individual in the tth generation parent population, rand is a decimal randomly taken from the interval [0, 1] and ratio means ratio of crossover operation. The $\pi - part$ of $o_{i,j,t}$ should be repaired after Intermediate crossover so that all components of the $\pi - part$ constitute a processing sequence with $n_o + n_N$ jobs. Also its $y - part$ and $m - part$ should be repaired so that components of $y - part$ are decimals taken from the interval [0, 1] and component of $m - part$ is taken from the set $\{1, 2, \ldots, n_o + n_N\}$.

5.3.1.5 Mutation Operation

When population evolution is at the early stage, using large perturbation like differential evolution for individual mutation will improve global optimization ability and speed up convergence, preventing getting stuck in local optimum [34]. And when the evolution reaches the late stage, using small perturbation will be helpful for improving the local search in a small neighborhood. Therefore, we will design differential evolution mutation operation and Gaussian mutation operator respectively for the above two stages of algorithm evolution.

We determine the boundary of two stages by calculating the improvement stagnation frequency denoted by *stagnationFrequencyLimit* in each generation based on the minimum distance to ideal point, which is obtained by optimally solving the original objective and deviation objective according to Lemma 5.2.1. The ideal point is usually not attainable. If *stagnationFrequencyLimit* reaches 6, we hold that the evolution comes to its late stage and Gaussian mutation should replace differential evolution mutation operation.

In the remaining of this subsection, we first introduce differential evolution mutation operator which contains three steps.

Step 1: Mutation based on difference vectors

Three terms are concerned for differential evolution mutation operation [31]: target vector (a parent vector from the current generation), donor vector (a mutant vector obtained through the differential evolution mutation operation), and trial vector (an offspring formed by recombining the donor with the target vector).

Here, we will perform differential evolution mutation operation on the $y - part$ and $m - part$ of the individual based on "$DE|rand|1|bin$" [154]. To create the donor vector $\vec{v}_{i,t}$ for the ith target vector $\vec{x}_{i,t}$ from the tth population, three other distinct parameter vectors, say $\vec{x}_{r_1,t}$, $\vec{x}_{r_2,t}$, and $\vec{x}_{r_3,t}$ are sampled randomly from the tth population. The indices r_1, r_2, and r_3 are mutually exclusive integers randomly chosen from the range $[1, pop]$, which are also different from the base vector index i. For each mutant vector, a group of r_1, r_2, and r_3 are randomly generated. Then we use a scalar number F to scale the difference between any two of these three vectors. After scaling, the difference would be added to the third vector to obtain the donor vector $\vec{v}_{i,t}$. We can express the process as follows:

$$\vec{v}_{i,t} = \vec{x}_{r_1,t} + F \cdot (\vec{x}_{r_2,t} - \vec{x}_{r_3,t}) \tag{5.3.3}$$

In this chapter, if the boundary constraint is violated for a component $\vec{v}_{i,j,t}$ of a mutant vector $\vec{v}_{i,t}$, it is reset as follows:

$$v_{i,j,t} = \begin{cases} \min\{U_j, 2L_j - v_{i,j,t}\}, & v_{i,j,t} < L_j \\ \max\{L_j, 2U_j - v_{i,j,t}\}, & v_{i,j,t} \geq L_j \end{cases} \tag{5.3.4}$$

For the $\pi - part$ we will use permutation-based operation [150], which has been shown to be effective for permutation-based solutions, to perform the differential evolution mutation operation. For two permutations, we define $\otimes$ operation to calculate the position difference of each job. $P_1 \otimes P_2$ returns a location offset vector L with the same dimension as P_1 and P_2. $\otimes$ operation is used to transfers the current permutation to a new one using the location offset vector L. Permutation-based differential evolution mutation operation performs global search effectively by avoiding the repair of unfeasible solutions to speed up evolution. This process could be represented as follows.

$$\vec{v}_{i,t} = \vec{x}_{r_1,t} + \otimes(\vec{x}_{r_2,t} \otimes \vec{x}_{r_3,t}) \tag{5.3.5}$$

After the above mutation process we could combine each updated component ($\pi - part$, $y - part$ and $m - part$) to get the corresponding donor vector $\vec{v}_{i,t}$.

Step 2: Crossover operation

To enhance the potential diversity of the population, a crossover operation is adopted after generating the donor vector $\vec{v}_{i,t}$ through mutation: select $\vec{x}_{i,t,best}$ randomly from current population or from the collection of current non-dominated individuals with 0.5 probability respectively, then exchange the three parts of $\vec{v}_{i,t}$ with those of $\vec{x}_{i,t,best}$. The exchange method we use is binomial crossover which is performed on each of the component whenever a randomly generated number from [0, 1] is less than or equal to crossover rate $C_r \in (0, 1)$. In this case, the number of parameters inherited from the donor has a binomial distribution. The scheme may be outlined as formula (5.3.6).

$$u_{i,j,t} = \begin{cases} v_{i,t,j}, & rand_j(0,1) \le C_r \quad or \quad j = j_{rand} \\ x_{i,j,t,best}, & otherwise \end{cases} \tag{5.3.6}$$

$$i = 1, 2, \ldots, pop, \ j = 1, 2, \ldots, n_o + n_N$$

where $rand_j(0, 1)$ is a uniformly distributed random number known as anew for each jth component of the ith parameter vector. $j_{rand} \in [1, n_o + n_N]$ is a randomly chosen index, which ensures that $\vec{u}_{i,t}$ gets at least one component from $\vec{v}_{i,t}$. Then we will get the processing sequence part, resource allocations part and maintenance position part of trial vector $\vec{u}_{i,t}$. The processing sequence part of $\vec{u}_{i,t}$ should be repaired so that components of them constitute a feasible processing sequence of $n_o + n_N$ jobs.

Crossover operations preserve good structures from current individuals by selecting the second parent individual from current parent population or current non-dominated solutions' collection, and the algorithm will converge rapidly. We could get the trial vector $\vec{u}_{i,t}$ by combining the updated three components obtained through crossover operation.

Step 3: Selection operation

We use tournament selection operation to determine which of trial vector $\vec{u}_{i,t}$ and target vector $\vec{x}_{i,t}$ would survive in next generation: dominance relationship is used in the first place; if $\vec{u}_{i,t}$ and $\vec{x}_{i,t}$ both are non-dominated solutions, the one closer to the ideal point would be selected.

After stating differential evolution mutation operation, we would describe Gaussian mutation as follows.

Perform Gaussian mutation with mutation probability $P_m = \frac{1}{(n_o+n_N)}$ on the component of resource allocations and maintenance position part of the individual. Gaussian mutation process is expressed as Formula (5.3.7),

$$x_{i,j,t} = x_{i,j,t} + \left(\text{scale} - \text{shrink} \cdot \text{scale} \cdot \frac{\text{currentiter}}{\text{Max}_{gen}}\right) \cdot (u_{\text{limit},j} - l_{\text{limit},j}) * randn \tag{5.3.7}$$

$$i = 1, 2, \ldots, pop, \ j = n_o + n_N + 1, n_o + n_N + 2, \ldots, 2(n_o + n_N) + 1, \ t = 1, 2, \ldots, Max_{gen}$$

where $scale$ represents scale of variation point, $shrink$ represents variation ratio of contraction, $currentIter$ represents current generation algebra, Max_{gen} represents the maximum of generation algebra, $u_{limit,j}$ and $l_{limit,j}$ represent the upper bound and lower bound of $x_{i,j,t}$ and $randn$ represents a decimal randomly generated from Gaussian distribution. We should repair each component so that its value remains in a given range. For the jobs sequence part of the individual, perform Gaussian mutation operation on each position, and swap its component with the one in a newly generated position.

5.3.2 *NSGA-II/DE + POSQ Algorithm*

In this subsection we will introduce Pareto Optimal Solution Quality (POSQ for short) into NSGA-II/DE algorithm, and propose Non-dominated Sorting Genetic Algorithm with Differential Evolutionary and Pareto Optimal Solution Quality (NSGA-II/DE + POSQ for short). Framework and solution representation of NSGA-II/DE + POSQ is the same with that of NSGA-II/DE.

5.3.2.1 Initial Solution

Similar to the NSGA-II/DE, NSGA-II/DE + POSQ also starts with an initial population of pop numbers of randomly generated solutions which consists of the three parts as in formula (5.3.1). But for each individual of the population, we should adjust its processing sequence part according to Theorem 5.2.3 after that. Thus, the original jobs and new jobs will be sorted separately according to the SPT rule with respect to $(\overline{p}_j - b_j u_j)$. The corresponding resource allocations part should be adjusted simultaneously.

5.3.2.2 Other Operations

Fitness value calculation, crossover operation and mutation operation of NSGA-II/DE + POSQ are also similar with those of NSGA-II/DE. The difference between the two is that, we should always adjust processing sequence part of each new generated individual after crossover or mutation operation according to Theorem 5.2.3, and adjust the corresponding resource allocation part.

5.3.3 *NSGA-II/DE + POSQ + AHS Algorithm*

In this subsection we will introduce Approximation Heuristic Strategy (AHS for short) mentioned in Theorem 5.2.4 into NSGA-II/DE + POSQ, and propose Non-dominated Sorting Genetic Algorithm with POSQ and Approximation Heuristic Strategy algorithm (NSGA-II/DE + POSQ + AHS for short). Framework of NSGA-II/DE + POSQ + AHS is the same with that of NSGA-II/DE + POSQ.

5.3.3.1 Solution Representation

Similar to the NSGA-II/DE and NSGA-II/DE + POSQ, solution of NSGA-II/DE + POSQ + AHS also follows the representation scheme in formula (5.3.1). But component of the resource allocations part of NSGA-II/DE + POSQ + AHS represents whether or not to allocate resource to the corresponding job: '1' means allocating the maximum resource amount, and '0' means allocating zero resource amount.

5.3.3.2 Initial Solution

Different from NSGA-II/DE + POSQ, NSGA-II/DE + POSQ + AHS algorithm starts with an initial population of $pop - 2$ number of randomly generated solutions which consists of the three parts, and its processing sequence and resource allocations parts are adjusted according to Theorem 5.2.3 and all jobs actual processing time ($\overline{p}_j - b_j u_j$) after resource allocation. Moreover, components of each solution's resource allocations part are randomly taken from {0, 1} set, thus to applicant approximation heuristic strategies proposed in Theorem 5.2.4 to the algorithm. The rest two solutions would be generated as follows: focusing solely on the total operational cost by solving an assignment model for $\{J_1, J_2, \ldots, J_{n_o+n_N}\}$ to obtain the first solution, and then only on the total deviation cost by keeping $\{J_1, J_2, \ldots, J_{n_o}\}$ unchanged and solving an assignment model for $\{J_{n_o+1)}, J_{n_o+2}, \ldots, J_{n_o+n_N}\}$ to obtain the second solution. Note that these two solutions form the ideal point in objective space.

5.3.3.3 Other Operations

Fitness value calculation, crossover operation and mutation operation of NSGA-II/DE + POSQ + AHS algorithm are also similar with that of NSGA-II/DE + POSQ algorithm. The difference between the two is that, we should do additional repair expressed in Formula (5.3.8) to the resource allocations part of each new generated individual after crossover or mutation operation according to Theorem 5.2.4. Thus, each component's value of this part is in the {0, 1} set range.

$$x_{i,j,t} = \begin{cases} 0, & x_{i,j,t} < 0.5 \\ 1, & x_{i,j,t} \geq 0.5 \end{cases} \tag{5.3.8}$$

$i = 1, 2, \ldots, pop,\ j = n_o + n_N + 1, n_o + n_N + 2, \ldots, 2(n_o + n_N),\ t = 1, 2, \ldots, N$

5.4 Comparative Studies

5.4.1 Parameter Setting

In order to examine the effectiveness of algorithm hybridization and the improvement impact of non-dominated solution property on algorithm performance, we design comparative studies categorized by problem size. Four rescheduling cases have been considered by assigning various values to the pair (n_o, n_N): (10, 5) for case 1, (30, 20) for case 2, (80, 35) for case 3, and (130, 55) for case 4.

From case 1 to case 4, the increase in problem size generally makes the problem become more difficult. The remaining parameters concerning jobs and PM are the same for all cases. The normal processing time $\bar{p}_j$ and compression cost coefficient c_j of all jobs are integers randomly generated from uniform distribution: $\bar{p}_j \in U[1, 100], c_j \in U[2, 9]$, and compression time coefficient b_j are decimals also randomly generated from given uniform distributions: $b_j \in U[0.6, 0.9]$.

The deteriorating rate shared by all jobs is $\alpha = 0.01$. As to PM, the basic maintenance duration is set as $M = 30$, and the deteriorating rate is set as $\gamma = 0.01$. The cost rate of maintenance q is set to 1. For each case, 30 problem instances are randomly generated following the given distribution, and each problem instance is solved by running the four MOEA algorithms. After that the average performance would be returned and compared.

Next the tuning process of parameters of the four algorithms (NSGA-II, NSGA-II/DE, NSGA-II/DE + POSQ, and NSGA-II/DE + POSQ + AHS) would be presented. The parameters in NSGA-II contain population size pop, crossover fraction P_c in Intermediate crossover, ratio of crossover operation $ratio$, mutation fraction in Gaussian mutation P_m, scale of variance point $scale$, ratio of mutation shrinks $shrink$ and maximum generation number Max_{gen}. Besides those parameters, NSGA-II/DE, NSGA-II/DE + POSQ, and NSGA-II/DE + POSQ + AHS share the same extra parameters like crossover fraction C_r in differential evolution mutation operation and scaling factor F. Since more parameters are concerned for NSGA-II/DE, we would report the tuning process of NSGA-II/DE and examine the impact of the parameter value on algorithm performance: the minimum distance of obtained Pareto front to ideal point. The smaller the distance value, the better the parameter would be. By searching related literatures [31, 33], we start with $pop = 50$, $P_c = \frac{2}{2n_o+2n_N+1}$, $ratio = 0.8$, $P_m = \frac{2}{2n_o+2n_N+1}$, $scale = 0.1$, $shrink = 0.5$, $C_r = 0.1$, and $F = 0.5$ for problem instance of case 3. Then we focus on the parameters one by one, examine the algorithm performance of parameters consecutively taking various values while keeping other parameters unchanged. The tuning results are shown in Table 5.2.

The proper parameter values could be determined based on the corresponding algorithm performance in bold font. By applying the same process, we could determine the appropriate parameters combination for cases 1, 2 and 4, the results of which are similar and omitted. During the pilot experiments, we find out that all four algorithms converge within 200 generations for four cases, therefore we set $Max_{gen} = 300$ to control algorithm termination. We would use the tuned parameters to solve all the problem instances of 4 cases respectively.

Table 5.2 Results of parameters tuning

Parameters	Alternative values	Algorithm performance ($\times 10^4$)	Parameters	Alternative values	Algorithm performance ($\times 10^4$)
Pop	50	7.03		(0.1, 0.5)	7.94
	100	5.44		(0.1, 0.9)	7.49
	150	5.67		(0.5, 0.1)	4.74
P_c	$\frac{2}{2n_o+2n_N+1}$	8.40		(0.5, 0.5)	5.09
	$\frac{4}{2n_o+2n_N+1}$	6.41		(0.5, 0.9)	5.59
	$\frac{6}{2n_o+2n_N+1}$	7.11		(0.9, 0.1)	4.52
	$\frac{8}{2n_o+2n_N+1}$	6.97		(0.9, 0.5)	4.09
Ratio	0.8	6.26		(0.9, 0.9)	4.56
	1.2	5.39	C_r	0.1	7.58
	1.6	5.69		0.3	5.73
P_m	$\frac{2}{2n_o+2n_N+1}$	5.43		0.5	7.28
	$\frac{4}{2n_o+2n_N+1}$	6.64		0.7	5.78
	$\frac{6}{2n_o+2n_N+1}$	7.74		0.9	8.03
	$\frac{8}{2n_o+2n_N+1}$	7.98	F	0.5	7.47
(*Scale*, *Shrink*)	(0.1, 0.1)	8.01		0.9	5.83

5.4.2 Performance Indicators of Pareto Fronts

The four proposed MOEA algorithms all return a Pareto front between total operational cost and total deviation. In order to quantitatively compare different Pareto front, we introduce several existing performance indicators of Pareto fronts. The title, optimal direction and implications of those metrics are summarized in Table 5.3, and would be used in Sect. 5.3.

The performance of a Pareto front is reflected in its convergence and diversity. Of the six metrics, $ONVG$ measures the diversity of solutions in Pareto front, whereas CM, IGD, D_{max} measures the convergence. And HV and AQ return the comprehensive performance of convergence and diversity in an integrated manner.

5.4.3 Results

After all the problem instances have been solved by using the tuned parameters in Sect. 5.4.1, we report the typical results of one instance of case 3 ($n_O = 80$, $n_N = 35$) by presenting the initial population, the convergence process and the variation of Pareto fronts during evolution in Figs. 5.1, 5.2, 5.3 and 5.4, in order to illustrate the effectiveness of algorithm hybridization The rest results of case 3 and the results of

Table 5.3 Summary of performance indicators of Pareto fronts

Title	Optimal direction	Implications
ONVG [144]	Max	The number of non-dominated solutions in a candidate Pareto front
CM [194]	Min	The percentage of solutions in one candidate Pareto front that is dominated by solutions in another Pareto front
IGD [180]	Min	The average distance of candidate Pareto front to the reference set of optimal Pareto front
D_{max} [142]	Min	The maximum distance of candidate Pareto front to the reference set of optimal Pareto front
HV [86]	Max	The area covered by a Pareto front in two-dimensional objective space, reflecting the convergence and diversity of Pareto front
AQ [67]	Min	The average value of weighted sum of distance and distribution over a representative sample of weight vector, reflecting the convergence and diversity of Pareto front

cases 1, 2 and 4 are similar therefore not included. Figures 5.1, 5.3 and 5.4 depict the objective space, where x-axis denotes the total operational cost of $n_0 + n_N$ jobs and y-axis denotes the total deviation of n_0 original jobs. Figure 5.2 reveals the convergence process of four algorithms by measuring the average and minimum distances of Pareto front in each generation to ideal point. Constant curve stretching over generation means the corresponding algorithm is converging.

From Fig. 5.1, we could make two major observations. On one hand, NSGA-II and NSGA-II/DE share the same initial population: the starting individuals of two algorithms are identical. With other parameters staying the same, the difference of the two algorithms' final results could only be explained by the hybridization of differential evolution mutation operation mechanism. On the other hand, by introducing the Pareto Optimal Solution Quality into population, the entire population has been obviously moved towards the left and lower area of the objective space. The validity of Theorem 5.2.1 could be verified from an experimental point of view. The impact of further adding Approximation Heuristic Strategy into NSGA-II/DE + POSQ is two-folded: first, two solutions of coordinates $(1.15 \times 10^5, 0.19 \times 10^5)$ and $(1.64 \times 10^5, 0)$ which dominate all other identified solutions in the objective space. The better objective values of these two points also constitute the unattainable ideal point. Second some solutions in the lower and right area have emerged, making the population distribute more sparsely and allowing the possibility that better solutions could be found.

Figure 5.2 directly shows that the minimum and average distance curves of NSGA-II/DE + POSQ + AHS constantly stay below the curves of the other three algorithms. Besides, the variation scope of NSGA-II/DE + POSQ + AHS is relatively small. This could be explained by that due to two high-quality solutions obtained based

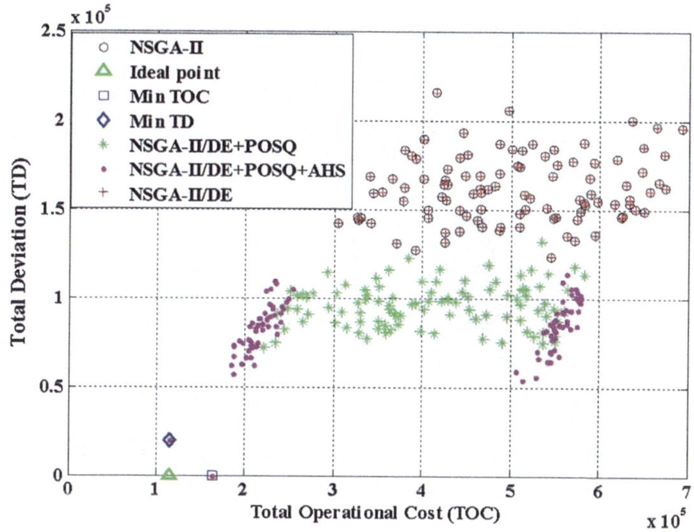

Fig. 5.1 Comparison of initial population

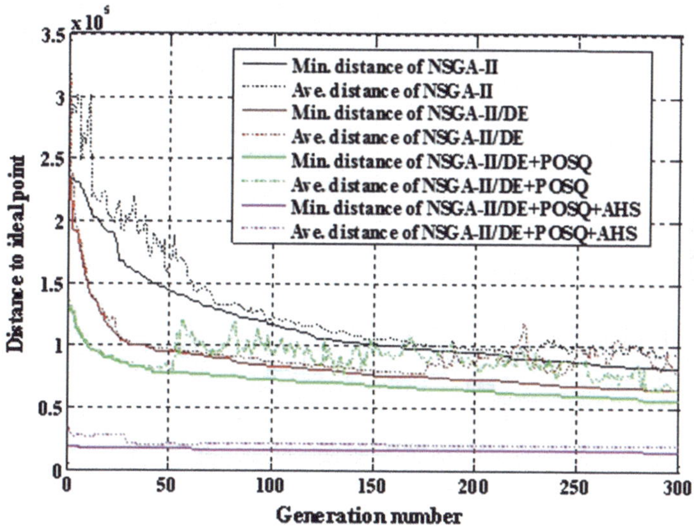

Fig. 5.2 Convergence analysis

on Lemma 5.2.1, the exploitation and exploration could be focused on the area $[1.15 \times 10^5, 1.64 \times 10^5] \times [0, 0.19 \times 10^5]$ in the objective space. Actually NSGA-II/DE + POSQ + AHS has converged around the 50th generation. The search improvement of NSGA-II through hybridization with DE mutation could be illustrated by comparing NSGA-II/DE with NSGA-II. The minimum distance curve of NSGA-II/DE decreases sharply from the beginning to around the 50th generation, then

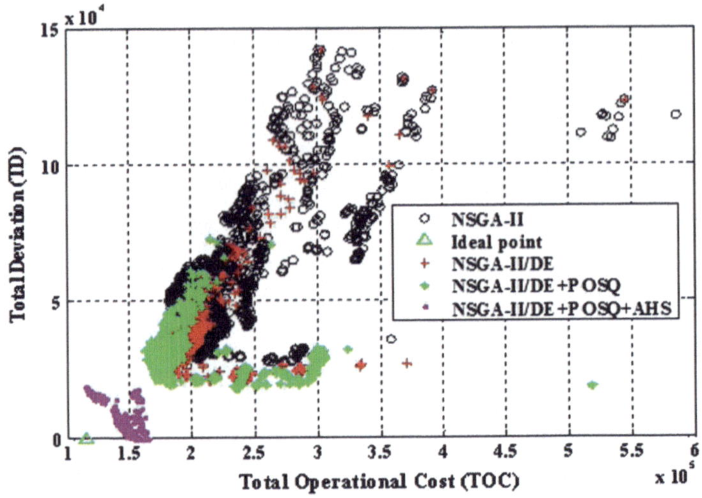

Fig. 5.3 Convergence process of Pareto fronts

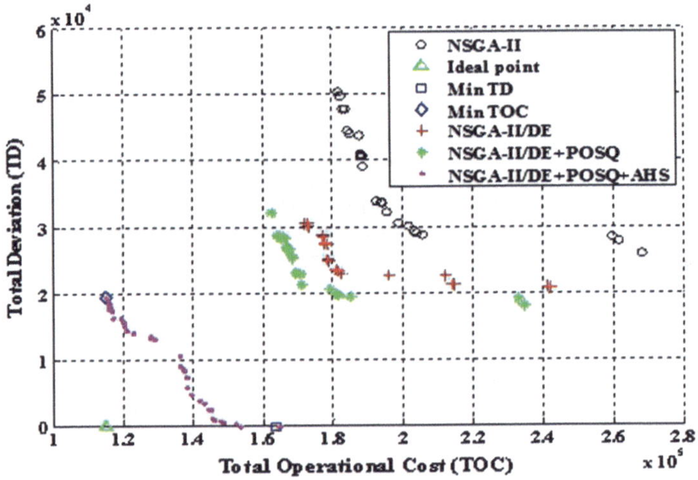

Fig. 5.4 The final Pareto fronts of 4 algorithms

the decreasing trend gradually slows down. This pattern could also be observed for NSGA-II/DE + POSQ. One explanation is that stagnationFrequencyLimit = 6 holds around the 50th generation, after which Gaussian mutation replaces differential evolution mutation operation. In combination of the evolution process of Pareto fronts in Fig. 5.3, we could observe that hybridization could speed up the convergence process of NSGA-II. The newly identified solutions of red cross marker in the area $[2 \times 10^5, 2.5 \times 10^5] \times [2 \times 10^4, 2.5 \times 10^4]$ of Fig. 5.3 illustrate that the DE mutation could enhance the population diversity. The finalized Pareto front outputted by

NSGA-II/DE in Fig. 5.4 could be partially attributed to those newly emerged solutions. To summarize, by balancing between exploration and exploitation through algorithm hybridization, NSGA-II/DE could improve the convergence and diversity of NSGA-II.

The exceptive phenomenon in Fig. 5.2 that the mean distance curves of NSGA-II/DE and NSGA-II/DE + POSQ are sometimes above NSGA-II could be attributed to improved population diversity. From Fig. 5.3, we could directly observe that the green star and red cross points are more evenly distributed. Larger number of solutions and more evenly distribution would naturally lead to larger average distance to ideal point. However, this does not affect the superiority of NSGA-II/DE's or NSGA-II/DE + POSQ's minimum distance over that of NSGA-II.

From the point of algorithm efficiency, we report the average running time over 30 runs of NSGA-II, NSGA-II/DE, NSGA-II/DE + POSQ and NSGA-II/DE + POSQ + AHS of Case 4 with maximum problem size respectively: 2.37, 3.01, 2.99 and 3.07 (s). We could conclude that the additional computational cost in NSGA-II/DE + POSQ + AHS in comparison with NSGA-II is reflected in the increased average 0.7 s. The increase in computational cost is worthwhile in consideration of the improved convergence process and obtained Pareto front.

After directly comparing the initial population, convergence process, and Pareto fronts of the four algorithms, we make use of performance indicators in Table 5.3 to measure the convergence and/or diversity of Pareto fronts and analyze the performance improvement brought by non-dominated solution property from a quantitative point of view. In order to examine the impact of analyzed property on performance improvement, we only compare the Pareto fronts of NSGA-II/DE + POSQ + AHS and NSGA-II/DE, and the results are shown in Table 5.4. The remaining results are similar therefore are not mentioned. We would be happy to share the results for algorithm verification and comparison purposes.

From Table 5.4, we could observe that NSGA-II/DE + POSQ + AHS outperforms NSGA-II/DE in almost every metric. By incorporating the analyzed property of the four partial SPT schedules with regards to maintenance position and new/old job category, certain area in objective space with inferior solution quality could be skipped during evolution. Therefore the convergence process could be speeded up and NSGA-II/DE + POSQ + AHS could return a better Pareto front within the same running time. This point could further be strengthened by adding two solutions which minimize the total operational cost and total deviation cost respectively into initial population, we could obtain a Pareto front uniformly distributed between those two points in the objective space. The search process could be directed towards exploring the area around those two good points, enhancing the probability that better results could be achieved. So adding two solutions serves the function of exploitation in our paper. This implies that another means besides algorithm hybridization to achieve balance between exploration and exploitation is to analyze the specific problem property and to make use of the property. Another major observation from Table 5.4

Table 5.4 Comparison of Pareto front performance metrics

		Case 1		Case 2		Case 3		Case 4	
		Ave	Std	Ave	Std	Ave	Std	Ave	Std
NSGA-II/DE + POSQ + AHS	ONVG	22.43	6.66	28.20	8.10	28.03	5.44	22.27	7.11
NSGA-II/DE		95.20	19.63	30.77	11.75	26.40	8.67	17.50	5.33
NSGA-II/DE + POSQ + AHS	CM	0.23	0.27	0.00	0.00	0.00	0.00	0.00	0.00
NSGA-II/DE		0.66	0.33	1.00	0.01	1.00	0.00	1.00	0.00
NSGA-II/DE + POSQ + AHS	IGD	0.02	0.02	0.00	0.00	0.00	0.00	0.00	0.00
NSGA-II/DE		0.06	0.05	0.30	0.12	0.45	0.14	0.68	0.08
NSGA-II/DE + POSQ + AHS	D_{max}	0.05	0.05	0.00	0.00	0.00	0.00	0.00	0.00
NSGA-II/DE		0.19	0.13	0.39	0.15	0.54	0.14	0.76	0.06
NSGA-II/DE + POSQ + AHS	HV	6.53×10^5	5.18×10^5	4.52×10^7	2.43×10^7	2.12×10^9	1.20×10^9	5.49×10^9	2.76×10^9
NSGA-II/DE		5.67×10^5	4.57×10^5	2.59×10^7	1.99×10^7	7.03×10^8	6.45×10^8	4.55×10^8	2.45×10^8
NSGA-II/DE + POSQ + AHS	AQ	2241.33	52.87	16524.31	337.28	73038.60	2429.53	194533.90	6879.96
NSGA-II/DE		2321.62	68.65	19028.19	567.00	91903.94	3457.79	241832.66	8181.48

is that the advantage of NSGA-II/DE + POSQ + AHS over NSGA-II/DE is robust against problem size variation from case 1 to case 4. The gap between performance metric values gradually enlarges as the problem size increases, implying our method is more appropriate for solving large-scale problem instances.

5.5 Summary

In this chapter we consider a rescheduling problem in the presence of new arrival jobs in the deteriorating production environments. The flexible strategies of preventive maintenance together with controllable processing time are adopted to reduce the negative impact of new arrival jobs and deterioration effect, where the machine could be totally recovered after being maintained. In response to this kind of disruption events, the unfinished and new arrived jobs should be scheduled to minimize the operational cost and disruption cost. To solve this bi-objective problem, we improve the widely-applied NSGA-II by balancing between exploration and exploitation in two aspects. On one hand, differential evolution mutation operation has been embedded into NSGA-II to increase population diversity, so that the tendency of producing identical individuals during evolution of NSGA-II could be eased. On the other hand, high-quality initial solution based on assignment model is constituted for exploitation, and analytic property of non-dominated solution is incorporated for exploration. Computational study verifies the effectiveness of our hybridized algorithm, which demonstrates that hybridized evolutionary algorithm could solve complicated rescheduling problem and the application of problem-specific information could enhance the performance of algorithm.

5.6 Bibliographic Remarks

A few years ago, researchers started taking machine states into consideration in scheduling research. The machines are often supposed to be in a perfect state at the times when they perform their work. In the last decade, machine scheduling problems with availability constraints due to maintenance activities, tool changes or breakdowns have been studied in the literature in different machine settings [77, 78, 94, 99–101, 188]. It is well known that proper machine maintenance helps improve production efficiency and product quality.

In order to be more realistic in modelling a production system, researchers have recently considered scheduling problems with simultaneous consideration of deteriorating jobs and maintenance activities. Kubzin and Strusevich [75, 76] introduce the concept of deteriorating maintenance activities whose durations depend on their start times into scheduling research. However, in their studies, the processing times of the jobs do not depend on their places with respect to a maintenance activity in a schedule. Yang and Yang [163] study a single-machine scheduling problem with job-dependent aging effects, multiple maintenance activities and variable maintenance durations to minimise the makespan. Yang et al. [164] investigate a due-window assignment and single-machine scheduling problem with job-dependent aging effects and a maintenance activity, where the objective is to find jointly the job sequence, the maintenance position and the due-window position to minimise a total cost function. They develop a polynomial time algorithm for it. Mosheiov and Sidney [101] investigate a single-machine scheduling problem with a maintenance activity which has a variable maintenance duration. They consider such objective functions as the makespan, total flowtime, maximum lateness, total earliness, tardiness and due-date cost, and number of tardy jobs, and provide polynomial time solutions for all these problems. Rustogi and Strusevich [123] present polynomial-time algorithms for single-machine scheduling problems with generalised positional deteriorating jobs and machine maintenance. They use general non-decreasing functions to model the deterioration rates of job processing times and assume that a maintenance activity does not necessarily restore the machine fully to its original perfects state. The objective is to find the job sequence and number of maintenance activities to minimise the makespan. They provide polynomial-time solution algorithms for various versions of the problem. Rustogi and Strusevich [123] extend their previous study to the case with unrelated parallel machines to minimise the total flow time. They show that this problem is also polynomially solvable. Rustogi and Strusevich [124] further study a more general case where the actual processing times of the jobs are subject to a combination of positional and time-dependent effects, which are job-independent. They provide solution algorithms for the problems to minimise the makespan and the sum of completion times, respectively. Yin et al. [172] address the scheduling problem with simultaneous consideration of due-date assignment, generalised position-dependent deteriorating jobs, and deteriorating maintenance activities. It is assumed that the actual processing time of a job is a general non-decreasing function depending on the number of maintenance activities performed before it and its position in a sequence. Moreover, the machine may be subject to several maintenance activities up to a limit over the scheduling horizon. The maintenance activities do not necessarily restore the machine fully to its original perfect state and the duration of a maintenance activity depends on its start time. They provide polynomial-time solution algorithms for various versions of the problem with the objective of minimizing an optimality criterion that includes the cost of due-date assignment, the cost of discarding jobs that cannot be completed by their due dates and the earliness of the scheduled jobs under the popular CON and SLK due-date assignment methods.

With a few exceptions, most single machine models with controllable processing time, PM and/or new orders are bi-objective in nature and $\mathcal{NP}$-hard in complexity. Such problems become increasingly intractable for exact algorithms as the problem size grows. By contrast, meta-heuristics such as multi-objective evolutionary algorithms (MOEAs) are well suited for NP-hard problems, which are able to generate uniformly distributed Pareto optimal solutions more efficiently [82, 105]. For comprehensive reviews of MOEAs and their applications in scheduling, refer to the review papers [17, 44].

This chapter considers arrival of new orders, which is a typical type of uncertainty in manufacturing systems. A survey of evolutionary algorithms (EAs) in the presence of uncertainty has been provided [68], summarizing four types of uncertainties: noise in fitness evaluations, design/environmental parameter variations, errors of approximation models, and dynamically changing environments. Among the many MOEAs, NSGA-II is believed to be able to find more uniform spread of solutions and better convergence to the true Pareto front compared to other popular algorithms such as Pareto-archived evolution strategy (PAES) and strength-Pareto evolutionary algorithm (SPEA) [33]. Therefore NSGA-II or enhanced versions of NSGA-II have been widely applied in production scheduling. Despite its attractive properties, NSGA-II is prone to produce identical solutions in selection, reducing its population diversity and leading to premature convergence [82]. One possible approach to address this issue is to hybridize various meta-heuristics. The similarities and differences of existing widely used meta-heuristics have been analyzed, and the importance of hybridization of meta-heuristics as well as the integration of meta-heuristics with other methods for optimization has been emphasized [16, 49]. Following this idea, NSGA-II has been modified by embedding a new mutation process to solve a parallel machine scheduling problem with three objectives and the modified NSGA-II performs better than the original NSGA-II and SPEA2 [12]. The role of geometric concepts has been investigated in combinatorial problems and a multi-objective scheduling problem is solved by use of a variant of NSGA-II constructed from geometry-based operators [139]. An improved NSGA-II algorithm has been proposed and applied to solve the lot-streaming flow shop scheduling problem with four criteria, which outperforms the compared algorithms demonstrated by a serial of experiments [52]. The better performance of hybridized algorithms can be attributed to a good balance between exploration and exploitation, which are the two cornerstones of problem solving in evolutionary search. A more comprehensive and systematic understanding of exploration and exploitation has been discussed [28]. In this work, we will improve the performance of NSGA-II by balancing exploration and exploitation through algorithm hybridization to address premature convergence.

Differential evolution (DE), which was initially proposed in 1997 [135] for optimization problems over continuous spaces, together with its various variants have been widely applied in engineering and optimization area [31]. It was used to solve no-idle permutation flow shop scheduling problem with tardiness criterion, which presented some efficient methods of converting a continuous vector to a discrete job permutation and vice versa [138]. Also a variable parameter search was introduced into DE to accelerate the search process for global optimization and enhance the solution quality. DE has also been hybridized to minimize the maximum completion time for a flow shop scheduling problem with intermediate buffers located between two consecutive machines [116]. They adopted job permutation to represent individuals and apply job-permutation-based mutation and crossover, and the effectiveness of hybrid algorithm has well been demonstrated. Inspired by Pan et al. [116]. In this paper we will introduce differential evolution mutation operation into NSGA-II in order to reduce the probability of premature convergence, and further accelerate the convergence and global search ability of NSGA-II. It should be pointed out that the purpose of this problem-oriented paper is not to design a state-of-the-art MOEA that outperforms all the rest of applicable MOEAs. Rather we focus on solving the proposed problem effectively base on a hybrid multi-objective evolutionary framework constructed from NSGA-II and DE, and examining the improvement brought by the analyzed properties of non-dominated solutions about job's sequence and approximation heuristic strategy for resource allocation of the problem, and the impact of non-dominated solutions obtained by solving the assignment model for two rescheduling special cases.

It is worth noting that the main results of this chapter come from Wang et al. [147].

Chapter 6
A Knowledge-Based Evolutionary Proactive Scheduling Approach in the Presence of Machine Breakdown and Deterioration Effect

This chapter considers proactive scheduling in response to stochastic machine breakdown under deteriorating production environments, where the actual processing time of a job gets longer along with machine's usage and age. It is assumed that job processing times are controllable by allocating extra resources and the machine breakdown can be described using a given probability distribution. If a machine breaks down, it needs to be repaired and is no longer available during the repair. To absorb the repair duration, the subsequent unfinished jobs are compressed as much as possible to match up the baseline schedule. This work aims to find the optimal baseline sequence and the resource allocation strategy to minimize the operational cost consisting of the total completion time cost and resource consumption cost of the baseline schedule, and the rescheduling cost consisting of the match-up time cost and additional resource consumption cost. To this end, an efficient multi-objective evolutionary algorithm based on elitist non-dominated sorting is proposed, in which a support vector regression (SVR) surrogate model is built to replace the time-consuming simulations in evaluating the rescheduling cost, which represents the solution robustness of the baseline schedule. In addition, a priori domain knowledge is embedded in population initialization and offspring generation to further enhance the performance of the algorithm. Comparative results and statistical analysis show that the proposed algorithm is effective in finding non-dominated tradeoff solutions between operational cost and robustness in the presence of machine breakdown and deterioration effect.

This part is composed of five sections. In Sect. 6.1 we formulate the proactive scheduling problem. In Sect. 6.2 we present a knowledge-based multi-objective evolutionary algorithm to solve the proposed proactive scheduling problem. In Sect. 6.3, we conduct extensive comparative studies to verify the effectiveness of the proposed algorithm. We conclude this chapter in Sect. 6.4, and end the chapter in Sect. 6.5 with bibliographic remarks.

D. Wang et al., *Rescheduling Under Disruptions in Manufacturing Systems*,
Uncertainty and Operations Research, https://doi.org/10.1007/978-981-15-3528-4_6

6.1 Problem Formulation

We consider scheduling a set of non-preemptive jobs $J = \{J_1, J_2, \ldots, J_n\}$ to be processed on a common machine that are all continuously available from time zero onwards. Each job J_j is initially available for processing at time zero. Analogous to the problem investigated in Chap. 4, the actual processing time of each job, which is subject to deterioration effect and could be compressed by allocating more resources, is denoted by $p_j = \overline{p}_j + \alpha t_j - b_j u_j$.

It is assumed that the decision maker is interested in finding a baseline schedule S to minimize the operational cost measured by the sum of the total completion time cost and resource consumption cost, which is one of the optimality criteria under consideration, and is denoted as follows:

$$f(S) = q \sum_{j=1}^{n} C_j + \sum_{j=1}^{n} c_j u_j. \tag{6.1.1}$$

where q is the unit completion time cost, C_j is the completion time of job J_j, and c_j denotes the unit resource cost of job J_j. Using the classical three-field notation, we can formally formulate our original operational cost minimization problem denoted by **P** as follows:

$$1|\bar{p}_j + \alpha t_j - b_j u_j|q \sum_{j=1}^{n} C_j + \sum_{j=1}^{n} c_j u_j. \tag{6.1.2}$$

The following result provides the time complexity needed for solving problem **P**.

Lemma 6.1.1 *Problem* **P** *can be solved in* $O(n^3)$ *time.*

Proof An optimal solution of problem **P** can be determined by the following steps:

(1) For job sequence $S = (J_{[1]}, J_{[2]}, \ldots, J_{[n]})$, the total operational cost can be formulated as follows:

$$\begin{aligned}
q \sum_{j=1}^{n} c_j + \sum_{j=1}^{n} c_j u_j &= q \sum_{j=1}^{n} c_{[j]} + \sum_{j=1}^{n} c_{[j]} u_{[j]} \\
&= q \left(C_{[1]} + C_{[2]} + \cdots + C_{[n]}\right] + \sum_{j=1}^{n} c_{[j]} u_{[j]} \\
&= q \sum_{j=1}^{n} (n+1-j) p_{[1]} + \sum_{j=1}^{n} c_{[j]} u_{[j]^+} \\
&= q \sum_{j=1}^{n} \tilde{w}_j p_{[j]} + \sum_{j=1}^{n} c_{[j]} u_{[j]}
\end{aligned}$$

where $\tilde{w}_j = n + 1 - j$, $j = 1, 2, \ldots, n$ denotes the position weight, $[j]$ represents the index of the job scheduled in the jth position of the schedule.

Now substituting $p_j = \overline{p}_j + \alpha t_j - b_j u_j$ into the above equation, we have

$$q\sum_{j=1}^{n} \tilde{w}_j p_{[j]} + \sum_{j=1}^{n} c_{[j]}u_{[j]} = q\sum_{j=1}^{n} W_j \left(\overline{p}_{[j]} - b_{[j]}u_{[j]}\right) + \sum_{j=1}^{n} c_{[j]}u_{[j]}$$

$$q\sum_{j=1}^{n} W_j \overline{p}_{[j]} + \sum_{j=1}^{n} \left(c_{[j]} - qW_j b_{[j]}\right) u_{[j]}$$

where $W_j = \sum_{i=j}^{n} \sum_{k=0}^{i-j} \mathbf{M}_{i-j+1,k+1}\alpha^k \tilde{w}_i$ and $\mathbf{M}_{i,j}$ can be iteratively calculated as $\mathbf{M}_{i,j} = \mathbf{M}_{i-1,j-1} + \mathbf{M}_{i-1,j}$ with $\mathbf{M}_{1,1} = 1 \cdot \mathbf{M}_{1,j} = 0, \mathbf{M}_{i,1} = 0$ for $i, j = 2, 3, \ldots, n$.

Therefore for the jth job in given schedule, when $c_{[j]} \geq qW_j b_{[j]}$ its optimal resource allocation amount should be $u_{[j]} = 0$, otherwise, its optimal resource allocation amount should be $u_{[j]} = \bar{u}_{[j]}$.

(2) For $1 \leq j, r \leq n$, let us define

$$C_{jr} = \begin{cases} W_r \overline{p}_j, & r = 1, 2, \ldots, n;\ c_j \geq qW_r b_j \\ W_r \overline{p}_j + \left(c_j - qW_r b_j\right)\overline{u}_j, & r = 1, 2, \ldots, n;\ c_j < qW_r b_j \end{cases}$$

where C_{jr} denotes the minimum possible cost resulting from assigning job J_j to position r in the sequence.

Here we introduce binary variable z_{jr} to denote whether job J_j is arranged at the rth position in the schedule: $z_{jr} = 1$ means 'yes' and $z_{jr} = 0$ means 'no'. Then the problem **P** can be transferred into the following assignment problem:

$$\min \sum_{m=1}^{n} \sum_{j=1}^{n} c_{r^2 r}$$

$$\text{s.t.} \sum_{r=1}^{n} z_{jr} = 1, \quad j = 1, 2, \ldots, n$$

$$\sum_{j=1}^{n} z_{jr} = 1, \quad r = 1, 2, \ldots, n$$

$$z_{jr} = 1 \text{ or } z_{jr} = 0, \quad r, j = 1, 2, \ldots, n$$

□

Once machine breakdown occurs, repairing of the machine will be undertaken immediately, resulting in an unavailability time interval during which no production can be carried out. Different from the strategies adopted in the previously chapters, a widely adopted approach to reducing the impact of machine breakdown, known as the proactive scheduling, is to generate a predictive schedule that is robust against anticipated disruptions that may occur during execution of the schedule, which means that the realized schedule stays in consistence with the baseline schedule as much as possible after disruptions. When machine maintenance is completed, it is desirable not to reschedule all remaining jobs to reduce computational burden and alleviate the negative impact on the entire production system resulting from the machine breakdown. To achieve this, we select a subset of subsequent unfinished jobs and fully compress them so that the repair duration can be compensated as soon as possible. As a result, the partially adjusted schedule will match up with the baseline schedule at a certain time point after the machine breakdown. In other words, from the match-up point on, the processing sequence and start-end time of each job will again become identical with the baseline schedule. The main criterion for the adjusted partial schedule, known as the rescheduling cost, is measured as the sum of the match-up time cost and the additional resource cost for the jobs to be further compressed. The rescheduling cost is formulated as follows:

$$g(S, \mathbf{B}) = mW_{\min} + f_{W_{\min}} \tag{6.1.3}$$

where $W_{\min}$ denotes the match-up time, m is the unit match-up time cost, and $f_{W_{\min}}$ represents the additional resource cost for further compressing job processing times. Since the unforeseen disruptions cause performance variability, the expectation of $g(S, \mathbf{B})$ denotes as $E(g(S, \mathbf{B}))$ is introduced as the robustness of the predictive schedule with stochastic machine breakdowns. Here, since no analytical function is available, the scenario-based evaluation approach is adopted to evaluate the solution robustness, which can be denoted as follows:

$$E(g(S, \mathbf{B})) = \frac{1}{s}\sum_{i=1}^{s} g(S, \mathbf{B}) \tag{6.1.4}$$

where s represents the size of the scenario set for scenario-based fitness evaluation of $E(g(S, \mathbf{B}))$, and $\mathbf{B_i}$ denotes the machine breakdown time of the ith scenario in the scenario set $g(S, \mathbf{B})$ and $E(g(S, \mathbf{B}))$ are simplified as g and $E(g)$ or E separately when there is no ambiguity. Note that such simulation based evaluations of the solution robustness may become computationally very intensive and surrogate-assisted evolutionary techniques will be helpful.

A proactive baseline schedule is expected to be not only advantageous in operational cost, but also robust against stochastic machine breakdown. Hence, it would be ideal if we can find an optimal scheduling sequence and a resource allocation strategy that simultaneously minimizes the initial operational cost and robustness in response to machine breakdown. Unfortunately, such an ideal solution does not exist and typically, there is a tradeoff between minimal initial operational cost and solution robustness. That is, the baseline schedule having the minimal initial operational cost may not be optimal in terms of solution robustness, vice versa. As a result, we can only find a set of so-called Pareto optimal solutions, i.e., a set of schedules that present different tradeoffs between the two objectives. Again by using the three-field notation, we formulate the above bi-objective scheduling problem denoted by **P1** as follows:

$$1|\bar{p_j} + \alpha t_j - b_j u_j, brkdwn, rs| \left(E(g(\pi, \mathbf{B})), q \sum_{j=1}^{n} C(\pi) + \sum_{j=1}^{n} c_j u_j \right) \quad (6.1.5)$$

where in the second field $brkdwn$ stands for the stochastic machine breakdown, and rs means robust scheduling.

6.2 A Knowledge-Based Multi-objective Evolutionary Algorithm

As stochastic machine breakdown is considered in this chapter to solve the proactive scheduling problem, no traditional mathematical programming methods can be directly used due to the unavailability of explicit analytic formulations for its robust objective [68]. For this reason, we decide to design a multi-objective evolutionary algorithm (MOEA) for solving this problem, since MOEAs have been proved to be effective in solving many scheduling problems [133], including dynamic scheduling problems [36, 126, 132], steelmaking casting problems [85], knowledge-based reactive scheduling system development for emergency departments [74] and semiconductor final testing scheduling problems [191]. However, for evaluating the robustness of each solution, a large number of time-consuming Monte Carlo simulations have to be performed, since a set of stochastic machine breakdown scenarios need to be sampled. Therefore, we resort to surrogate-assisted evolutionary algorithms to reduce computation cost [5, 115, 158, 184].

Surrogate-assisted evolutionary algorithms use surrogate models to replace computationally expensive real fitness evaluations, which have attracted increasing attention of researchers working on optimization of real-world applications involving expensive computation or physical simulation for evaluating the fitness of candidate solutions [71, 73, 91, 136]. Many surrogate models have been employed to assist evolutionary algorithms, such as Gaussian process modeling, artificial neural networks, support vector regressions and radial basis functions, through which the computational cost can be reduced significantly due to the surrogate-assisted fitness evaluation instead of exact real fitness evaluation [70, 86, 115].

In the following, we propose a knowledge-based, surrogate-assisted multi-objective evolutionary algorithm using elitist non-dominated sorting, termed ADK/SA-NSGA-II to solve the proactive scheduling problem. The original elitist non-dominated sorting genetic algorithm, known as NSGA-II [33], is a popular multi-objective evolutionary algorithm that has been successfully used for a variety of optimization problems. Within NSGA-II, we introduce a support vector regression model as the surrogate to evaluate the solution robustness to replace the time-consuming simulations. To further enhance the search efficiency of the evolutionary search,

Fig. 6.1 Flow diagram of ADK/SA-NSGA-II

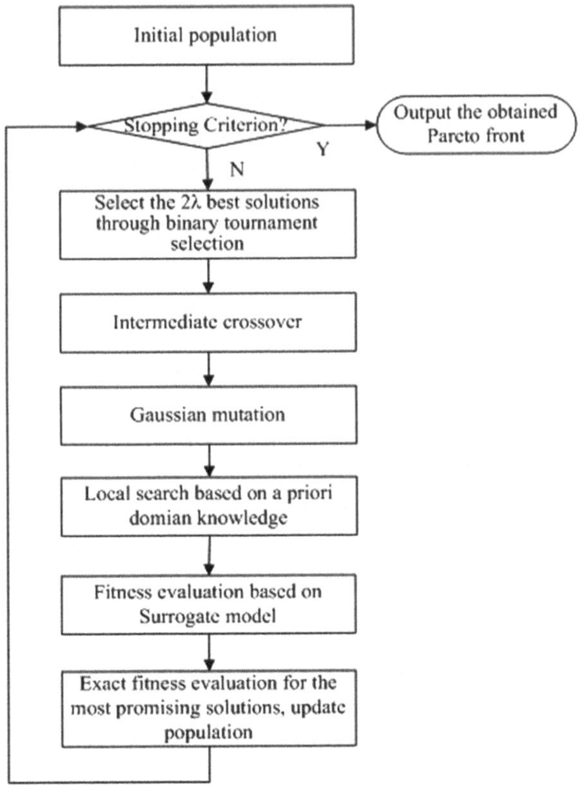

the structural property based a priori domain knowledge is embedded in population initialization and offspring generation. The main steps of the proposed ADK/SA-NSGA-II algorithm are summarized in the following steps, also as illustrated in Fig. 6.1.

Step 1: Let $T = 1$, randomly sample *pop* solutions to form the initial population P_T, and evaluate each individual through simulation based real fitness evaluation method.

Step 2: If the problem related stopping criterion is met, output the obtained Pareto front; otherwise go to Step 3.

Step 3: Select λ pairs of best solution through tournament selection to form a parent population P_P, where λ is an integer with $\lambda \geq 1$ and is set as $pop/2$ by default.

Step 4: Apply Intermediate crossover and Gaussian mutation on P_P to generate the offspring population P_O with 2λ individuals.

Step 5: Improve P_O through a priori domain knowledge based local search where the analytical structural property of problem **P1** is considered.

Step 6: Take the exact fitness values in the first *TrainScale* number of generations as the training data to prescreen P_O using support vector regression (SVR) model in the

original space. The training data is updated in the following every *TrainingInternal* generations using the newly achieved 2λ exact fitness values, so is the SVR model.

Step 7: Evaluate the real fitness value of the estimated *SimulateRatio* percent best offspring from Step 6, and combine it with P_T to obtain P_{T+1}. Go back to Step 2.

The following remarks on the proposed ADK/SA-NSGA-II algorithm can be made.

- Simulation-based real fitness evaluations and fitness evaluations based on the surrogate are mainly for estimating the solution robustness $E(g)$ of a schedule for problem **P1** since no analytic formulations are available for $E(g)$. Efficient surrogate model is used to replace the computationally expensive real fitness evaluations, which can significantly reduce the computational cost. Here we assume that the computational cost for building the surrogates is negligible compared to the expensive simulation based fitness evaluations.
- We assume that the computational budget is limited and high quality solutions should be obtained given limited computational budget to meet the increasingly stringent industry requirements. Consequently, the stopping criterion is set as the number of simulation-based real fitness evaluations which is the product of maximum generation number N, exact evaluated offspring number in each generation *SimulateRatio* $\times$ *pop* and scenario set size *simulationTimes* for robustness evaluation.
- It is desirable to construct a good surrogate model for locating the most promising candidate solutions within a reasonable amount of computational effort. Although we assume that the computational cost of model construction is far less than that of the simulation-based real fitness evaluation, it is not realistic to use too many training data to train the surrogate model and reconstruct the model very often. On the other hand, using too few training data and insufficient reconstruction may deteriorate the reliability of the surrogate model and thus the solution quality.
- After the surrogate model is used to prescreen the offspring population, simulations will be used to re-evaluate part of population, which are typically the most promising solutions in the current population. The ratio of individuals to be re-evaluated is defined by a parameter *simulationRatio*. Re-evaluation of part of solutions can help prevent the search from being misled by the approximation errors of the surrogate models.
- All individuals in the first *TrainSetScale* generations of the evolution will be evaluated using the expensive simulations to collect data for training the surrogates. Once the surrogate is trained, it will replace the simulations to reduce computation time. In addition, all individuals in the last generation will also be evaluated using simulations to ensure that the fitness values of the Pareto optimal solutions obtained by the algorithm are correct.

6.2.1 Encoding Scheme

The chromosome encoding the solutions to problem **P1** contains $2n$ elements, in which the first n elements form a permutation of n jobs and the following n elements correspond to a sequence of real numbers from the interval [0, 1]. The encoding scheme is formulated as follows.

$$\mathbf{x}_{i,t} = (\overbrace{x_{i,1,t}, x_{i,2,t}, \ldots, x_{i,n,t}}^{\pi\text{-part}}, \underbrace{x_{i,n+1,t}, x_{i,n+2,t}, \ldots, x_{i,2n,t}}_{y\text{-part}}) \tag{6.2.1}$$

$$i = 1, 2, \ldots, pop; t = 1, 2, \ldots, N$$

where pop stands for the population size, N stands for the maximum generation number, and $\mathbf{x}_{i,t}$ stands for the ith individual of the population in the tth generation. π-part of $\mathbf{x}_{i,t}$ directly encodes the sequence of all the jobs, and y-part denotes the percentage of the pre-allocated resource to the corresponding job sequenced in π-part.

6.2.2 Main Evolutionary Operations

6.2.2.1 Intermediate Crossover

With a probability of $CrossFraction$, the following intermediate crossover operation is applied on the π-part and y-part of two selected individuals indicated by subscripts $r1$ and $r2$, respectively.

$$o_{i,j,t} = p_{r1,j,t} + rand \cdot Ratio \cdot (p_{r2,j,t} - p_{r1,j,t}) \tag{6.2.2}$$

$$i = 1, 2, \ldots, pop; j = 1, 2, \ldots, 2n; t = 1, 2, \ldots, N$$

where $o_{i,j,t}$ denotes the jth entry of the ith offspring individual in the tth generation, $p_{r1,j,t}$ and $p_{r1,j,t}$ represent the jth entries of two selected individuals in the tth generation. $rand$ is a decimal randomly generated from the interval [0, 1], and $Ratio$ is the parameter called 'ratio' to control the intermediate crossover process.

After adjusting each entry achieved through the above operation within its feasible interval, the π-part of each chromosome should be further repaired to fix infeasible solutions, for example those containing duplicated jobs in the sequence. The duplicated jobs should be replaced with missing ones.

6.2.2.2 Gaussian Mutation

With a probability of *MutateFraction*, the following Gaussian mutation is applied on the π-part and y-part of the selected individual, respectively

$$\tilde{o}_{i,j,t} = o_{i,j,t} + rand \cdot \left(Scale - Shrink \cdot Scale \cdot \frac{t}{N} \right) \cdot (u_{limit,j} - l_{limit,j}) \tag{6.2.3}$$

$$i = 1, 2, \ldots, pop;\ j = 1, 2, \ldots, 2n;\ t = 1, 2, \ldots, N$$

where $rand$ is a decimal, uniformly generated number within the interval [0, 1], *Scale* is used to control the mutation scale, $Shrink$ represents the mutation shrink coefficient, $u_{limit,j}$ and $l_{limit,j}$ are the upper and lower bound of $o_{i,j,t}$. Repair should be applied on $\tilde{o}_{i,j,t}$ similar to the intermediate crossover operation to guarantee the feasibility of the solution.

6.2.2.3 Selection Based on Non-dominated Sorting and Crowing Distance

After $E(g)$ and f re-estimated for each individual, based on the dominance relationship between individuals, the current population is divided into K non-dominated fronts $\{PF_1, PF_2, \ldots, PF_K\}$. For any two fronts PF_i and PF_j, if $i < j$, then any individual in PF_j is dominated by some individual in PF_i. For individuals in the same front, a crowding distance is calculated to measure the degree of diversity of each individual. Fitness is assigned according to two criteria: individuals having a smaller front number are preferred in selection, and for individuals in the same front, those having a larger crowding distance will be prioritized. Refer to Deb et al. [33] for details about non-dominated sorting and crowding distance calculation.

6.2.3 *Support Vector Regression Model*

6.2.3.1 Principles of Support Vector Regression

It is assumed that a number of training data $\{(x_1, y_1), (x_2, y_2), \ldots, (x_l, y_l)\} \subset \mathbf{X} \times \mathbf{R}$ is available for constructing the support vector regression model, where l is the size of the training data, and $\mathbf{X}$ denotes the space of the input patterns $\mathbf{X} = \mathbf{R}^d$. The main idea behind SVR is to map $X \in \mathbf{R}^d$ into some feature space by a non-linear mapping $\phi(\cdot)$, and to find a linear function $f(x)$ that has at most ε deviation from the actually obtained targets y_i for all the training data [22]. The linear function $f(x)$ is formulated as follows:

$$f(x) = \omega^T \phi(x) + b \tag{6.2.4}$$

where ω is the weight vector, and b is the threshold value.

In SVR method [22], the vector ω and the threshold b can be obtained via the following optimization:

$$\begin{aligned} &\min \frac{1}{2}|\omega|^2 + C\sum_{i=1}^{l}(\xi_i + \xi_i^*) \\ &\text{s.t.} y_i - K(\omega, x_i) - b \le \varepsilon + \xi_i \\ &\quad K(\omega, x_i) + b - y_i \le \varepsilon + \xi_i^* \\ &\quad \xi_i, \xi_i^* \ge 0 \end{aligned} \tag{10}$$

where C determines the tolerated deviation between the flatness of $f(x)$ and ε, $K(x_k, x) = \phi(x_k)^T\phi(x)$ is the kernel function. Here, the radial basis function is chosen as the kernel function $K(x_i, x_j)$, defined as $K(x_i, x_j) = e^{-\gamma|x_i - y_i|^2}$ [22].

6.2.3.2 Management of Support Vector Regression Model

By managing the SVR model, we mean the initial training of the surrogate in the beginning of the optimization and the control of the frequency of updating the SVR model during evolutionary optimization. In this work, we simply pre-specify that the surrogate is updated in every *TrainInternal* generations. If the surrogate is to be updated, the population in that generation is used to update the training data, and the newly generated data will be used to update the surrogate.

Step 1: Initialize the training data set with those individuals generated in the first *TrainSetScale* generations. All these individuals are exactly evaluated using the simulation-based real fitness evaluation method. Thus a training data set formulated is achieved as follows:

$$\begin{aligned} trainingSet = \{&(x_{11}, x_{12}, \ldots, x_{1,2n}, E_1), \ldots, (x_{i1}, x_{i2}, \ldots, x_{i,2n}, E_i), \ldots, \\ &(x_{l1}, x_{l2}, \ldots, x_{l,2n}, E_l)\} \quad i = 1, 2, \ldots, l \end{aligned}$$

where $l = TrainSetScal \times pop$ denotes the row of the matrix, and $(x_{i1}, x_{i2}, \ldots, x_{i,2n}, E_i)$ represents the training data corresponding to the ith individual $(x_{i1}, x_{i2}, \ldots, x_{i,2n})$ with E_i as its robustness objective.

Step 2: Tune the two key parameters C and γ of the SVR model based on the training data using cross validation. The exponential grid interval for C is set as $[C_{\min}, C_{\max}]$, and the moving step is set as C_{step}, meaning C takes a series of values $\{2^{C_{\min}}, 2^{C_{\min}+C_{\text{step}}}, \ldots, 2^{C_{\max}}\}$. $C_{\min}$, $C_{\max}$ and C_{step} are defaulted as -5, 5, 1, respectively. The alternative values for γ are similar with respect to $\gamma_{\min}$, $\gamma_{\max}$ and γ_{step} of the same default values. The training data is divided into three parts for cross validation, and the combination of C and γ with the most accurate estimation is selected.

Step 3: Construct the SVR model based on principles of support vector regression, where the training data obtained in Step 1 and the parameters tuned in Step 2 are adopted.

Step 4: After every *TrainInternal* number of generations, *trainingSet* should be updated by replacing the dominated individuals with those of higher qualities in the current generation. Consequently, the SVR model should be updated with the same method mentioned in its construction based on the updated training data and the tuned parameters.

6.2.3.3 SVR Model Based Fitness Evaluation

The constructed SVR model is embedded into the evolutionary algorithm to pre-screen the obtained offspring population in each generation. Based on the evaluation results given by SVR model, $SimulateRatio \in [0, 1]$ percentage of the promising individuals are re-evaluated through simulation-based real fitness evaluation so as to prevent the search process from being misled to a false optimum [70, 115].

6.2.4 Structural Property Based a Priori Domain Knowledge

The following lemma defines the structure property that will be used as a priori domain knowledge of problem **P1** in ADK/SA-NSGA-II to enhance its search capability.

Lemma 6.2.1 *For a given resource allocation strategy, the objective of operational cost can be minimized by sequencing the jobs according to the non-decreasing order of* $\bar{p}_j - b_j u_j$.

Proof Given the resource allocation amount for each job, the decision of sequencing jobs clearly does not affect the resource cost part of $f(\pi)$. For any two adjacent jobs violating the non-decreasing order of $\bar{p}_j - b_j u_j$, applying the pairwise exchange technique clearly reduces the total completion objective part. Therefore Lemma 6.2.1 holds. □

According to Lemma 6.2.1, sequencing jobs in the non-decreasing order of $\bar{p}_j - b_j u_j$ with a given resource allocation strategy will improve the total completion time. Therefore, we apply this as a priori domain knowledge to the population initialization and part of the obtained offspring individuals by adjusting their π-parts to minimize their initial operational cost. Their y-parts are also adjusted accordingly to keep the sequence in consistency with the π-parts.

6.3 Comparative Studies

6.3.1 Experimental Design

In order to examine the efficiency of the proposed knowledge-based surrogate-assisted multi-objective evolutionary algorithm (ADK/SA-NSGA-II), ten problem cases of randomly generated numerical instances are considered. The problem cases are categorized based on the number of jobs, and labeled as Case 1 to 10 for 30, 50, 70, 90, 110, 130, 150, 200, 300 and 500 jobs, respectively. For each case, 100 numerical test instances are randomly generated, resulting in a total of 1000 test instances. All the algorithms are implemented in MATLAB and run on a PC with 4G RAM, Intel Core i5 CPU 2.5 GHz. In each problem case, the parameter settings are as follows:

- The normal processing time $\bar{p}_j$, positive compression rate b_j, unit resource cost c_j of each job are all decimals randomly generated from different uniform distributions $U[1, 100]$, $U[0, 1]$ and $U[2, 9]$, respectively, where $j = 1, 2, \ldots, n$. The maximum available resource amount $\bar{u}_j$ of each job is a decimal randomly generated from the corresponding uniform distribution $U[0.6\bar{p}_j/b_j, 0.9\bar{p}_j/b_j]$.
- The deterioration rate is set as $\alpha = 0.01$, the parameter of the exponential distribution of machine breakdown is set as $E(\mathbf{B}) = 100$, the basic maintenance duration is set as $M = 30$, the deterioration rate of repairing is set as $\gamma = 0.01$, the unit completion time cost is set as $q = 1$ and the unit match-up time cost is set as $m = 100$ according to the empirical data in practice.
- The size of scenario set is set as $SimulationTimes = 30$ to evaluate the solution robustness of the candidate schedule.

In order to examine the performance of the proposed ADK/SA-NSGA-II, two other NSGA-II based algorithms are compared on the above test instances. One is NSGA-II using simulations only for fitness evaluations (denoted as NSGA-II), the other is NSGA-II assisted by a SVR model for fitness evaluations, which is termed as SA-NSGA-II. The encoding schemes and evolutionary operators of NSGA-II and SA-NSGA-II are same as those of ADK/SA-NSGA-II for the fairness of the comparison. We first compare SA-NSGA-II with NSGA-II to examine the efficiency of the proposed SVR model, and compare ADK/SA-NSGA-II with SA-NSGA-II to understand the improvement offered by a priori domain knowledge. In addition, we compare our algorithms with MOEA/D [84, 185], another popular multi-objective evolutionary algorithm, which has been successfully applied to solve various discrete and continuous multi-objective problems [84, 185]. The encoding schemes and evolutionary operators of MOEA/D are also the same as those of ADK/SA-NSGA-II for the fairness of the comparison.

To understand the search capabilities of the four algorithms under comparison, we will present the initial population, convergence curves and the obtained Pareto front of each algorithm from one typical run, respectively. For benchmarking, we also apply the assignment model proposed in Lemma 6.2.1 to solve the test instance.

This solution will serve as a reference, which only minimizes the operational cost of the problem.

6.3.2 Parameters Tuning

The parameters of ADK/SA-NSGA-II algorithm, such as population size *pop*, the maximum number of generations N, SVR model related parameters (*TrainSetScale*, *TrainInternal*, and *SimulateRatio*) and evolutionary operation related parameters (*CrossFraction*, *Ratio*, *MutateFraction*, *Scale* and *Shrink*) will certainly influence its performance. Therefore, parameters are first tuned based on the performance of the results from 50 runs on Case 2. The average minimum distance of the obtained Pareto front to the ideal point is used as an indicator for the performance of each tuned value of the parameter, where the ideal point is constructed by the minimal operational cost of the predictive schedule and the lower bound of the robustness objective. The tuned results are shown in Table 6.1, and the highlighted values are chosen for the subsequent comparisons. NSGA-II, MOEA/D and SA-NSGA-II share the same parameter values with ADK/SA-NSGA-II if needed to ensure fair comparison. In MOEA/D, the number of weight vectors in the neighborhood of each weight vector T is set to be 30 based on the results of our pilot studies.

Note that $N = 200$ is the tuned value of the maximum number of generations. The corresponding computational cost of ADK/SA-NSGA-II measured by the number of fitness evaluations using simulations can be calculated as $N \times pop \times SimulateRatio \times SimulationTimes$, where $pop \times SimulateRatio \times SimulationTimes$ is the number of simulations employed in each generation. For fair comparison, the maximum number of generations of NSGA-II and MOEA/D is set as $N \times SimulateRatio$, so that the number of expensive simulations it uses is the same as ADK/SA-NSGA-II. And SA-NSGA-II takes the same maximum number of generations as ADK/SA-NSGA-II for its surrogate-assisted fitness evaluations.

6.3.3 Results

(1) Optimization process of one typical test instance

The initial populations, convergence processes and the obtained Pareto fronts of the four compared algorithms in solving one typical test instance of Case 2 are shown in Figs. 6.2, 6.3 and 6.4, respectively. We use these as examples of illustrating the contribution of SVR model and the improvement gained by incorporating domain knowledge in evolution. The results of Cases 1, 3–10 are similar to Case 2, and therefore are not shown here. From Fig. 6.2, we can observe that SA-NSGA-II, NSGA-II and MOEA/D have the same initial population, and the initial population

Table 6.1 The results of parameters tuning

Parameters	Options	Distances	Parameters	Options	Distances
pop	50	3154	*N*	150	2069
	100	18612		200	1853
	150	2037		250	1853
TrainSetScale	1	4876	*MutateFraction*	1/n	2760
	3	4429		2/n	2163
	5	2123		3/n	3053
	7	3101		4/n	4181
TrainInternal	3	4622	Ratio	0.8	2760
	5	5712		1.2	2163
	7	4475		1.6	3053
	9	5430	(*Scale*, *Shrink*)	(0.1, 0.1)	5065
SimulateRatio	0.3	2014		(0.1, 0.5)	5885
	0.5	1981		(0.1, 0.9)	8128
	0.7	2793		(0.5, 0.1)	2423
	0.9	3786		(0.5, 0.5)	1732
CrossFraction	1/n	2628		(0.5, 0.9)	2787
	2/n	2739		(0.9, 0.1)	2089
	3/n	3790		(0.9, 0.5)	2171
	4/n	3326		(0.9, 0.9)	2217

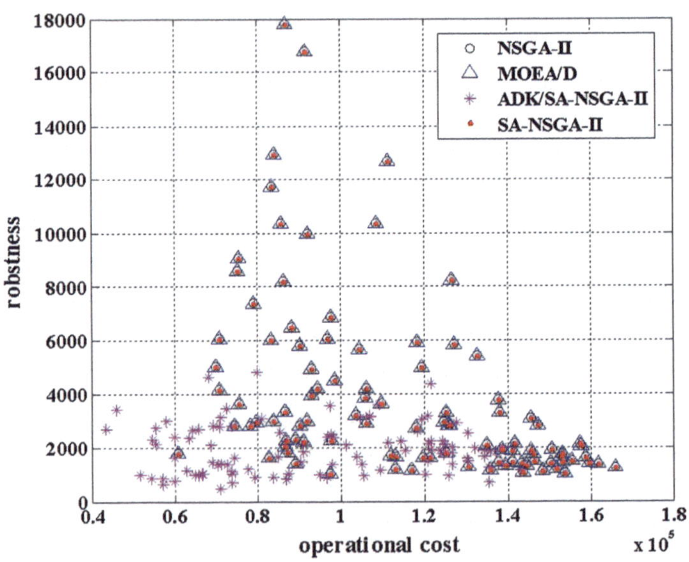

Fig. 6.2 The initial populations of NSGA-II, MOEA/D, SA-NSGA-II and ADK/SA-NSGA-II

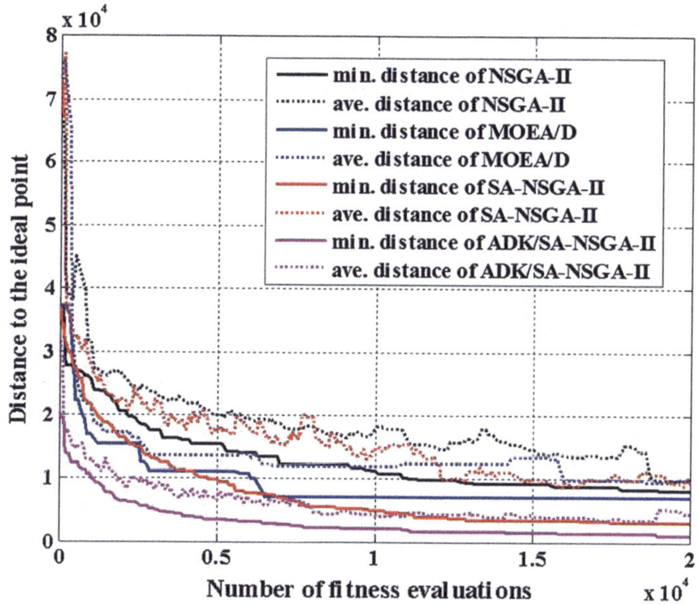

Fig. 6.3 The convergence processes of NSGA-II, MOEA/D, SA-NSGA-II and ADK/SA-NSGA-II

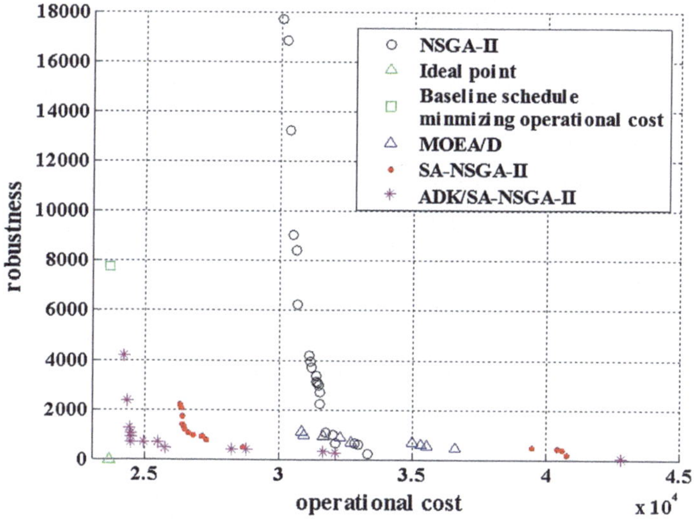

Fig. 6.4 The obtained Pareto fronts of the four algorithms

of ADK/SA-NSGA-II is improved owing to the adjustment done by incorporating a priori domain knowledge.

The convergence processes of NSGA-II, MOEA/D, SA-NSGA-II and ADK/SA-NSGA-II under the same computational cost are shown in Fig. 6.3. The convergence curves show that fitness values converge rapidly in the four algorithms from the beginning to 5000 simulation-based fitness evaluations. SA-NSGA-II outperforms NSGA-II with any number of exact fitness evaluations. MOEA/D is competitive with respect to SA-NSGA-II in the early stage of the search. However, as the evolution continues, the advantage of SA-NSGA-II becomes more obvious. These indicate the efficiency of the constructed SVR model in speeding up the convergence. The convergence curves of ADK/SA-NSGA-II shows clear advantages over NSGA-II, MOEA/D and SA-NSGA-II during the entire optimization process, which shows that a priori domain knowledge leads to great improvement in the convergence speed of the proposed algorithm.

Figure 6.4 shows the obtained Pareto fronts from the four compared algorithms. It is observed that SA-NSGA-II achieves a better Pareto front in comparison with NSGA-II. MOEA/D achieves similar robustness objectives to that of SA-NSGA-II, but has a much larger operational cost on average. These indicate that the SVR model can efficiently improve the operational cost of the schedules as well as their robustness in response to machine breakdown. By comparing the Pareto fronts approximated by ADK/SA-NSGA-II and SA-NSGA-II, we can see the Pareto optimal solutions obtained by ADK/SA-NSGA-II are further improved. Based on these observations, we conclude that a priori domain knowledge has significantly enhanced the searching capability of the evolutionary algorithm.

By examining the optimal solution obtained by solving problem **P** through the assignment model proposed in Lemma 6.2.1 and those Pareto optimal solutions approximated by ADK/SA-NSGA-II, we can see that the robustness of the solution will be very poor if only the operational cost is minimized in response to machine breakdown. It is indeed very helpful to make use of information about machine breakdown to find non-dominated solutions that also take schedule robustness into account. From the Pareto optimal solutions obtained by the proposed ADK/SA-NSGA-II, it is very straightforward for the decision-maker to pick out a solution that has an acceptable operational cost but considerably reduced rescheduling cost, for example the one indicated by the arrow in Fig. 6.4.

(2) Quantitative comparisons

Convergence and diversity of the obtained Pareto optimal solutions are two most important aspects for measuring the quality of the solutions. Among many others, inverted generational distance (*IGD*) and hyper-volume (*HV*) are two popular performance indicators. *IGD* measures the average distance between the obtained Pareto front denoted by PF to the optimal Pareto front denoted by PF^* [192]:

$$IGD(PF^*, PF) = \frac{\sum_{v \in PF^*} d(v, PF)}{|PF^*|} \tag{6.3.1}$$

where v represents a Pareto solution in the obtained Pareto front PF, $d(v, PF)$ represents the distance between v and PF, and $|PF^*|$ denotes the number of different Pareto solutions in PF^*, which is either a representative set chosen from a known theoretical Pareto, or a set of non-dominated solutions selected from the combination of all Pareto fronts to be compared, if the theoretical Pareto front is unknown. The *IGD* metric mainly reflects the convergence of a Pareto front, and a smaller value indicates better convergence. The *HV* metric calculates the area dominated by the obtained Pareto front [193], which can account for both convergence and diversity of the obtained solution set, referring to [193] for details. The larger the *HV* value, the better the performance.

The results of the four algorithms in terms of *IGD* and *HV* are presented in Tables 6.2, 6.3, 6.4 and 6.5, respectively. The results are averaged over 100 independently generated test instances for each case. From Table 6.2, we can see that the mean *IGD* values of SA-NSGA-II are lower than those of NSGA-II on all ten problem cases with a smaller or similar standard deviation, and the mean *HV* values of SA-NSGA-II are also better than those of NSGA-II. The improvement in *IGD* metric becomes more obvious as the problem size increases. Thus, it is evident that SA-NSGA-II outperforms NSGA-II, demonstrating that the use of surrogates can efficiently improve the performance. This improvement becomes more significant as the problem size increases.

Table 6.2 Comparative results between SA-NSGA-II and NSGA-II

		IGD		HV	
		Ave.	Std.	Ave.	Std.
Case 1	NSGA-II	0.04	0.03	2.19×10^7	3.14×10^7
	SA-NSGA-II	0.01	0.01	2.22×10^7	3.14×10^7
Case 2	NSGA-II	0.08	0.06	3.77×10^9	3.04×10^{10}
	SA-NSGA-II	0.02	0.03	3.78×10^9	3.04×10^{10}
Case 3	NSGA-II	0.15	0.09	9.19×10^7	2.29×10^8
	SA-NSGA-II	0.01	0.01	1.11×10^8	2.79×10^8
Case 4	NSGA-II	0.26	0.13	1.92×10^8	1.18×10^9
	SA-NSGA-II	0.01	0.02	2.33×10^8	1.35×10^9
Case 5	NSGA-II	0.34	0.15	1.40×10^8	6.30×10^8
	SA-NSGA-II	0.00	0.01	2.29×10^8	1.00×10^9
Case 6	NSGA-II	0.46	0.20	6.93×10^7	1.77×10^8
	SA-NSGA-II	0.01	0.03	1.39×10^8	2.25×10^8
Case 7	NSGA-II	0.44	0.18	1.43×10^8	3.08×10^8
	SA-NSGA-II	0.01	0.03	2.77×10^8	4.33×10^8
Case 8	NSGA-II	0.60	0.16	1.14×10^9	7.49×10^9
	SA-NSGA-II	0.00	0.01	2.52×10^9	1.04×10^{10}
Case 9	NSGA-II	0.69	0.14	7.84×10^8	8.32×10^8
	SA-NSGA-II	0.00	0.00	4.35×10^9	2.20×10^9
Case 10	NSGA-II	0.74	0.10	2.83×10^{10}	2.51×10^{10}
	SA-NSGA-II	0.00	0.00	2.37×10^{11}	9.74×10^{10}

Table 6.3 Comparative results between MOEA/D and NSGA-II

		IGD		HV	
		Ave.	Std.	Ave.	Std.
Case 1	MOEA/D	0.13	0.06	1.20×10^{7}	1.85×10^{7}
	NSGA-II	0.00	0.00	1.49×10^{7}	2.12×10^{7}
Case 2	MOEA/D	0.08	0.06	3.76×10^{9}	3.03×10^{10}
	NSGA-II	0.01	0.02	3.76×10^{9}	3.03×10^{10}
Case 3	MOEA/D	0.03	0.05	9.03×10^{7}	1.99×10^{8}
	NSGA-II	0.13	0.12	9.25×10^{7}	2.21×10^{8}
Case 4	MOEA/D	0.01	0.01	4.76×10^{8}	3.26×10^{9}
	NSGA-II	0.29	0.17	4.58×10^{8}	3.27×10^{9}
Case 5	MOEA/D	0.00	0.00	2.80×10^{8}	1.06×10^{9}
	NSGA-II	0.42	0.16	1.79×10^{8}	6.76×10^{8}
Case 6	MOEA/D	0.00	0.01	1.45×10^{8}	1.24×10^{8}
	NSGA-II	0.60	0.16	4.07×10^{7}	6.65×10^{7}
Case 7	MOEA/D	0.00	0.00	3.66×10^{8}	4.80×10^{8}
	NSGA-II	0.61	0.15	1.26×10^{8}	3.03×10^{8}
Case 8	MOEA/D	0.00	0.00	3.92×10^{9}	1.30×10^{10}
	NSGA-II	0.75	0.13	1.21×10^{9}	7.51×10^{9}
Case 9	MOEA/D	0.00	0.00	1.21×10^{10}	8.66×10^{9}
	NSGA-II	0.85	0.07	9.00×10^{8}	2.50×10^{9}
Case 10	MOEA/D	0.00	0.00	7.54×10^{11}	2.10×10^{11}
	NSGA-II	0.89	0.05	2.77×10^{10}	2.53×10^{10}

Table 6.4 Comparative results between ADK/SA-NSGA-II and MOEA/D

		IGD		HV	
		Ave.	Std.	Ave.	Std.
Case 1	ADK/SA-NSGA-II	0.00	0.00	1.23×10^{7}	2.37×10^{7}
	MOEA/D	0.25	0.09	9.00×10^{6}	2.07×10^{7}
Case 2	ADK/SA-NSGA-II	0.00	0.01	4.46×10^{8}	3.33×10^{9}
	MOEA/D	0.36	0.14	3.91×10^{8}	2.98×10^{9}
Case 3	ADK/SA-NSGA-II	0.01	0.02	6.40×10^{7}	1.96×10^{8}
	MOEA/D	0.40	0.16	3.11×10^{7}	1.19×10^{8}
Case 4	ADK/SA-NSGA-II	0.02	0.04	1.02×10^{8}	4.19×10^{8}
	MOEA/D	0.39	0.21	7.25×10^{7}	3.67×10^{8}
Case 5	ADK/SA-NSGA-II	0.04	0.10	1.37×10^{8}	5.38×10^{8}
	MOEA/D	0.28	0.22	7.79×10^{7}	2.65×10^{8}
Case 6	ADK/SA-NSGA-II	0.15	0.18	4.64×10^{7}	9.48×10^{7}
	MOEA/D	0.14	0.19	5.60×10^{7}	1.38×10^{8}
Case 7	ADK/SA-NSGA-II	0.29	0.20	4.46×10^{7}	7.16×10^{7}
	MOEA/D	0.04	0.11	6.69×10^{7}	6.63×10^{7}
Case 8	ADK/SA-NSGA-II	0.50	0.24	4.36×10^{8}	2.05×10^{9}
	MOEA/D	0.01	0.05	6.19×10^{8}	2.31×10^{9}
Case 9	ADK/SA-NSGA-II	0.50	0.22	9.22×10^{8}	3.08×10^{9}
	MOEA/D	0.01	0.06	1.95×10^{9}	3.00×10^{9}
Case 10	ADK/SA-NSGA-II	0.02	0.07	4.68×10^{10}	3.89×10^{10}
	MOEA/D	0.50	0.29	1.19×10^{10}	1.08×10^{10}

Table 6.5 Comparative results between ADK/SA-NSGA-II and SA-NSGA-II

		IGD		HV	
		Ave.	Std.	Ave.	Std.
Case 1	ADK/SA-NSGA-II	0.02	0.02	1.85×10^7	3.00×10^7
	SA-NSGA-II	0.07	0.05	1.81×10^7	3.14×10^7
Case 2	ADK/SA-NSGA-II	0.02	0.02	4.86×10^8	3.34×10^9
	SA-NSGA-II	0.17	0.09	4.65×10^8	3.21×10^9
Case 3	ADK/SA-NSGA-II	0.02	0.04	6.55×10^7	1.66×10^8
	SA-NSGA-II	0.23	0.14	4.64×10^7	1.26×10^8
Case 4	ADK/SA-NSGA-II	0.01	0.02	1.20×10^8	5.56×10^8
	SA-NSGA-II	0.32	0.19	7.93×10^7	3.67×10^8
Case 5	ADK/SA-NSGA-II	0.02	0.04	7.44×10^7	8.60×10^7
	SA-NSGA-II	0.32	0.19	4.49×10^7	6.32×10^7
Case 6	ADK/SA-NSGA-II	0.02	0.05	1.01×10^8	1.69×10^8
	SA-NSGA-II	0.32	0.22	8.00×10^7	1.77×10^8
Case 7	ADK/SA-NSGA-II	0.02	0.05	1.45×10^8	2.53×10^8
	SA-NSGA-II	0.35	0.22	7.37×10^7	1.13×10^8
Case 8	ADK/SA-NSGA-II	0.02	0.06	3.13×10^8	3.76×10^8
	SA-NSGA-II	0.41	0.21	1.59×10^8	2.34×10^8
Case 9	ADK/SA-NSGA-II	0.00	0.00	3.57×10^9	2.20×10^9
	SA-NSGA-II	0.70	0.13	5.52×10^8	5.64×10^8
Case 10	ADK/SA-NSGA-II	0.00	0.00	4.18×10^{11}	1.27×10^{11}
	SA-NSGA-II	0.88	0.07	1.68×10^{10}	1.58×10^{10}

Table 6.3 indicates that NSGA-II has a better performance in terms of convergence and solution diversity when the problem size is relatively small (30 and 50 jobs). As the problem size increases to 500 jobs, MOEA/D becomes more competitive with better mean IGD and HV values. However, ADK/SA-NSGA-II can still outperform MOEA/D, as shown in Table 6.4.

From Table 6.5, we can see that the *IGD* values of ADK/SA-NSGA-II are much better than SA-NSGA-II. So are the *HV* values. The improvement of the *IGD* and the *HV* values also becomes more obvious with the increase of problem size. Consequently, we can conclude that ADK/SA-NSGA-II outperforms SA-NSGA-II thanks to the incorporation of a priori domain knowledge for guiding the search process. The improvement resulting from the embedding of a priori domain knowledge becomes more significant as the problem size increases, which implies that such domain knowledge will be increasingly helpful in solving large scheduling problems.

The runtime comparisons between NSGA-II, MOEA/D, SA-NSGA-II and ADK/SA-NSGA-II are presented in Table 6.6. Each reported value denotes a relative time indicator (RTI) calculated by $(RT_1 - RT_2)/RT_2$, where RT_1 and RT_2 represent the runtime of the two compared algorithms, respectively. So a negative value indicates the first algorithm is faster. From these results, we can see that NSGA-II takes less time than MOEA/D, and ADK/SA-NSGA-II takes less time than SA-NSGA-II. These results demonstrate that the proposed algorithm ADK/SA-NSGA-II is effective in reducing computational time.

Table 6.6 Comparison of relative runtime of the four algorithms

Cases	Compared algorithms	RTI
Case 1	NSGA-II & MOEA/D	−0.33
	ADK/SA-NSGA-II & SA-NSGA-II	−0.05
Case 2	NSGA-II & MOEA/D	−0.34
	ADK/SA-NSGA-II & SA-NSGA-II	−0.02
Case 3	NSGA-II & MOEA/D	−0.33
	ADK/SA-NSGA-II & SA-NSGA-II	−0.03
Case 4	NSGA-II & MOEA/D	−0.33
	ADK/SA-NSGA-II & SA-NSGA-II	−0.03
Case 5	NSGA-II & MOEA/D	−0.34
	ADK/SA-NSGA-II & SA-NSGA-II	−0.06
Case 6	NSGA-II & MOEA/D	−0.32
	ADK/SA-NSGA-II & SA-NSGA-II	−0.08
Case 7	NSGA-II & MOEA/D	−0.33
	ADK/SA-NSGA-II & SA-NSGA-II	−0.04
Case 8	NSGA-II & MOEA/D	−0.34
	ADK/SA-NSGA-II & SA-NSGA-II	−0.10
Case 9	NSGA-II & MOEA/D	−0.36
	ADK/SA-NSGA-II & SA-NSGA-II	−0.12
Case 10	NSGA-II & MOEA/D	−0.39
	ADK/SA-NSGA-II & SA-NSGA-II	−0.17

(3) The ANOVA results

The analysis of variance (ANOVA) is implemented using the commercial software SPSS (Version 17.0) to analyze the *IGD* and *HV* values obtained by the compared algorithms. The resulting F-ratios and p-values of ANOVA are shown in Tables 6.7 and 6.8. The difference is considered to be statistically significant if the p-value is less than 0.05. From Tables 6.7 and 6.8, we can draw the following conclusions. First, for the *IGD* measure, the algorithm factor has a statistically significant impact for nearly all cases. ADK/SA-NSGA-II performs significantly better than MOEA/D and SA-NSGA-II in terms of convergence. This is also true for MOEA/D against NSGA-II, and SA-NSGA-II against NSGA-II. Second, for the *HV* measure, the impact of the algorithm factor is not significant for small cases with 30 to 200 jobs (Cases 1–8). But the impact becomes significant for 300 and 500 jobs (Cases 9–10), indicating that improvement in computational efficiency achieved by the proposed algorithm is more significant for solving larger problems.

Table 6.7 The ANOVA result for the IGD performance measure

	SA-NSGA-II & NSGA-II		MOEA/D & NSGA-II		ADK/SA-NSGA-II & MOEA/D		ADK/SA-NSGA-II & SA-NSGA-II	
	F-ratio	p-value	F-ratio	p-value	F-ratio	p-value	F-ratio	p-value
Case 1	23.37	0.000	371.19	0.000	510.69	0.000	61.10	0.000
Case 2	55.74	0.000	64.37	0.000	420.05	0.000	184.40	0.000
Case 3	145.33	0.000	39.67	0.000	394.89	0.000	146.88	0.000
Case 4	238.95	0.000	186.22	0.000	195.52	0.000	176.30	0.000
Case 5	333.95	0.000	426.76	0.000	62.25	0.000	163.62	0.000
Case 6	332.81	0.000	931.21	0.000	0.14	0.000	115.47	0.000
Case 7	361.71	0.000	1142.45	0.000	84.34	0.000	141.98	0.000
Case 8	902.40	0.000	2252.67	0.000	265.66	0.000	211.50	0.000
Case 9	1579.44	0.000	9822.67	0.000	297.20	0.000	1796.25	0.000
Case 10	3389.11	0.000	18097.48	0.000	166.47	0.000	9401.54	0.000

Table 6.8 The ANOVA result for the HV performance measure

	SA-NSGA-II & NSGA-II		MOEA/D & NSGA-II		ADK/SA-NSGA-II & MOEA/D		ADK/SA-NSGA-II & SA-NSGA-II	
	F-ratio	p-value	F-ratio	p-value	F-ratio	p-value	F-ratio	p-value
Case 1	0.00	0.96	0.70	0.403	0.73	0.395	0.00	0.947
Case 2	0.00	1.00	0.00	0.999	0.01	0.921	0.00	0.970
Case 3	0.19	0.67	0.00	0.950	1.35	0.247	0.56	0.457
Case 4	0.03	0.85	0.00	0.974	0.19	0.667	0.25	0.619
Case 5	0.38	0.54	0.43	0.512	0.63	0.427	5.07	0.026
Case 6	3.98	0.05	36.63	0.000	0.21	0.644	0.50	0.480
Case 7	4.21	0.04	11.84	0.001	3.44	0.066	4.40	0.038
Case 8	0.76	0.38	2.13	0.146	0.23	0.631	7.99	0.005
Case 9	151.12	0.00	105.35	0.000	3.78	0.004	116.99	0.000
Case 10	284.18	0.00	778.33	0.000	49.04	0.000	650.05	0.000

6.4 Summary

In this paper we address the proactive scheduling problem in the presence of stochastic machine breakdown in the deteriorating production environments. A knowledge-based multi-objective evolutionary algorithm is proposed to solve the problem, where support vector regression based surrogate models are employed to reduce the computation cost resulting from the extra time-consuming simulations for evaluating the solution robustness, and analytical a priori domain knowledge is introduced to guide the searching process. Comparative results clearly show that both surrogate-assisted techniques and analytical a priori domain knowledge are effective in enhancing the time efficiency and search capability of the evolutionary algorithm. Our algorithm is very generic and applicable to other computationally expensive black-box optimization problems, such as aerodynamic design optimization problems and energy performance optimization of building, just to name a few.

The proposed algorithm has been shown to be efficient and promising in handling stochastic machine breakdown, where the SVR-based surrogate model plays an important role in reducing the computational cost resulting from the simulation-based fitness evaluations. On the other hand, we note that NSGA-II is outperformed by MOEA/D, indicating that NSGA-II may be replaced by other state-of-the-art multi-objective evolutionary algorithms.

6.5 Bibliographic Remarks

In scheduling literature, proactive scheduling approaches to handling uncertainties aim to prepare a baseline schedule which can be easily adjusted within little performance degradation [47, 48, 127]. Aytug et al. [8] review existing literature on scheduling in the presence of unforeseen disruptions and robust scheduling approaches focusing on predictive schedules that minimize the effect of disruptions. Sabuncuoglu and Goren [125] summarize existing robustness and stability measures for proactive scheduling and endeavor to understand the philosophy of proactive and reactive approaches by analyzing the major issues in a scheduling process under uncertainties and studying how different policies are generated for handling these issues.

The buffering approach is the most frequently used proactive approach to minimizing the impact of stochastic disruptions, through which idle times are inserted into the predictive schedules [18, 47, 90, 96, 109], which has been examined as an efficient proactive approach to generating a robust baseline schedule with fixed processing times. However, inserting idle times will degrade the performance of the baseline schedule and if no disruption occurs, the inserted idle time becomes useless and the limited capacity of production resources is wasted. By assuming that the job processing time can be compressed with certain extra resource cost [131], several researchers consider absorbing disruptions by extensively compressing a set of jobs in the schedule to catch up with the baseline schedule at a certain point. For example, Akturk et al. [2] study a scheduling problem on non-identical parallel machines with disruptions, where the processing time of each job is controllable at a certain manufacturing cost. They generate reactive schedules to catch up with the baseline schedule as soon as possible in response to disruptions with a slight increase in manufacturing cost. Gurel et al. [51] consider anticipative scheduling problems on non-identical parallel machines with disruptions and controllable processing times. Distributions of uncertain events and flexibilities of jobs are considered for making the anticipative schedule, and a match-up strategy is used to catch up with the predictive schedule at some certain point with compression of processing times for the remaining jobs. Al-Hinai and ElMekkawy [5] address flexible job shop scheduling problems with random machine breakdowns to find robust and stable solutions. Several bi-objective measures along with the robustness and stability of the predictive schedule are investigated.

It is worth noting that the main results of this chapter come from Wang et al. [148].

References

1. Adiri, I., Bruno, J., Frostig, E., & RinnooyKan, A. H. G. (1989). Single machine flow-time scheduling with a single breakdown. *Acta Informatica, 26*, 679–696.
2. Akturk, M. S., Atamturk, A., & Gurel, A. (2010). Parallel machine match-up scheduling with manufacturing cost considerations. *Journal of Scheduling, 13*(1), 95–110.
3. Agnetis, A., Billaut, J. C., Gawiejnowicz, S., Pacciarelli, D., & Soukhal, A. (2014). *Multiagent scheduling: Models and algorithms*. Heidelberg.
4. Aho, A. V., Hopcroft, J. E., & Ullman, J. D. (1974). *The design and analysis of computer algorithms*. Reading: Addison-Wesley.
5. Al-Hinai, N., & ElMekkawy, T. Y. (2011). Robust and stable flexible job shop scheduling with random machine breakdowns using a hybrid genetic algorithm. *International Journal of Production Economics, 132*(2), 279–291.
6. Ali, M., Siarry, P., & Pant, M. (2012). An efficient differential evolution based algorithm for solving multi-objective optimization problems. *European Journal of Operational Research, 217*, 404–416.
7. Aragon, V., Esquivel, S., & Coello, C. C. (2005). Evolutionary multiobjective optimization in non-stationary environments. *Journal of Computer Science and Technology, 5*(3), 133–143.
8. Aytug, H., Lawley, M. A., McKay, K., Mohan, S., & Uzsoy, R. (2005). Executing production schedules in the face of uncertainties: A review and some future directions. *European Journal of Operational Research, 161*, 86–110.
9. Azevedo, C., & Araujo, A. (2011). Generalized immigration schemes for dynamic evolutionary multiobjective optimization. In *Proceedings of the IEEE Congress on Evolutionary Computation* (pp. 2033–2040).
10. Baker, K. R. (1974). *Introduction to sequencing and scheduling*. New York: Wiley.
11. Ballestin, F., & Leus, R. (2008). Meta-heuristics for stable scheduling on a single machine. *Computers and Operations Research, 35*(7), 2175–2192.
12. Bandyopadhyay, S., & Bhattacharya, R. (2013). Solving multi-objective parallel machine scheduling problem by a modified NSGA-II. *Applied Mathematical Modelling, 37*, 6718–6729.
13. Bartal, Y., Leonardi, S., Marchetti-Spaccamela, A., Sgall, J., & Stougie, L. (2000). Multiprocessor scheduling with rejection. In *Proceedings of the Seventh Annual ACM-SIAM Symposium on Discrete Algorithms* (pp. 95–103).
14. Bean, J. C., Birge, J. R., Mittenthal, J., & Noon, C. E. (1991). Matchup scheduling with multiple resources, release dates and disruptions. *Operations Research, 39*, 470–483.
15. Billaut, J. C., Sanlaville, E., & Moukrim, A. (2002). *Flexibilite et Robustesse en Ordonnancement*. France: Hermes.
16. Blum, C., & Roli, A. (2003). Metaheuristics in combinatorial optimization: Overview and conceptual comparison. *ACM Computing Surveys, 35*, 268–308.

D. Wang et al., *Rescheduling Under Disruptions in Manufacturing Systems*, Uncertainty and Operations Research, https://doi.org/10.1007/978-981-15-3528-4

17. Boussaid, I., Lepagnot, J., & Siarry, P. (2013). A survey on optimization metaheuristics. *Information Sciences*, *237*, 82–117.
18. Briskorn, D., Leung, J., & Pinedo, M. L. (2011). Robust scheduling on a single machine using time buffers. *IIE Transactions*, *43*(6), 383–398.
19. Browne, S., & Yechiali, U. (1990). Scheduling deteriorating jobs on a single processor. *Operational Research*, *38*, 495–498.
20. Brucker, P. (2007). *Scheduling algorithms* (5th ed.). Berlin: Springer.
21. Cesaret, B., Oguz, C., & Salman, F. S. (2012). A tabu search algorithm for order acceptance and scheduling. *Computers and Operations Research*, *39*(6), 1197–1205.
22. Chang, C., & Lin, C. (2011). LIBSVM: A library for support vector machines. *ACM Transactions on Intelligent Systems and Technology*, *2*(3), 1–27.
23. Cheng, Y., & Sun, S. (2007). Scheduling linear deteriorating jobs with rejection on a single machine. *European Journal of Operational Research*, *194*, 18–27.
24. Cheng, T. C. E., Ding, Q., & Lin, B. M. T. (2004). A concise survey of scheduling with time-dependent processing times. *European Journal of Operational Research*, *152*, 1–13.
25. Cheng, R., Jin, Y., Narukawa, K., & Sendhoff, B. (2015). A multiobjective evolutionary algorithm using Gaussian process based inverse modeling. *IEEE Transactions on Evolutionary Computation*, *19*(6), 838–856.
26. Chiu, Y. F., & Shih, C. J. (2012). Rescheduling strategies for integrating rush orders with preventive maintenance in a two-machine flow shop. *International Journal of Production research*, *50*, 5783–5794.
27. Clausen, J., Hansen, J., Larsen, J., & Larsen A. (2001, October). Disruption management. *OR/MS Today*, *28*, 40–43.
28. Črepinšek, M., Liu, S., & Mernik, M. (2013). Exploration and exploitation in evolutionary algorithms. *ACM Computing Surveys*, *45*, 1–33.
29. Cormen, T. H., Leiserson, C. E., & Rivest, R. L. (1994). *Introduction to algorithms*. Cambridge: MIT.
30. Dahal, K., Al-Arfaj, K., & Paudyal, K. (2015). Modelling generator maintenance scheduling costs in deregulated power markets. *European Journal of Operational Research*, *240*, 551–561.
31. Das, S., & Suganthan, P. N. (2011). Differential evolution: A survey of the state-of-the-art. *IEEE Transactions on Evolutionary Computing*, *15*, 4–31.
32. Deb, K., Rao, U., & Karthik, S. (2007). Dynamic multiobjective optimization and decision-making using modified NSGA-II: A case study on hydro-thermal power scheduling. In *Evolutionary Multi-criterion Optimization: 4th International Conference, EMO* (pp. 803–817).
33. Deb, K., Pratap, A., Agarwal, S., & Meyarivan, T. (2002). A fast and elitist multiobjective genetic algorithm: NSGA-II. *IEEE Transactions on Evolutionary Computation*, *6*(2), 182–197.
34. Dong, M. G., & Wang, N. (2012). A novel hybrid differential evolution approach to scheduling of large-scale zero-wait batch processes with setup times. *Computers and Chemical Engineering*, *45*, 72–83.
35. Dubois-Lacoste, J., Lopez-Ibanez, M., & Stutzle, T. (2011). A hybrid TP+PLS algorithm for bi-objective flow-shop scheduling problems. *Computers and Operations Research*, *38*(8), 1219–1236.
36. Duc-Hoc, T., Cheng, M., & Minh-Tu, C. (2015). Hybrid multiple objective artificial bee colony with differential evolution for the time-cost-quality tradeoff problem. *Knowledge-Based Systems*, *74*, 176–186.
37. Elmaghraby, S. E., & Park, S. H. (1974). Scheduling jobs on a number of identical machines. *AIIE Transactions*, *6*, 1–13.
38. Emmons, H. (1969). One-machine sequencing to minimize certain functions of job tardiness. *Operations Research*, *17*, 701–715.
39. Farina, M., Deb, K., & Amato, P. (2004). Dynamic multiobjective optimization problems: Test cases, approximations, and aplications. *IEEE Transactions on Evolutionary Computation*, *8*(5), 425–442.

40. Farley, A. A. (1990). A note on bounding a class of linear programming problems, including cutting stock problems. *Operations Research, 38*, 922–923.
41. Gawiejnowicz, S. (2008). *Time-dependent scheduling: EATCS monographs in theoretical computer science*. Berlin/New York: Springer.
42. Graham, R. L., Lawler, E. L., Lenstra, J. K., & Rinnooy Kan, A. H. G. (1979). Optimization and approximation in deterministic machine scheduling: A survey. *Annals of Discrete Mathematics, 5*, 287–326.
43. Garey, M. R., & Johnson, D. S. (1979). *Computers and intractability: A guide to the theory of NP-completeness*. New York: W.H. Freeman and Company.
44. Gogna, A., & Tayal, A. (2013). Metaheuristics: Review and application. *Journal of Experimental and Theoretical Artificial Intelligence, 25*, 503–526.
45. Gopalakrishnan, M., Ahire, S. L., & Miller, D. M. (1997). Maximizing the effectiveness of a preventive maintenance system: An adaptive modeling approach. *Management Science, 43*, 827–840.
46. Gordon, V. S., Potts, C. N., Strusevich, V. A., & Whitehead, J. D. (2008). Single machine scheduling models with deterioration and learning: Handling precedence constraints via priority generation. *Journal of Scheduling, 11*, 357–370.
47. Goren, S., & Sabuncuoglu, I. (2008). Robustness and stability measures for scheduling: Single-machine environment. *IIE Transactions, 40*(1), 66–83.
48. Goren, S., & Sabuncuoglu, I. (2010). Optimization of schedule robustness and stability under random machine breakdowns and processing time variability. *IIE Transactions, 42*(3), 203–220.
49. Gu, F. Q., Liu, H. L., & Tan, K. C. (2015). A hybrid evolutionary multiobjective optimization algorithm with adaptive multi-fitness assignment. *Soft Computing, 19*(11), 3249–3259.
50. Gunasekaran, A. (1998). Agile manufacturing: Enablers and an implementation framework. *International Journal of Production Research, 36*, 1223–1247.
51. Gurel, I. S., Korpeoglu, E., & Akturk, M. S. (2010). An anticipative scheduling approach with controllable processing times. *Computers and Operations Research, 37*(6), 1002–1013.
52. Han, Y., Gong, D., Sun, X., & Pan, Q. (2014). An improved NSGA-II algorithm for multi-objective lot-streaming flow shop scheduling problem. *International Journal of Production Research, 52*, 2211–2231.
53. Hall, N. G., Liu, Z. X., & Potts, C. N. (2007). Rescheduling for multiple new orders. *INFORMS Journal on Computing, 19*, 633–645.
54. Hall, N. G., & Potts, C. N. (2004). Rescheduling for new orders. *Operations Research, 52*, 440–453.
55. Hall, N. G., & Potts, C. N. (2010). Rescheduling for job unavailability. *Operations Research, 58*, 746–755.
56. Hatzakis, I., & Wallace, D. (2006). Dynamic multiobjective optimization with evolutionary algorithms: A forward-looking approach. In *Proceedings of Genetic and Evolutionary Computation Conference* (pp. 1201–1208).
57. Hatzakis, I., & Wallace, D. (2006). Topology of anticipatory populations for evolutionary dynamic multiobjective optimization. In *Proceedings of 11th AIAA/ISSMO Multidisciplinary Analysis and Optimization Conference* (pp. 1944–1950).
58. He, Y., & Sun, L. (2015). One-machine scheduling problems with deteriorating jobs and position dependent learning effects under group technology considerations. *International Journal of Systems Science, 46*, 1319–1326.
59. Helo, P. (2004). Managing agility and productivity in the electronics industry. *Industrial Management and Data Systems, 104*, 567–577.
60. Helbig, M., & Engelbrecht, A. (2012). Analyses of guide update approaches for vector evaluated particle swarm optimisation on dynamic multiobjective optimisation problems. In *Proceedings of IEEE World Congress on Computational Intelligence* (pp. 2621–2628).
61. Herroelen, W., & Leus, R. (2004). Robust and reactive project scheduling: A review and classification of procedures. *International Journal of Production Research, 42*(8), 1599–1620.

62. Jin, Y., & Branke, H. (2005). Evolutionary optimization in uncertain environments—A survey. *IEEE Transactions on Evolutionary Computation, 9*(3), 303–317.
63. Hoogeveena, H., Lentéb, C., & T'kindtb, V. (2012). Rescheduling for new orders on a single machine with setup times. *European Journal of Operational Research, 223*, 40–46.
64. Huo, Y., & Zhao, H. (2018). Two machine scheduling subject to arbitrary machine availability constraint. *Omega, 76*, 128–136.
65. Jain, S., & Foley, W. J. (2016). Dispatching strategies for managing uncertainties in automated manufacturing systems. *European Journal of Operational Research, 248*, 328–341.
66. Jakobovic, D., & Budin, L. (2006). *Dynamic scheduling with genetic programming*. Lecture Notes in Computer Science (Vol. 3905, pp. 73–84). Berlin, Heidelberg: Springer.
67. Jaszkiewicz, A. (2003). Do multiple-objective metaheuristcs deliver on their promises? A computational experiment on the set-covering problem. *IEEE Transactions on Evolutionary Computation, 7*(2), 133–143.
68. Jin, Y., & Branke, H. (2005). Evolutionary optimization in uncertain environments—A survey. *IEEE Transactions on Evolutionary Computation, 9*(3), 303–317.
69. Jin, Y., & Sendhoff, B. (2004). Constructing dynamic test problems using the multi-objective optimization concept. *Applications of Evolutionary Computing, 3005*, 525–536.
70. Jin, Y. (2011). Surrogate-assisted evolutionary computation: Recent advances and future challenges. *Swarm and Evolutionary Computation, 1*(2), 61–70.
71. Jin, Y., Olhofer, M., & Sendhoff, B. (2002). A framework for evolutionary optimization with approximate fitness functions. *IEEE Transactions on Evolutionary Computation, 6*(5), 481–494.
72. Karimi, H., Rahmati, S. H. A., & Zandieh, M. (2012). An efficient knowledge-based algorithm for the flexible job shop scheduling problem. *Knowledge-Based Systems, 36*, 236–244.
73. Kattan, A., & Ong, Y. S. (2015). Surrogate genetic programming: A semantic aware evolutionary search. *Information Sciences, 296*, 345–359.
74. Kiris, S., Yuzugullu, N., Ergun, N., & Cevik, A. A. (2010). A knowledge-based scheduling system for emergency departments. *Knowledge-Based Systems, 23*, 890–900.
75. Kubzin, M. A., & Strusevich V. A. (2005). Two-machine flow shop no-wait scheduling with machine maintenance. *4OR: A Quarterly Journal of Operations Research, 3*, 303–313.
76. Kubzin, M. A., & Strusevich, V. A. (2006). Planning machine maintenance in two-machine shop scheduling. *Operations Research, 54*, 789–800.
77. Lee, C. Y., & Leon, V. J. (2001). Machine scheduling with a rate-modifying activity. *European Journal of Operational Research, 128*, 119–128.
78. Lee, C. Y., & Lin, C. S. (2001). Single-machine scheduling with maintenance and repair rate-modifying activities. *European Journal of Operational Research, 135*, 493–513.
79. Leon, V. J., Wu, S. D., & Storer, R. H. (1994). Robustness measures and robust scheduling for job shops. *IIE Transactions, 26*, 32–43.
80. Leus, R., & Herroelen, W. (2007). Scheduling for stability in single-machine production systems. *Journal of Scheduling, 10*(3), 223–235.
81. Levin, A., Mosheiov, G., & Sarig, A. (2009). Scheduling a maintenance activity on parallel identical machines. *Naval Research Logistics, 56*, 33–41.
82. Li, B., & Wang, L. (2007). A hybrid quantum-inspired genetic algorithm for multiobjective flow shop scheduling. *IEEE Transactions on Systems, Man, and Cybernetics, Part B, 37*, 576–591.
83. Li, D., & Lu, X. (2017). Two-agent parallel-machine scheduling with rejection. *Theoretical Computer Science, 703*, 66–75.
84. Li, H., & Zhang, Q. (2009). Multiobjective optimization problems with complicated Pareto sets, MOEA/D and NSGA-II. *IEEE Transactions on Evolutionary Computation, 13*(2), 284–302.
85. Li, J., Pan, Q., Mao, K., & Suganthan, P. N. (2014). Solving the steelmaking casting problem using an effective fruit fly optimisation algorithm. *Knowledge-Based Systems, 72*, 28–36.
86. Lim, D., Jin, Y., Ong, Y. S., & Sendhoff, B. (2010). Generalizing surrogate-assisted evolutionary computation. *IEEE Transactions on Evolutionary Computation, 14*(3), 329–355.

87. Liu, F., Wang, J. J., & Yang, D. L. (2013). Solving single machine scheduling under disruption with discounted costs by quantum-inspired hybrid heuristics. *Journal of Manufacturing Systems*, *32*, 715–723.
88. Liu, Z., & Ro, Y. K. (2014). Rescheduling for machine disruption to minimize makespan and maximum lateness. *Journal of Scheduling*, *17*, 339–352.
89. Liu, L., & Zhou, H. (2015). Single-machine rescheduling with deterioration and learning effects against the maximum sequence disruption. *International Journal of Systems Science*, *46*(14), 2640–2658.
90. Liu, L., Gu, H. Y., & Xi, Y. G. (2007). Robust and stable scheduling of a single machine with random machine breakdowns. *International Journal of Advanced Manufacturing Technology*, *31*(7–8), 645–654.
91. Liu, B., Zhang, Q., & Gielen, G. G. E. (2014). A Gaussian process surrogate model assisted evolutionary algorithm for medium scale expensive optimization problems. *IEEE Transactions on Evolutionary Computation*, *18*(2), 180–192.
92. Loukil, T., Teghem, J., & Tuyttens, D. (2005). Solving multi-objective production scheduling problems using metaheuristics. *European Journal of Operational Research*, *161*(1), 42–61.
93. Luo, W., & Liu, F. (2017). On single-machine scheduling with workload-dependent maintenance duration. *Omega*, *68*, 119–122.
94. Ma, Y., Chu, C., & Zuo, C. (2010). A survey of scheduling with deterministic machine availability constraints. *Computers and Industrial Engineering*, *58*, 199–211.
95. Manavizadeh, N., Goodarzi, A. H., Rabbani, M., & Jolai, F. (2013). Order acceptance/rejection policies in determining the sequence in mixed model assembly lines. *Applied Mathematical Modelling*, *37*(4), 2531–2551.
96. Mehta, S. V., & Uzsoy, R. M. (1998). Predictable scheduling of a job shop subject to breakdowns. *IEEE Transactions on Robotics and Automation*, *14*(3), 365–378.
97. Minella, G., Ruiz, R., & Ciavotta, M. (2008). A review and evaluation of multiobjective algorithms for the flowshop scheduling problem. *INFORMS Journal on Computing*, *20*(3), 451–471.
98. Mosheiov, G. (1991). V-shaped policies for scheduling deteriorating jobs. *Operational Research*, *39*, 979–991.
99. Mosheiov, G., & Oron, D. (2006). Due-date assignment and maintenance activity scheduling problem. *Mathematical and Computer Modelling*, *44*, 1053–1057.
100. Mosheiov, G., & Sarig, A. (2009). Scheduling a maintenance activity and due-window assignment on a single machine. *Computers and Operations Research*, *36*, 2541–2545.
101. Mosheiov, G., & Sidney, J. B. (2010). Scheduling a deteriorating maintenance activity on a single machine. *Journal of the Operational Research Society*, *61*, 882–887.
102. Munari, P., & Gondzio, J. (2013). Using the primal-dual interior point algorithm within the branch-price-and-cut method. *Computers and Operations Research*, *40*, 2026–2036.
103. Nguyen, S., Zhang, M., Johnston, M., & Tan, K. C. (2014). Automatic design of scheduling policies for dynamic multi-objective job shop scheduling via cooperative coevolution genetic programming. *IEEE Transactions on Evolutionary Computation*, *18*(2), 193–208.
104. Nguyen, S., Zhang, M., Johnston, M., & Tan, K. C. (2015). Automatic programming via iterated local search for dynamic job shop scheduling. *IEEE Transactions on Cybernetics*, *45*(1), 1–14.
105. Nguyen, S., Zhang, M., Johnston, M., & Tan, K. C. (2014). Genetic programming for evolving reusable due-date assignment models in job shop environment. *Evolutionary Computation*, *22*(1), 105–138.
106. Nguyen, T. T., Yang, S., & Branke, J. (2012). Evolutionary dynamic optimization: A survey of the state of the art. *Swarm and Evolutionary Computation*, *6*, 1–24.
107. Nie, L., Shao, X., Gao, L., & Li, W. (2010). Evolving scheduling rules with gene expression programming for dynamic single-machine scheduling problems. *The International Journal of Advanced Manufacturing Technology*, *58*, 729–747.
108. Nobibon, F. T., & Leus, R. (2011). Exact algorithms for a generalization of the order acceptance and scheduling problem in a single-machine environment. *Computers and Operations Research*, *38*, 367–378.

109. O'Donovan, R., Uzsoy, R., & McKay, K. N. (1999). Predictable scheduling of a single machine with breakdowns and sensitive jobs. *International Journal of Production Research, 37*(18), 4217–4233.
110. Oron, D. (2014). Scheduling controllable processing time jobs in a deteriorating environment. *Journal of the Operational Research Society, 65*, 49–56.
111. Ou, J., & Zhong, X. (2017). Bicriteria order acceptance and scheduling with consideration of fill rate. *European Journal of Operational Research, 262*, 904–907.
112. Ou, J., Zhong, X., & Wang, G. (2015). An improved heuristic for parallel machine scheduling with rejection. *European Journal of Operational Research, 241*(3), 653–661.
113. Ouelhadj, D., & Petrovic, S. (2009). A survey of dynamic scheduling in manufacturing systems. *Journal of Scheduling, 12*, 417–431.
114. Ozlen, M., & Azizoğlu, M. (2011). Rescheduling unrelated parallel machines with total flow time and total disruption cost criteria. *Journal of the Operational Research Society, 62*, 152–164.
115. Paenke, I., Branke, J., & Jin, Y. (2006). Efficient search for robust solutions by means of evolutionary algorithms and fitness approximation. *IEEE Transactions on Evolutionary Computation, 10*(4), 405–420.
116. Pan, Q., Wang, L., Gao, L., & Li, W. D. (2011). An effective hybrid discrete differential evolution algorithm for the flow shop scheduling with intermediate buffers. *Information Sciences, 181*, 668–685.
117. Papadimitriou, C. M. (1994). *Computational complexity*. Reading: Addison Wesley.
118. Pickardt, C. W., Hildebrandt, T., Branke, B., Heger, J., & Scholz-Reiter, B. (2013). Evolutionary generation of dispatching rule sets for complex dynamic scheduling problems. *International Journal of Production Economics, 145*, 67–77.
119. Pinedo, M. L. (2016). *Scheduling: Theory, algorithms, and systems* (5th ed.). Berlin: Springer.
120. Qi, X., Bard, J. F., & Yu, G. (2006). Disruption management for machine scheduling: The case of SPT schedules. *International Journal of Production Economics, 103*, 166–184.
121. Rahimi-Vahed, A. R., & Mirghorbani, S. M. (2006). A multi-objective particle swarm for a flow shop scheduling problem. *Journal of Combinatorial Optimization, 13*(1), 79–102.
122. Rinnooy Kan, A. H. G. (1976). *Machine scheduling problems: Classification, complexity and computations*. The Hague, The Netherlands: Nijhoff.
123. Rustogi, K., & Strusevich, V. A. (2012). Single machine scheduling with general positional deterioration and rate-modifying maintenance. *Omega, 40*, 791–804.
124. Rustogi, K., & Strusevich, V. A. (2014). Combining time and position dependent effects on a single machine subject to rate-modifying activities. *Omega, 42*, 166–178.
125. Sabuncuoglu, I., & Goren, S. (2009). Hedging production schedules against uncertainty in manufacturing environment with a review of robustness and stability research. *International Journal of Computer Integrated Manufacturing, 22*(2), 138–157.
126. Schneider, E. R. F. A., & Krohling, R. A. (2014). A hybrid approach using TOPSIS, Differential Evolution, and Tabu Search to find multiple solutions of constrained non-linear integer optimization problems. *Knowledge-Based Systems, 62*, 47–56.
127. Sevaux, M., & Rensen, K. S. (2004). A genetic algorithm for robust schedules in a one-machine environment with ready times and due dates. *4OR: A Quarterly Journal of Operations Research, 2*(1), 129–147.
128. Shabtay, D. (2014). The single machine serial batch scheduling problem with rejection to minimize total completion time and total rejection cost. *European Journal of Operational Research, 233*, 64–74.
129. Shabtay, D., Gaspar, N., & Kaspi, M. (2013). A survey on offine scheduling with rejection. *Journal of Scheduling, 16*(1), 3–28.
130. Shabtay, D., Gaspar, N., & Yedidsion, L. (2012). A bicriteria approach to scheduling a single machine with job rejection and positional penalties. *Journal of Combinatorial Optimization, 23*, 395–424.
131. Shabtay, D., & Steiner, G. (2007). A survey of scheduling with controllable processing times. *Discrete Applied Mathematics, 155*, 1643–1666.

132. Shen, X., & Yao, X. (2015). Mathematical modeling and multi-objective evolutionary algorithms applied to dynamic flexible job shop scheduling problems. *Information Sciences, 298*, 198–224.
133. Shen, J., Wang, L., & Wang, S. (2015). A bi-population EDA for solving the no-idle permutation flow-shop scheduling problem with the total tardiness criterion. *Knowledge-Based Systems, 74*, 167–175.
134. Slotnick, S. A. (2011). Order acceptance and scheduling: A taxonomy and review. *European Journal of Operational Research, 212*(1), 1–11.
135. Storn, R., & Kenneth, P. (1997). Differential evolution—A simple and efficient heuristic for global optimization over continuous Spaces. *Journal of Global Optimization, 11*, 341–359.
136. Sun, C., Zeng, J., Pan, J., Xue, S., & Jin, Y. (2013). A new fitness estimation strategy for particle swarm optimization. *Information Sciences, 221*, 355–370.
137. Tang, L., Zhao, Y., & Liu, J. (2014). An improved differential evolution algorithm for practical dynamic scheduling in steelmaking-continuous casting production. *IEEE Transactions on Evolutionary Computation, 18*, 209–225.
138. Tasgetiren, M. F., Pan, Q., Suganthan, P. N., & Jin Chua, T. (2011). A differential evolution algorithm for the no-idle flowshop scheduling problem with total tardiness criterion. *International Journal of Production Research, 49*, 5033–5050.
139. Tepedino, A. C. M. A., Takahashi, R. H. C., & Carrano, E. G. (2013). Distance based NSGA-II for earliness and tardiness minimization in parallel machine scheduling. In *IEEE Congress on Evolutionary Computation* (pp. 317–324).
140. Thevenin, S., Zufferey, N., & Widmer, M. (2015). Metaheuristics for a scheduling problem with rejection and tardiness penalties. *Journal of Scheduling, 18*, 89–105.
141. Thevenin, S., Zufferey, N., & Widmer, M. (2016). Order acceptance and scheduling with earliness and tardiness penalties. *Journal of Heuristics, 22*(6), 849–890.
142. Ulungu, E. L., Teghem, J., & Ost, C. (1998). Efficiency of interactive multiobjective simulated annealing through a case study. *Journal of the Operational Research Society, 49*(10), 1044–1050.
143. Unal, A. T., Uzsoy, R., & Kiran, A. S. (1997). Rescheduling on a single machine with part-type dependent setup times and deadlines. *Annals of Operations Research, 70*, 93–113.
144. Van Veldhuizen, D. A. (1999). *Multiobjective evolutionary algorithms: Classifications, analyses, and new innovations*. Ph.D. dissertation, Department of Electrical and Computer Engineering, Graduate School of Engineering, Air Force Institute of Technology, Wright-Patterson AFB, OH.
145. Vieira, G. E., Herrmann, J. W., & Lin, E. (2003). Rescheduling manufacturing systems: A framework of strategies, policies, and methods. *Journal of Scheduling, 6*, 39–62.
146. Wang, D., Liu, F., & Jin, Y. (2016). A multi-objective evolutionary algorithm guided by directed search for dynamic scheduling. *Computers and Operations Research, 9*, 279–290.
147. Wang, D., Liu, F., Wang, J., & Wang, Y. Z. (2016). Integrated rescheduling and preventive maintenance for arrival of new jobs through evolutionary multi-objective optimization. *Soft Computing, 20*(4), 1635–1652.
148. Wang, D., Liu, F., Wang, Y. Z., & Jin, Y. (2015). A knowledge-based evolutionary proactive scheduling approach in the presence of machine breakdown and deterioration effect. *Knowledge-Based Systems, 90*, 70–80.
149. Wang, D., Yin, Y., & Cheng, T. C. E. (2018). Parallel-machine rescheduling with job unavailability and rejection. *Omega, 81*, 246–260.
150. Wang, L., Pan, Q., Suganthan, P. N., Wang, W., & Wang, Y. (2010). A novel hybrid discrete differential evolution algorithm for blocking flow shop scheduling problems. *Computers and Operations Research, 37*(3), 509–520.
151. Wang, J., & Guo, Q. (2010). A due-date assignment problem with learning effect and deteriorating jobs. *Applied Mathematical Modelling, 34*, 309–313.
152. Wang, J., & Wang, C. (2011). Single-machine due-window assignment problem with learning effect and deteriorating jobs. *Applied Mathematical Modelling, 35*, 4017–4022.

153. Wang, J. J., Wang, J. B., & Liu, F. (2011). Parallel machines scheduling with a deteriorating maintenance activity. *Journal of the Operational Research Society*, *62*, 1898–1902.
154. Wang, Y., & Cai, Z. X. (2012). Combining multiobjective optimization with differential evolution to solve constrained optimization problems. *IEEE Transactions on Evolutionary Computing*, *16*, 117–134.
155. Wu, S. D., Storer, R. H., & Chang, P. C. (1993). One-machine rescheduling heuristics with efficiency and stability as criteria. *Computers and Operations Research*, *20*, 1–14.
156. Wu, Y., Jin, Y., & Liu, X. (2015). A directed search strategy for evolutionary dynamic multiobjective optimization. *Soft Computing*, *19*(11), 3221–3235.
157. Xiong, J., Yang, K., Liu, J., Zhao, Q., & Chen, Y. (2012). A two-stage preference-based evolutionary multi-objective approach for capability planning problems. *Knowledge-Based Systems*, *31*, 128–139.
158. Xiong, J., Xing, L. N., & Chen, Y. W. (2013). Robust scheduling for multi-objective flexible job-shop problems with random machine breakdowns. *International Journal of Production Economics*, *141*(1), 112–126.
159. Xu, D., Wan, L., Liu, A., & Yang, D. L. (2015). Single machine total completion time scheduling problem with workload-dependent maintenance duration. *Omega*, *52*, 101–106.
160. Yan, P., Che, A., Cai, X., & Tang, X. (2014). Two-phase branch and bound algorithm for robotic cells rescheduling considering limited disturbance. *Computers and Operations Research*, *50*, 128–140.
161. Yang, B. (2007). Single machine rescheduling with new jobs arrivals and processing time compression. *International Journal of Advanced Manufacturing Technology*, *34*, 378–384.
162. Yang, S., Cheng, H., & Wang, F. (2010). Genetic algorithms with immigrants and memory schemes for dynamic shortest path routing problems in mobile ad hoc networks. *IEEE Transactions on Systems, Man, and Cybernetics, Part C*, *40*, 52–63.
163. Yang, S., & Yang, D. (2010). Minimizing the makespan on single-machine scheduling with aging effect and variable maintenance activities. *Omega*, *38*, 528–533.
164. Yang, S., Yang, D., & Cheng, T. C. E. (2010). Single-machine due-window assignment and scheduling with job-dependent aging effects and deteriorating maintenance. *Computers and Operations Research*, *37*, 1510–1514.
165. Yang, B., & Geunes, J. (2008). Predictive-reactive scheduling on a single resource with uncertain future jobs. *European Journal of Operational Research*, *189*(3), 1267–1283.
166. Yin, Y., Liu, M., Hao, J., & Zhou, M. (2012). Single-machine scheduling with job-position-dependent learning and time-dependent deterioration. *IEEE Transactions on Systems Man and Cybernetics—Part A Systems and Humans*, *42*(1), 192–200.
167. Yin, Y., Cheng, T. C. E., Cheng, S. R., & Wu, C. C. (2013). Single-machine batch delivery scheduling with an assignable common due date and controllable processing times. *Computers and Industrial Engineering*, *65*, 652–662.
168. Yin, Y., Cheng, T. C. E., Wu, C. C., & Cheng, S. R. (2014). Single-machine due window assignment and scheduling with a common flow allowance and controllable job processing time. *Journal of the Operational Research Society*, *65*, 1–13.
169. Yin, Y., Cheng, T. C. E., & Wu, C. (2014). Scheduling with time dependent processing times. *Mathematical Problems in Engineering*, 1–2.
170. Yin, Y., Wu, W., Cheng, T. C. E., & Wu, C. (2015). Single-machine scheduling with time-dependent and position-dependent deteriorating jobs. *International Journal of Computer Integrated Manufacturing*, *28*(7), 10.
171. Yin, Y., Wu, W., Cheng, T. C. E., & Wu, C. (2014). Due date assignment and single-machine scheduling with generalized positional deteriorating jobs and deteriorating multi-maintenance activities. *International Journal of Production Research*, *52*, 2311–2326.
172. Yin, Y., Cheng, T. C. E., Wu, C., & Cheng, S. (2014). Single-machine batch delivery scheduling and common due-date assignment with a rate-modifying activity. *International Journal of Production Research*, *52*, 5583–5596.
173. Yin, Y., Cheng, S. R., Chiang, J. Y., Chen, J. C. H., Mao, X., & Wu, C. (2015). Scheduling problems with due date assignment. *Discrete Dynamics in Nature and Society* (Article ID 683269).

174. Yin, Y., Wang, D., Cheng, T. C. E., & Wu, C. (2016). Bi-criterion single-machine scheduling and due-window assignment with common flow allowances and resource-dependent processing times. *Journal of the Operational Research Society, 67*(9).
175. Yin, Y., Cheng, T. C. E., Wang, J., & Wu, C. (2016). Improved algorithms for single-machine serial-batch scheduling with rejection to minimize total completion time and total rejection cost. *IEEE Transactions on Systems, Man and Cybernetics: Systems, 46*, 1578–1588.
176. Yin, Y., Wang, J., & Cheng, T. C. E. (2016). Rescheduling on identical parallel machines with machine disruptions to minimize total completion time. *European Journal of Operational Research, 252*, 737–749.
177. Yin, Y., Wang, Y., Cheng, T. C. E., Liu, W., & Li, J. (2017). Parallel-machine scheduling of deteriorating jobs with potential machine disruptions. *Omega, 69*, 17–28.
178. Yu, G., Argello, M., Song, G., McCowan, S. M., & White, A. (2003). A new era for crew recovery at Continental Airlines. *Interfaces, 33*, 5–22.
179. Yuan, J. J., & Mu, Y. D. (2007). Rescheduling with release dates to minimize makespan under a limit on the maximum sequence disruption. *European Journal of Operational Research, 182*(2), 936–944.
180. Zhou, A., Jin, Y., & Zhang, Q. (2014). A population prediction strategy for evolutionary dynamic multiobjective optimization. *IEEE Transactions on Cybernetics, 44*(1), 40–53.
181. Zhou, A., Jin, Y., Zhang, Q., Sendhoff, B., & Tsang, E. (2007). Prediction based population re-initialization for evolutionary dynamic multiobjective optimization. *Evolutionary Multi-criterion Optimization, 4403*, 832–846.
182. Zhang, L., Lu, L., & Yuan, J. (2010). Single-machine scheduling under the job rejection constraint. *Theoretical Computer Science, 411*, 1877–1882.
183. Zhang, Q., Zhou, A., & Jin, Y. (2008). RM-MEDA: A regularity model-based multiobjective estimation of distribution algorithm. *IEEE Transactions on Evolutionary Computation, 12*(1), 41–63.
184. Zhang, R., Song, S., & Wu, C. (2012). A two-stage hybrid particle swarm optimization algorithm for the stochastic job shop scheduling problem. *Knowledge-Based Systems, 27*, 393–406.
185. Zhang, Q., & Li, H. (2007). MOEA/D: A multiobjective evolutionary algorithm based on decomposition. *IEEE Congress on Evolutionary Computation, 11*(6), 712–731.
186. Zhao, C. L., & Tang, H. Y. (2010). Rescheduling problems with deteriorating jobs under disruptions. *Applied Mathematical Modelling, 34*(1), 238–243.
187. Zhao, Q. L., & Yuan, J. J. (2013). Pareto optimization of rescheduling with release dates to minimize makespan and total sequence disruption. *Journal of Scheduling, 16*(3), 253–260.
188. Zhao, C., & Tang, H. (2010). Single machine scheduling with general job-dependent aging effect and maintenance activities to minimize makespan. *Applied Mathematical Modelling, 34*, 837–841.
189. Zhao, C. L., & Tang, H. Y. (2010). Rescheduling problems with deteriorating jobs under disruptions. *Applied Mathematical Modelling, 34*, 238–243.
190. Zhao, C. L., & Tang, H. Y. (2010). Scheduling deteriorating jobs under disruption. *International Journal of Production Economics, 125*, 294–299.
191. Zheng, X., Wang, L., & Wang, S. (2014). A novel fruit fly optimization algorithm for the semiconductor final testing scheduling problem. *Knowledge-Based Systems, 57*, 95–103.
192. Zhou, A., Zhang, Q., & Jin, Y. (2009). Approximating the set of Pareto-optimal solutions in both the decision and objective spaces by an estimation of distribution algorithm. *IEEE Congress on Evolutionary Computation, 13*(5), 1167–1189.
193. Zitzler, E., & Thiele, L. (1998). Multiobjective optimization using evolutionary algorithms—A comparative case study. *International Conference on Parallel Problem Solving from Nature, 1498*(3), 292–301.
194. Zitzler, E. (1999). *Evolutionary algorithms for multiobjective optimization: Methods and applications*. Ph.D. dissertation, Swiss Federal Institute of Technology (ETH), Zurich, Switzerland.
195. Zweben, M., Davis, E., Daun, B., & Deale, M. J. (1993). Scheduling and rescheduling with iterative repair. *IEEE Transactions on Systems, Man, and Cybernetics, 23*, 1588–1596.

The manufacturer's authorised representative in the EU is Springer Nature Customer Service Centre GmbH, Europaplatz 3, 69115 Heidelberg, Germany. If you have any concerns regarding our products, please contact ProductSafety@springernature.com

Printed and bound by CPI Group (UK) Ltd, Croydon, CR0 4YY
25/09/2026
02222901-0018